THE ART OF GRAHAM GREENE

Islay Lyons, Capri

GRAHAM GREENE

THE ART OF GRAHAM GREENE

BY

KENNETH ALLOTT

AND

MIRIAM FARRIS

NEW YORK

RUSSELL & RUSSELL · INC

1963

FIRST PUBLISHED IN 1951
REISSUED, 1963, BY RUSSELL & RUSSELL, INC.
BY ARRANGEMENT WITH KENNETH ALLOTT AND MIRIAM FARRIS
L. C. CATALOG CARD NO: 63—15146
PRINTED IN THE UNITED STATES OF AMERICA

TO

L. C. MARTIN

ACKNOWLEDGMENTS

The quotations from the novels, entertainments and travel-books of Graham Greene are used by the courtesy of William Heinemann Ltd. The authors (the 'I' of the text) also wish to thank Mr. Greene for the loan of books, manuscripts and the photograph used as a frontispiece, and for his kindness and patience in answering their inquiries.

CONTENTS

THE ART OF GRAHAM GREENE

CHAPTER ONE

INTRODUCTION: THE TERROR OF LIFE

> . . . the two great popular statements of faith are 'What a small place the world is' and 'I'm a stranger here myself.'
>
> *The Ministry of Fear*, GRAHAM GREENE

FOR some years I have known that this book was going to be written: I wanted to write it because Graham Greene's novels and 'entertainments' have interested me and given me pleasure since I began early in the nineteen thirties to read them as they appeared; and, now that it exists, it seems to me a natural outgrowth of the reflective process that went along with the earlier reading of *A Gun for Sale*, for example, or *Brighton Rock*. From time to time, too, I have felt like answering some common objections to Greene's work which seem to rest on confusions and misunderstandings—such objections, for instance, as its morbidity of imagination and melodramatic flavour.

After all, to take these in reverse order, there is a sizable quantity of melodrama in much of what passes for the world's important literature from Greek epic to Elizabethan tragedy. Greene cannot be blamed merely for making use of *grand guignol*, although he may be criticized for his melodramatic treatment of particular scenes—it should be noted that the objection is not usually accompanied by a serious attempt to describe how he handles melodrama or what special effects it enables him to obtain.

Similarly, the objection to morbidity of imagination is puzzling. One might quote T. S. Eliot and leave it at that:

> [His] morbidity of temperament cannot, of course, be ignored . . . We should be misguided if we treated it as an unfortunate ailment or attempted to detach the sound from the unsound in his work. Without the morbidity none of his work would be possible or significant.

It has always been clear that some considerable artists have influenced their fellows precisely by squinting rather than looking at reality. Mr. Eliot was writing about Baudelaire —I am not comparing Greene with Baudelaire, perhaps I ought to add—but the point is that morbidity of imagination is not, any more than the use of melodrama, in itself a reason for having a high or low opinion of a writer's work. It may be that some kinds of morbidity are less than useful to an artist, or that morbidity beyond a certain degree is disabling, but again nobody yet seems to have given so exact an attention to Greene's writings as to justify such a pronouncement in his case.

These remarks are so obvious that the two objections still puzzle me, but there is nothing puzzling about the further less openly-voiced objection on the score of popularity. There is no blinking Greene's success. His books have large sales in Great Britain and the United States, and translations of them can be found with as much ease in the bookshops of Stockholm and Helsinki as in those of Paris, Rome and Vienna. His stories are serialized, filmed, and adapted for the stage. And what might once have been a recommendation is now an embarrassment. It is not logical at all, but it is natural enough today to be suspicious of enormous popularity.

If these objections can be properly met, if the questions my reading and re-reading of Graham Greene have faced me with can be answered, they will be met and answered by this book as a whole. Here I wish to dispose of certain preliminaries. This is not a biography of Greene, nor an examination of his religious or philosophical convictions, nor even a critique of his entire published work—or it is only incidentally these things when they appear to throw light on his fiction. It is an evaluation of the novels and entertainments as full and as documented as possible. I have tried to be strict about this and to avoid the wider and wilder speculations a writer's work can excite—of which some recent French studies of Greene afford dismal examples—but with the best intentions there are certain topics that fall to be dealt with in an introductory chapter.

Let me say at once that I find Greene the most interesting English novelist writing today (Mr. E. M. Forster no longer writes novels or he would be the obvious exception), but my starting-point is less the interest of the novels, for the kind and quality of this interest might be questioned, than the remarkable family likeness they bear to each other, which cannot be questioned at all. The comparison is exact: *The Man Within*, *England Made Me* and *The Power and the Glory* differ as widely as do the members of any large family, but they are stamped nevertheless with 'shared' features by which they can be identified.

'Every creative writer worth our consideration; every writer who can be called in the wide eighteenth century use of the term a poet, is a victim: a man given over to an obsession', Greene writes in a tribute to Walter de la Mare, and in various places he has suggested the preoccupations which can be detected in the novels of Conrad, Hardy and Henry James. In what is one of the best short pieces of criticism on Henry James[1], he has described how a ruling passion may unify the work of a writer, binding the story-telling together by recurrences of theme, incident and image, and giving it weight, direction and 'a symmetry of thought' that lends to half a shelf of novels 'the importance of a system'. All but the most disgruntled will agree that there has been plenty of talent and sensitivity (and some intelligence) in the English novel in the last twenty years—Greene published *The Man Within*, his

[1] See *The English Novelists*, ed. D. Verschoyle.

first novel, in 1929—but these are qualities that give us novels, not novelists. Talent, sometimes of a very high order, produced *High Wind in Jamaica*, *Darkness at Noon*, *A Handful of Dust*. Much rarer is the obsessional compulsion which I meet in the novels, travel-books and even the occasional criticism of Graham Greene; which distinguishes his work from that of equally adroit contemporaries; and which I agree with him in thinking the hallmark of the poet as distinct from the journeyman in fiction. I hardly know where else to find it among English novelists today.

The fact of obsession is my present concern, not the degree of success with which in particular novels the leading preoccupations are fitted into a picture of ordinary life, and the most cursory reading of Greene's novels and entertainments is enough to establish that everything he writes is discoloured by an original hurt to his sensibility. Characters recur in his books: the lonely, isolated man perpetually engrossed in his own childhood, like Andrews in *The Man Within* or Arthur Rowe in *The Ministry of Fear*[1]; the plain pathetic child-woman, like Milly Drover in *It's a Battlefield* or Helen Rolt in *The Heart of the Matter*; the masculine gargoyle, like Acky the epileptic unfrocked Anglican clergyman with a knuckleduster in *A Gun for Sale*, or Minty in *England Made Me*, the ex-Harrovian penny-a-liner in Stockholm whose malevolence is vented in such expletives as 'Holy Cnut'. Certain types of incident are also repeated, such as the pursuit, which Walter Allen has described as almost a formula for a Greene fiction and which turns up in 'early', 'middle' and 'late' novels, for example, *Rumour at Nightfall*, *The Confidential Agent* and

[1] Morton Zabel is interesting on the lineage of Greene's 'hunted Ishmaelites' in an article contributed to *Forms of Fiction: essays collected in honour of J. W. Beach* (1948). He notes the link with Conrad's Lord Jim, Heyst and Razumov and the more distant affinities (not to beg any questions) with Gide's Lafcadio, Kafka's 'K' and Dostoievsky's Raskolnikov. Morton Zabel and Walter Allen are in my opinion the only English-speaking critics of Greene whom the reader will find it very profitable to consult.

The Power and the Glory; or acts of suicide, brutal violence and voluntary or involuntary betrayal. There is very little gaiety in the Greene world (which is so often an underworld), but there is tenderness: the darkness is never pushed back far or for long. There is a blanketing sense of cruelty's omnipresence and the inevitability of failure, and very frequently this mood is symbolized by a peculiar background of squalor, urban and suburban in many novels but primitive and semi-tropical in *The Power and the Glory*, evoked with scrupulous care.

Characters, incidents and background constitute a mythology, which is the vehicle for Greene's obsessional ideas. Some of these run unchanged through all his fiction—escape and betrayal are good examples. Others, like 'the divided mind' in the three early immature novels or the theme of pity as a destructive passion in *The Ministry of Fear* and *The Heart of the Matter*, belong to one phase of his work distinctly, though they may be present more subtly in disguised forms elsewhere. The full range of these ideas, together with the varying emphasis attending their appearance in different books, will only gradually appear from the detailed study of the novels; but the separate obsessions are all related to each other by being connected with an unchanging general outlook. This may be the thought of as a key obsession, or as a sun from which the satellite obsessions derive their luminosity and their capacity to sustain the life of the stories in which they appear.

There is a sentence by Gauguin, quoted approvingly by Greene, that comes near to expressing his main obsessional outlook: 'Life being what it is, one dreams of revenge.' A terror of life, a terror of what experience can do to the individual, a terror at a predetermined corruption, is the motive force that drives Greene as a novelist. With different degrees of plausibility in his various books Greene is continually saying that happiness is unusual and anxious routine nearer the disappointing 'natural' state of man, that experience saddens, that we must bear rather than rejoice because, in Matthew

Arnold's words, of a 'something that infects the world'. Failure,[1] ugliness, the primitive are in some sense truer than success, beauty and civilization with their deceptive gloss. The little boy gazing at an electric train in the uncollected short story 'The Hint of an Explanation'[2] is a true citizen of Greeneland: 'The tears of longing came into my eyes when I looked at the turntable. It was my favourite piece—it looked so ugly and practical and true.'

It should be stressed that Greene's reading of experience is not abnormal—it is a simple Declaration of the Wrongs of Man to which most intelligent people would subscribe. William James in *Varieties of Religious Experience* distinguishes between two ways of regarding life, 'the healthy-minded way' and 'the way that takes all . . . experience of evil as something essential'. He continues:

> To this latter way, the morbid-minded way, as we might call it, healthy-mindedness pure and simple seems unspeakably blind and shallow. To the healthy-minded way, on the other hand, the way of the sick soul seems unmanly and diseased.

But he is unable to maintain that these two attitudes are in all respects equally valid. Speaking as an 'impartial onlooker' he comments:

> It seems to me that we are bound to say that morbid-mindedness ranges over the wider scale of experience, and that its

[1] The autobiographical article 'The Revolver in the Corner Cupboard' is revealing on the love of failure. Speaking of being hopelessly in love and in love with the hopelessness, Greene writes:

> 'At that age [seventeen] one may fall irrevocably in love with failure, and success of any kind loses half its savour before it is experienced. Such a love is surrendered once and for all to the singer at the pavement's edge, the bankrupt, the old school friend who wants to touch you for a dollar. Perhaps in many so conditioned it is the love for God that mainly survives, because in His eyes they can imagine themselves to remain always drab, seedy, unsuccessful, and therefore worthy of notice.'

[2] Uncollected in this country. It appears in the American edition of *Nineteen Stories*. See the bibliography p. 247.

> survey is the one that overlaps. . . . The normal process of life contains moments as bad as any of those which insane melancholy is filled with, moments in which radical evil gets its innings and takes its solid turn. . . . Our civilization is founded on the shambles. . . .

Goethe is usually thought of as 'healthy-minded', but at the age of seventy-five he wrote: 'I will say nothing against the course of my existence. But at bottom it has been nothing but pain and burden. . . . It is but the perpetual rolling of a rock that must be raised up again forever.'

This pessimistic view of life is in the long run simply an adult view. Youth, physical well-being, success may temporarily blunt the sharpness of our perception of its truth, but the optimism dependent on these accidents is always precarious. Job, Aeschylus, Dante, Pascal—the creative artist or thinker is not a Cheeryble Brother. But, if healthy-mindedness to most mature minds seems 'unspeakably blind and shallow', we do go about our business without too much discomfort ignoring the suspended sword. It is the intensity of the feelings amounting to nausea aroused in Greene by this outlook that gives it importance in relation to the novels. It is as if he had been born with an abnormally thin skin so that the anomalies and paradoxes of existence continually irritate his attention. The vertigo of the abyss is not necessarily religious at all, but there is a whiff of it to be found in Calvinism and Jansenism—we have our nostrils tickled by it occasionally in Stevenson: which may explain why Greene has words like Augustinian, Jansenist and even Manichee hurled at him sometimes by reviewers (including, too, his fellow-Catholics).

The notion of evil as an essential element of life makes hay of the simple-minded judgment that Greene is really a social critic who has somehow regrettably become mixed up with religion. There is a sense in which Greene's Catholicism is the least important thing about his outlook, that is to say, in connection with his books, but this affords no excuse for critics like George Woodcock and Arthur Calder-Marshall, who seem to hold that Greene's criticism of life is valuable in so far as it is a criticism of a badly organized society, but beyond that reactionary if not neurotic. Such criticism was more popular in the nineteen-thirties than it is today. It reminds one of the regrets then expressed by intellectuals for Mr. Eliot's movement from *The Waste Land* to *Ash-Wednesday* and 'Burnt Norton', the first of the *Four Quartets.* In *Journey Without Maps* Greene separates himself fastidiously from Utopian thinkers and the whole cheerful bumble of progressive thought.

> There are others, of course, who prefer to look a stage ahead, for whom Intourist provides cheap tickets into a plausible future, but my journey represented a distrust of any future based on what we are.

There is social criticism and hatred of avoidable cruelty and injustice in Greene's novels, but such injustice is always seen as part of a wider reference to the 'injustice' of life as a whole. The theme is explored most fully in *It's a Battlefield.*

It should be added that this view of Greene as a revolutionary writer who has taken the wrong turning ignores his impatience with the equation 'Evil=Social Maladjustment', expressed in so many barbed portraits of idealists, progressives and liberals. An example is Mr. Hands in the unfinished 'The Other Side of the Border' whose 'old tired grey face had peculiar nobility. For nearly seventy years he had been believing in human nature, against every evidence—it hadn't been good for his promotion in the bank. He was a Liberal, he thought men could govern themselves if they were left alone to it, that wealth did not corrupt and that statesmen loved their country. All that had marked his face until it was a kind of image of what he believed the world to be. But it was breaking up now. . . . If he lived long enough his face might become more probable, more like the other people's world.' If Greene's pity towards a class of person is ever narrowly circumscribed, it is towards the well-meaning woolly idealist, the believer in committees, protest meetings, petitions and week-end conferences.[1] There is often a streak of malice in his treatment of the critical self-righteous leaven in society which keeps itself 'well-informed' in international politics, has no time for religion, is usually emancipated about sex and child-rearing, and may be imagined in moments of inspiration devising international languages[2] and planning masculine dress reform. The malice throws Greene off his balance once or twice in *The Ministry of Fear*, in which there is a hint of war-time highbrow-baiting.

It would be possible to illustrate both the reading of experience and the resultant 'terror of life' from any of the novels, but the terror is not everywhere equally apparent. It leaps out of *Brighton Rock*: in other novels it is implied or emerges with comparative obliquity from the treatment of minor characters and events. It is mentioned by name in *The Man Within* (1929) when the 'hero', the young coward Andrews, speaks of 'a terror of life, of going on soiling himself and repenting and soiling himself again', and this passage can be set beside Scobie's reflections in *The Heart of the Matter* (1948).

> It seemed . . . that life was immeasurably long. Couldn't the test of man have been carried out in fewer years? Couldn't we have committed our first major sin at seven, have ruined ourselves for love or hate at ten, have clutched at redemption on a fifteen year-old death-bed?

Another of Scobie's reflections gives us the reading of life plainly—he is deputy-commissioner of police in Freetown. Why, he wonders, am I so fond of the place?

> Is it because here human nature hasn't had time to disguise itself? Nobody here could ever talk about a heaven on earth.

[1] He has not much patience with the 'bondieuserie' of respectable complacent middle-aged women. See the remarks of the whisky-priest in *The Power and the Glory*.

[2] See the 'Entrenationo' centre in *The Confidential Agent*.

Heaven remained rigidly in its proper place on the other side of death, and on this side flourished the injustices, the cruelties, the meannesses, that elsewhere people so cleverly hushed up. Here you could love human beings nearly as God loved them, knowing the worst.

Both the reading of life and the terror are found together in the following passage from *The Ministry of Fear*. Arthur Rowe, the central character of the book, has lost his adult memories as a result of a bomb explosion in London, and the clue to an important part of the book's meaning is in our understanding of the antithesis established between childish expectations of life and adult resignation to its real nature.

> In childhood we live under the brightness of immortality—heaven is as near and actual as the seaside. Behind the complicated details of the world stand the simplicities: God is good, the grown-up man or woman knows the answers to every question, there is such a thing as truth, and justice is as measured and faultless as a clock. Our heroes are simple: they are brave, they tell the truth, they are good swordsmen and they are never in the long run really defeated. That is why no later books satisfy us like those which were read to us in childhood—for those promised a world of great simplicity of which we knew the rules, but the later books are complicated and contradictory with experience: they are formed out of our contradictory memories—of the V.C. in the police-court dock, of the faked income-tax returns, the sins in corners, and the hollow voice of men we despise talking to us of courage and purity. The little duke is dead and betrayed and forgotten: we cannot recognize the villain and we suspect the hero and the world is a small cramped place. That is what people are saying all the time everywhere: the two great popular statements of faith are 'What a small place the world is' and 'I'm a stranger here myself'.

The experience here can be linked with various satellite obsessions. Emphasize the gap between real and ideal and we have an idea connected with that of man's double nature in *The Man Within* and *Rumour at Nightfall*: emphasize the corruption of youth and we have a preoccupation important in *England Made Me*, *Brighton Rock* and elsewhere.

I have said that the terror of life is expressed with grimmest force in *Brighton Rock*. Pinkie Brown, the proud warped adolescent gangster, whose sex-revulsion drives him to monstrous cruelties and whose reckless confidence has given him the leadership of a race-course gang, at one point turns on the little waitress Rose savagely for her pathetic 'Life's not so bad' with: 'I'll tell you what life is. It's jail. It's not knowing where to get some money. Worms and cataract, cancer. You hear 'em shrieking from the upper window—children being born. It's dying slowly.' And in the same novel the dreadful seediness which seems to Greene the most honest representation of the true nature of things is rendered with macabre intensity in the figure of the shyster lawyer Mr. Drewitt. He has come down in the world since his beginning at a minor public school ('Lancaster College. Not one of the great schools, but you'll find it in the Public Schools Year Book.'); his yellow middle-aged face is lined with legal decisions and the rebukes of magistrates. He lives in a soot-grimed house near the railway, shaken by shunting engines at all hours, hating his wife in the basement.

> 'I married beneath me,' Mr. Drewitt said. 'It was my tragic mistake. I was young. An affair of uncontrollable passion. I was a passionate man,' he said, wriggling with indigestion. 'You've seen her,' he said, 'now. My God.' He leant forward and said in a whisper: 'I watch the little typists go by carrying their little cases. I'm quite harmless. A man may watch . . . Listen to the old mole down there. She's ruined me.' His old lined face had taken a holiday—from bonhomie, from cunning, from the legal jest. It was a Sunday and it was itself. Mr. Drewitt said: 'You know what Mephistopheles said to Faustus when he asked where Hell was? He said: "Why, this is Hell, nor are we out of it"'.

Drewitt is another Greene grotesque. He reminds us of Acky, Minty and the more genially imagined, absurd Mr. Rennit of the Orthotex Inquiry Bureau, whose vision of a post-war 'brave new world' is of more broken lives and more divorces. His bitterest complaint is against identity cards, which make registration at hotels so difficult—'You can't prove anything from cars.' These stunted perverse natures come from the same black places of the imagination as Dickens's Quilp or Krook, but Greene is more aware of their origin and the serious use to be made of them.

'Why, this is Hell, nor are we out of it.' It would have been natural to recall the famous description of a fallen world in Newman's *Apologia Pro Vita Sua* even if it had not appeared as one of the epigraphs to *The Lawless Roads*. 'To consider the world,' writes Newman, '. . . the greatness and littleness of man, his far-reaching aims, his short duration, the curtain hung over his futurity, the disappointments of life, the defeat of good, the success of evil, physical pain, mental anguish, the prevalence and intensity of sin, the pervading idolatries, the corruptions, the dreary hopeless irreligion, that condition of the whole race, so fearfully yet exactly described in the Apostle's words, "having no hope, and without God in the world"—all this is a vision to dizzy and appal . . .' Like Greene, Newman finds the nature of existence 'heartpiercing, reason-bewildering'.

> I can only answer, that either there is no Creator, or this living society of men is in a true sense discarded from His presence . . . *if* there be a God, *since* there is a God, the human race is implicated in some terrible aboriginal calamity.

So close indeed are Newman's and Greene's pictures of a fallen world that it may be asked how I could assert earlier that Greene's Catholicism is of minor importance in studying his main outlook on which the obsessions in the novels depend. The answer is a simple matter of timing.

The evidence of passages in *Journey Without Maps* and *The Lawless Roads*, together with that of certain less well-known essays, notably 'Heroes are Made in Childhood' and 'The Revolver in the Corner Cupboard', proves that what is substantially the Greene outlook exists at much earlier date than his conversation to Catholicism, which took place in 1926. It springs ultimately from the unhappiness probed by him in childhood—he was, it should be remembered, a schoolboy at Berkhamsted, where his father was headmaster.[1] An extract from 'Heroes Are Made in Childhood' will help to make the chronology clear. Greene is recalling the reading of Marjorie Bowen's historical romance *The Viper of Milan* and asking why it was so important to him.

> On the surface *The Viper of Milan* is only the story of a war between Gian Galeazzo Visconti, Duke of Milan, and Mastino della Scala, Duke of Verona, told with zest and cunning and an amazing pictorial sense. Why did it creep in and colour and explain the terrible living world of the stone stairs and the never quiet dormitory? It was no good in that real world to dream that one would ever be a Sir Henry Curtis, but della Scala who at last turned from an honesty that never paid and betrayed his friends and died dishonoured and a failure even at treachery—it was easier for a child to escape behind his mask. As for Visconti, with his beauty, his patience and his genius for evil, I had watched him pass by many a time in his black Sunday suit smelling of mothballs. His name was Carter. He exercised terror from a distance like a snowcloud over the young fields. Goodness has only once found a perfect incarnation in a human body and never will again, but evil can always find a home there. Human nature is not black and white but black and grey. I read all that in *The Viper of Milan* and I looked round and I saw that it was so.
>
> There was another theme I found there. At the end of *The Viper of Milan* you will remember if you have once read it the great scene of complete success—della Scala is dead, Ferrara, Verona, Novara, Mantua have all fallen . . . Visconti sits and jokes in the wine light. I was not on the classical side or I would have discovered, I suppose, in Greek literature instead of in Miss Bowen's novel, the sense of doom that lies over success—

[1] See Greene's contribution, 'The Last Word', to *The Old School* (1934), an anthology of school reminiscences by various writers, edited by him.

> the feeling that the pendulum is about to swing. That too made sense; one looked around and saw the doomed everywhere—the champion runner who would one day sag over the tape; the head of the school who would atone, poor devil, during forty dreary undistinguished years. . . . *Anyway she had given me my pattern—religion later might explain it to me in other terms, but the pattern was already there*—perfect evil walking the world where perfect good can never walk again, and only the pendulum ensures that after all in the end justice is done.

This sets echoes ringing from our reading of all the later Greene novels[1], but I have italicized the lines with the strongest bearing on the present argument. Obsessions as strong as Greene's have deeper roots than can be traced to a course of apologetics on the top of a Nottingham tram and a religious conversion in one's early twenties[2]: they go back at least as far as 'the terrible living world of the stone stairs and the never quiet dormitory.' The first chapter of *The Lawless Roads* makes clear the singularity of Greene's position as a schoolboy at Berkhamsted, living 'on the border', poised between the two adjoining but utterly different countries of home and school, and divided in his allegiance because hate is 'quite as powerful a tie' as love. He tells us of the horrors of classroom and pitchpine-partitioned dormitory from which he would escape surreptitiously to darkness and solitude with the rabbit 'restlessly cropping near the croquet hoops'. It was then that 'faith came to one—shapelessly without dogma . . .' The Penny Catechism declares that man is prone to evil from his very childhood, but before Greene had ever heard of the catechism he had 'looked round and seen that it was so'. It is because all his ideas have been conceived personally and proved on his pulses that he is not so much a 'Catholic novelist', even

[1] To take a single example: 'forty dreary undistinguished years'—and we think of Buddy Ferguson, the popular bouncing medical student in *A Gun for Sale,* living in his 'vivid vulgar way for five years before the long provincial interment of a life-time'.

[2] *Journey Without Maps,* Pt. II, Chap. I, 'New Country'.

in the later books where Mauriac is a master, as, in his own words, a 'novelist who is a Catholic'.[1]

The importance of the idea of childhood to any appraisal of Greene's work should be evident from much of this introductory chapter. It was the aptness of Marjorie Bowen's portrait of Renaissance Italy to his own experience of school-life at Berkhamsted that made the reading of *The Viper of Milan* the moment when 'the future for better or worse really struck'. Greene goes along with innumerable poets and other writers in accepting a golden age of innocence in earliest years, but what he stresses is how soon it is threatened even in childhood—'Hell lay about them in their infancy'—and how quickly and inevitably innocence and the capacity for simple, uncomplicated happiness leak away.

There are few novelists who have been so content as Greene simply to explore in their books the meaning of the 'certainties' given to them in their early years: it is a kind of fidelity less unusual among poets. 'I do not know for whom it is I write,' says Bernanos in *Les Enfants Humiliés*, 'but I do know why I write. I write to justify myself. In whose eyes? I have told you before . . . in the eyes of the child that I was. Whether that child speaks to me any longer or not, I shall never acknowledge his silence; I shall keep on answering him'. Greene might have said this. Pinkie and Rose in *Brighton Rock*, Anthony Farrant in *England Made Me*, Rose Cullen in *The Confidential Agent*, Helen Rolt in *The Heart of the Matter*—these are only a few of the characters understood in terms of childhood with its phobias, disciplines and secrecies. 'People change,' says Rose in *Brighton Rock*. 'Oh, no they

[1] These phrases are quoted from Greene's first letter in *Why Do I Write?* (1948), an exchange of views between Elizabeth Bowen, Greene and V. S. Pritchett. Greene acknowledges that the attempt to deal with Catholic themes in his novels is owed to the reading of Mauriac. As a director of Messrs. Eyre and Spottiswoode he was responsible for the project of an English edition of all Mauriac's novels. Several volumes have now appeared.

don't', replies the comfortable Ida. 'Look at me. I've never changed. It's like those sticks of rock: bite it all the way down, you'll still read Brighton. That's human nature.'[1]

People do not change: they grow older and accumulate memories. If childhood is 'that time of life when, however miserable we are, we have expectations', then to be mature is to know that the future has already struck—

In the lost boyhood of Judas
Christ was betrayed

—that a life and (Greene would add) a death have been chosen. We remember the unhappy dentist in *The Power and the Glory*, an exile in a fever-ridden Mexican state, separated from wife and children, drained of all initiative by the heat and the prevailing shoddiness, a typical Greene figure of decay.

> Mr. Tench's father had been a dentist too—his first memory was finding a discarded cast in a waste-paper basket—the rough toothless gaping mouth of clay, like something dug up in Dorset—Neanderthal or Pithecanthropus. It had been his favourite toy: they tried to tempt him with Meccano: but fate had struck. There is always one moment in childhood when the door opens and lets the future in.

Whenever we read about children or the state of childhood in Greene's novels we are near to his central obsession with the terror of life and its origin in his early years. If it should still appear rash to suggest such a direct relationship between Greene's life and fiction, then the reading of 'The Revolver in the Corner Cupboard' is recommended. Both Andrews and Scobie, heroes respectively of his first and his latest novel,

[1] Cf. Mauriac, *A Woman of the Pharisees*: 'People do not change. At my age one can have no illusions on that point: but they do quite often turn back to what they were once and show again those very characteristics which they have striven tirelessly, through a whole lifetime, to suppress. This does not mean that they necessarily end by succumbing to what is worst in themselves. God is very often the good temptation to which many human beings in the long run yield.'

commit suicide. Suicide is the ultimate escape—life, not the police or a political rival, is the enemy evaded. In 'The Revolver in the Corner Cupboard' Greene takes us behind the scenes of his adolescence. He describes how at the age of seventeen, bored and miserably and romantically in love with his sister's governess, he played a 'game' with a revolver and a single live charge. The charge was inserted without looking, the chambers twirled, the revolver put to the head and the trigger pulled. Greene had discovered 'that it was possible to enjoy again the visible world by risking its total loss'. This is not unconnected with the acceptance of the rigours of the Liberian journey[1], and I believe it is relevant to an understanding of *The Power and the Glory* and *The Heart of the Matter* where experience becomes significant because of the possibility of damnation, of risking (in the theological sense) a total loss; but, more simply, here we have in Greene's own experience a preoccupation attributed to several of his fictitious characters. The ambiguous attempt at suicide was not an isolated act. Greene tells us that he went on playing this 'game' even as an Oxford undergraduate, and that before the first attempt with the revolver there was a series of acts 'which my elders would have regarded as neurotic, but which I still consider to have been under the circumstances highly reasonable'.

> There had been for example, perhaps five or six years before, the disappointing morning in the dark room by the linen cupboard on the eve of term when I had patiently drunk a quantity of hypo under the impression that it was poisonous: on another occasion the blue glass bottle of hay-fever lotion which as it contained a small quantity of cocaine had probably been good

[1] Cf. *Journey Without Maps*, Pt. III, Chap. 1, 'The Lowland': 'The pain I had been feeling for some days now in my stomach seemed to get worse at the news . . . I was scared in the same way as I had been in England when I suddenly found that my plans had gone too far for me to back out of the Liberian journey . . . I was discovering in myself a thing I thought I had never possessed: a love of life.'

> for my mood: the bunch of deadly nightshade that I had eaten with only a slight narcotic effect: the twenty aspirin I had taken before swimming in the empty out-of-term school baths (I can still remember the curious sensation of swimming through wool) . . .

All these acts were rebellious protests against 'the horrible confinement and publicity of school'. They culminated in Greene's running away—he hid on Berkhamsted Common where he went with the revolver a few years later. The misery of school stretched out to spoil even the holidays. The first few days were 'light, space and silence', a rest for jangled nerves, but after that boredom set in—freedom, lacking misery's intensity, was tedious. Some ex-servicemen find peace tedious in the same way.

This boredom, a poor relation of Baudelaire's *ennui* and Leopardi's *noia*, is a definite part of the obsessional terror of life. It was fixed, Greene explains, by the psycho-analysis that followed his running away from school.

> For years, it seems to me, I could take no aesthetic interest in any visual thing at all: staring at a sight that others assured me was beautiful I would feel nothing.

Existence became a tedious routine, a migraine punctuated by the stabs of active fears. The notion can be related to something said in the previous paragraph. One reason for Greene's constant use of melodrama is his feeling, whether fully conscious or not, that existence can only be dramatic when routine is broken. For example, the recurrent pursuit formula takes a central character across other people's routine lives, but his life is one in which the unexpected always happens. Now that Greene consciously poses the actions of his characters against a supernatural screen which magnifies them and 'taints' the most ordinary scenes and conversations with eternity, there may be less need for the melodramatic. Certainly melodrama was less in evidence in *The Heart of the Matter*, which owed its sustained interest as much to the method of storytelling as to the story told.[1]

It is not easy to discuss Greene's interest in the form of the novel without dividing his work into phases of development which, like all such divisions, have only a very shadowy reality. The first phase is the most distinct and to it belong the three immature novels *The Man Within*, *The Name of Action* and *Rumour at Nightfall*, in which the obsessions are sometimes at war with the probability of the narrative. The second phase begins with *Stamboul Train*, the first entertainment and the first book really to employ a contemporary setting, and extends to the publication of *Brighton Rock*. *England Made Me* is the most successful novel of this phase. The third and last phase includes *Brighton Rock* and, among later books, *The Power and the Glory* and *The Heart of the Matter*.

The three novels of the last phase are associated by their common interest in the theme of damnation—their central characters are Catholics—and by the greater explicitness of the 'Morality' element when they are compared with *England Made Me*. This would be enough to distinguish them, but there is the added fact that by 1938 Greene had finished assimilating influences. The echoes of Conrad, Joyce, James and Virginia Woolf to be detected in *It's a Battlefield* and *England Made Me* no longer occur. Yet in some ways *Brighton Rock* hovers between the two groups; for example, in dealing with Brighton racecourse gangs it employs a topical subject, just as in *England Made Me* Greene uses Kreuger, the Swedish match-king, for his portrait of the imaginary capitalist Krogh.[2]

In Greene's second phase the obsessional ideas in the novels and entertainments are sunk further into the texture of the life described than in the third phase. At first sight this looks like a distortion of the usual course of a writer's development by

[1] Mr. Greene tells me that he has made a positive attempt to exclude melodrama from the novel now being written.

[2] For convenience *Brighton Rock* is discussed in Chapter 4 with two 'entertainments', rather than in Chapter 5.

which theme and representation of reality increasingly tend to interpenetrate as he matures. I explain the discrepancy by noticing that the 'heroes' of the last group of novels—Pinkie, the whisky priest, Scobie—are capable, for all their mutual disparity, of being identified with Greene himself with a directness that does not exist for any characters in the novels of the second period. Conrad Drover in *It's a Battlefield* may be partly a projection of Greene's experience in the sense mentioned, but the significant interest in this novel is shared between Conrad, the Commissioner and one or two other figures. Again, although Kate's 'point of view' may be said to furnish a unity for *England Made Me*, at different times the centrality of the viewing consciousness is possessed by Krogh and Anthony Farrant. It is at this point that the division of Greene's work into phases begins to seem high-handed. It is fatally easy to impose an order on the novels for the sake of finding consistency in their author's development. Critics are apt to forget that inconsistency itself may be quite normal.

The names of the novelists spoken of by Greene with affection and admiration—Conrad, Ford Madox Ford (for *The Good Soldier*), Henry James and François Mauriac—suggest closely enough the kind of novel approved by him. If one may speak loosely, he by-passes the experimental novel of the nineteen-twenties and early nineteen-thirties, where in the more obvious senses moral preoccupations are at a minimum, and form is either lyrical, a matter of mood, or is artificially imposed on material that hardly appears to be selected at all. Equally he rejects what is unfortunately still widely known as 'the traditional English novel'.

There is a simple way of making clear what I mean by this phrase. In reading *Passage to India*, *The Spoils of Poynton*, *Sons and Lovers* or *Under Western Eyes* we need to pay the kind of attention to verbal and structural niceties that we pay as a matter of course even to minor poetry, but rightly consider inappropriate in reading Smollett and Thackeray or, to take more recent examples, Galsworthy and Arnold Bennett.

Greene requires to be read with this 'poetic' attention. This is not to compare him in esteem with James or Conrad, but it is to rank him with them as a poet-novelist, a writer seriously and devotedly concerned with the artistic problems arising from the wish to express a way of looking at the world. From the technical point of view Greene has probably learnt most from these two writers[1]: the influence of Mauriac appears mainly in the choice of subject.

The question of the attention with which the 'poetic' novel needs to be read is not directly concerned with the degree to which the obsessional ideas are obtrusive in any particular piece of fiction. I should not like to be dogmatic about the depth at which a novelist should bury his obsessions. Hardy's recurrent themes, as Greene has pointed out, can be isolated fairly easily, whereas the care Henry James took to dramatize his material makes the investigation of them in his novels a business of some delicacy. In my view Henry James is a greater novelist than Thomas Hardy, but I am not sure that this has much to do with unobtrusiveness of theme. I observe that in Greene, as in Hardy and Conrad, the obsessions are always near the surface and provide the flavour of the Morality that seems to cling to their novels; that in Mauriac, as in James, the obsessions are much less visible. Mauriac is an important illustration because his reading of experience is as idiosyncratic as Greene's, indeed not unlike it, yet in his books the ruling ideas are less imposed, the Morality flavour much fainter. On the whole I incline to think that the great novelists bury their obsessional themes as nearly out of sight as possible, but I have to remind myself that very remarkable novels may be written on the compositional

[1] For the influence of James, see Greene's remark in Paul Rostenne's *Graham Greene, témoin des temps tragiques* (1949). In the Lettre-Préface he speaks of 'l'énorme influence exercée en Angleterre sur ma génération par le livre de M. Percy Lubbock: *The Craft of Fiction* par lequel tant d'entre nous furent initiés à la technique de Henry James et à l'importance du "point de vue".'

principle that the ruling ideas should be plainly visible, and that part of our legitimate pleasure in form may derive from their visibility. In both types of poetic novel—that in which the obsessions are more and that in which they are less evident—reading involves our being alive to the meaning that is danced, so to speak, by the form of the novel: that form may be looked on as a movement, including the larger structural gestures made by the grouping of characters and incidents for parallel and contrast, and the smaller ones made by related images and various verbal refinements.

Greene's novels from *It's a Battlefield* onward belong to the type of poetic novel in which the obsessions are close to the surface: in them structure is used emphatically alongside character and situation to project the total poetic meaning. The recipe is near enough to a commonly accepted view of Elizabethan and Jacobean drama to make a statement of it in Greene's *The British Dramatists* apposite here:

> It must be remembered that we are still within the period of the Morality: they are being acted yet in the country districts: they had been absorbed by Shakespeare, just as much as he absorbed the plays of Marlowe, and the abstraction . . . still rules the play. And rightly. Here is the watershed between the morality and the play of character: the tension between the two is perfectly kept: there is dialectical perfection. After Shakespeare, character—which was to have its dramatic triumphs—won a too-costly victory.

It may be, of course, that the greater fluidity of the novel form makes it advisable for the novelist to do what is not required of the poetic dramatist—to hide his themes and disguise the structure of his books. It may be that the most ambitious kind of novel can only be created in this way—I am inclined, as I say, to think so—but I can see no reason why a novelist should not employ with the necessary variations the method of the poetic dramatist. In reading Greene's novels and entertainments it may be more useful to think of the structure of *The Duchess of Malfi* than that of *Barchester Towers* or *The Newcomes*.[1]

[1] Webster's play is not chosen quite at random. See 'John Webster' in Lord David Cecil's *Poets and Story-tellers*:

> A hostile critic might say that the impression [the plays] make is all the same, extravagant, irrational and melodramatic . . . good Grand Guignol is bad tragedy. Once again such a criticism shows a failure to grasp the nature of Webster's art . . . the battle of heaven and hell cannot be convincingly conveyed in a mode of humdrum everyday realism. . . . The wild and bloody conventions of Elizabethan melodrama provided a most appropriate vehicle for conveying his hell-haunted vision of human existence.

CHAPTER TWO

THE DIVIDED MIND

The Man Within (1929)
The Name of Action (1931)
Rumour at Nightfall (1932)

There must be sorrow if there can be love.

W. H. AUDEN

It was on the moral side, and in my own person, that I learned to recognize the thorough and primitive duality of man; I saw that, of the two natures that contended in the field of my consciousness, even if I could rightly be said to be either, it was only because I was radically both; and from an early date . . . I had learned to dwell with pleasure, as a beloved daydream, on the thought of the separation of these elements.

The Strange Case of Dr. Jekyll and Mr. Hyde,
R. L. STEVENSON

I

THE actual bulk of Graham Greene's work sets a problem of division and grouping to the commentator, but there are good reasons for isolating the three early novels and examining them separately. Anyone familiar with one or two of the later novels, say *A Gun for Sale* and *England Made Me*, and having therefore a definite but unanalysed and only partially correct sense of what constitutes their author's world—the understanding and misunderstanding we have of a writer who is at once highly individual and imperfectly known to us—will feel lost if he picks up *The Man Within*, *The Name of Action* or *Rumour at Nightfall*; indeed, at a first reading, he may not recognize the same hand. This is the most general form our excuse for isolating the early books can take, but it is useful to particularize.

In the first place, then, Greene himself looks on them as *juvenilia* and has not allowed them to be included in the collection of his novels now being issued by William Heinemann. The collected edition offers a revised text and Greene felt that no revision of these early books, short of a complete re-writing, would be satisfactory.[1] He would not be sorry, I fancy, to have them forgotten, and two, *The Name of Action* (1930) and *Rumour at Nightfall* (1932), are nearly forgotten—it was not easy to come by copies of them for this study—though *The Man Within* (1929), his first novel, can still be found in lending libraries and has had a new lease of life since the film version with the same title.

Again, all three novels pre-date Greene's division of his fiction into novels and 'entertainments', and, while their backgrounds are various, they do possess a sameness, partly thematic, partly due to a lack of complication in plot, a somewhat phosphorescent romantic sensibility, and an indulged fondness for 'fine writing'. This indulgence slows the tempo of the storytelling unbearably, so that in *Rumour at Nightfall* the action often seems to be taking place in slow motion.

A third reason for segregating the early novels lies in their settings. *The Man Within* and *Rumour at Nightfall*, unlike any of the later books, are historical novels, while *The Name of Action*, nominally set in the nineteen-twenties, is a Ruritanian fantasy almost equally divorced from the representation of the contemporary scene. *The Man Within* is placed in Sussex at the beginning of the nineteenth century with smug-

[1] Revision of the novels in the collected edition is mainly stylistic, but extends to the reconstruction of whole episodes—an example is the Communist meeting in *It's a Battlefield*.

glers and Bow Street Runners, and care has evidently been taken to avoid anachronisms in the court procedure of one of the principal scenes. *Rumour at Nightfall* deals with a newspaper correspondent in Spain in the eighteen-seventies and what happens to him in the aftermath of the Carlist troubles. This matter of historical setting is worth a moment's pause, because the 'single-minded attempt to render the highest kind of justice to the visible universe'—Conrad's definition of art—is certainly not made easier by placing characters who are to project the author's ideas dramatically in what must be, for all his care, a blurred and unreal background, and by having them speak in phrases and idioms which cannot be checked by the rise and fall of any living voice. Instead of the verisimilitude of the contemporary scene being employed to suggest the 'truth' of the author's attitudes—that is to say, their relevant richness in a particular context—we have the historical setting creating problems of its own.

Finally, the early novels form a separate unit of Greene's work because of the nature of the literary influences which have helped to fashion them. With greater or less degrees of certainty we can observe the shadows of Mauriac, Péguy and Henry James lying across the later novels, but they do not fall here. Greene did not begin to read James seriously until the middle of the nineteen-thirties, or French writers of the Catholic literary renaissance until a little later again. The most important positive influences to be detected are those of Stevenson and Conrad. Greene's family-tie with Stevenson has been noted, and in 1949 he announced his intention of producing a new Stevenson biography. He writes about Walter de la Mare's prose as 'unequalled in its richness since the death of James, or dare one, at this date, say Robert Louis Stevenson', and he goes on to admire Stevenson's interest in language and his consciousness that there is a question of vocabulary for the writer. But Stevenson was appreciated in these early Greene novels for more than style, for more, too, than romantic panache and a storytelling gift:

there was the 'sense of good and evil' spoken of in a review of film-versions of *Treasure Island* and *Midshipman Easy*.

> *Treasure Island* contains, as *Midshipman Easy* does not, a sense of good and evil. Even a child can recognize the greater dignity and depths of this Scottish presbyterian's *Mansoul* written in terms of an adventure story for a boy's magazine.

Further, the three early Greene novels deal with man's double nature, and he was inevitably interested therefore in the author of *The Strange Case of Dr. Jekyll and Mr. Hyde* and *Weir of Hermiston*. Greene's preoccupation with the theme of the divided mind is, of course, more than literary in origin, and it continues more subtly in his later books, but in the special form it takes in the early novels it owes something to a reading of Stevenson.

Like Stevenson, Conrad appealed to Greene for various reasons. I have mentioned the phosphorescent romantic sensibility of the early novels, and whatever Greene can now find to say dispassionately in praise of Stevenson's language, I feel that a naive liking for mannerism in style was one of the things that attracted him to both these writers while he was at work on *Rumour at Nightfall*. In this novel, undoubtedly Greene's worst, the influence of the dangerous, romantic Conrad of *The Arrow of Gold* can be felt immediately. Both stories have their connection with the attempt of Don Carlos de Bourbon on the Spanish throne; both have irritating romantic heroines—Greene's Eulelia Monti has something of Doña Rita's 'mystery' and 'unfathomable appeal' in spite of the obvious differences between the two characters; and in each a similar inflation of style can be found at climactic moments. Here, for example, is Conrad spreading the butter too thick in *The Arrow of Gold*—the phrase is M. C. Bradbrook's:

> But there was an invincible need of gaiety in her heart. She said funnily, looking at the arrow sparkling in the gas light: 'Ah! That poor philistinish ornament!'

An echo of our early days, not more innocent but so much more youthful, was in her tone; and we both, as if touched with poignant regret, looked at each other with enlightened eyes.

'Yes,' I said, 'how far away all this is. And you wouldn't leave that object behind when you came last in here. Perhaps it is for that reason it haunted me—mostly at night. I dreamed of you sometimes as a huntress nymph gleaming white through the foliage and throwing this arrow like a dart straight at my heart. But it never reached it. It always fell at my feet as I woke up. The huntress never meant to strike down that particular quarry.'

'The huntress was wild but she was not evil. And she was no nymph, but only a goatherd girl. Dream of her no more, my dear.'

I had the strength of mind to make a sign of assent and busied myself arranging a couple of pillows at one end of the sofa. 'Upon my soul, goatherd, you are not responsible,' I said, 'you are not! Lay down that uneasy head', I continued, forcing a half-playful note into my immense sadness, 'that has even dreamed of a crown—but not for itself.'

In *Rumour at Nightfall* Greene spreads the same butter:

'Of course you are afraid,' she said. 'So am I afraid. That is why we will do it.' She laughed at him, mocked the shadow on his mind, his sense of responsibility. 'It will be fun. Two cowards pulling—what is your phrase?—his ear.' He tried with heavy steps to climb to her mood of laughter, but found the ledge insecure, the foothold treacherous, the fall too terrifying. She said, with laughter again, but laughter so low and natural and unconscious of itself that it seemed the abstract form of mirth, 'For me. For my sake. You have never even told me that you love me.'

He said in a passing reflection of her own light mood. 'It seemed unnecessary.' She protested: 'You leave so much to me.' It was evident that she considered the lightness of his reply a victory, which must be pressed home with mockery. 'You are so superior. You keep so silent, taking our love, my love, your friend's love. We do not get much in return for it. What are you doing all the time?'

These passages have been chosen almost at random, but in

both there is the same painful, operatic archness and the same straining after effect. 'Forcing a half-playful note into my immense sadness', writes Conrad, but the dialogue does not give us the sadness and we have to guess what 'a half-playful note' would be. Greene is playing the same confidence trick with Eulelia Monti's extraordinary laughter, 'laughter so low and natural and unconscious of itself that it seemed the abstract form of mirth'. In the pamphlet *Why do I Write?* Greene speaks of the writer's duty of 'telling the truth'.

> I don't mean anything flamboyant by the phrase 'telling the truth': I don't mean exposing anything. By truth I mean accuracy—it is largely a matter of style. It is my duty to society not to write: 'I stood above a bottomless gulf' or 'going downstairs, I got into a taxi', because these statements are untrue. My characters must not go white in the face or tremble like leaves, not because these phrases are clichés but because they are untrue. This is not only a matter of the artistic conscience but of the social conscience too. We already see the effect of the popular novel on popular thought. Every time a phrase like one of these passes into the mind uncriticized, it muddies the stream of thought.

In the three early novels characters do stand above bottomless gulfs and go white in the face. The style of *Rumour at Nightfall* particularly is as often an obstacle to communication as an instrument of it. It was proper enough for the younger Greene to wish to write prose and not simply to throw down words on a page, and reasonable to see what he could pick up from Conrad and Stevenson. That must be the excuse for the Brumma'gem jewellery of the worst parts of the early books: the badness sprang not from indifference or carelessness, but from a desire to write well.

It would be intolerable to limit Conrad's influence on Greene even at this period to support for an impulse to overwrite. The justification for discussing first the effect on style is that it is the most obvious effect, but Conrad's *The Secret Sharer* may have done as much as *Dr. Jekyll and Mr. Hyde* to turn Greene's attention to the theme of the *alter ego*, while the theme of man's double nature in a less specialized form is evident in *Lord Jim*, where it is explored, as in *The Man Within*, in terms of cowardice and conscience. More broadly, Greene may be said to have been drawn to Conrad because of the latter's feeling for the novel as something to be made artfully, a piece of craftmanship—and in these early novels the contrivance of the story (the balancing of one section of the tale against another, the use of contrast, the placing of minor climaxes and so on) is sound if still in a rudimentary way. There is at least nothing of the *Bildungsroman* about them, as there is about the first novels of so many writers who are not really novelists at all. The self-consciousness that betrayed Greene into over-writing acted in this matter as a safeguard. He was not able to confuse an easy 'sensitive' transcript of experience with a novel.

The question of form in Conrad's novels is closely connected with his way of interpreting human experience, and Greene was also drawn to the Conrad who was busy with the moral implications of 'a few simple ideas'. In a review of Chaplin's film *Modern Times* he writes:

> Mr. Chaplin has, like Conrad, 'a few simple ideas'; they could be expressed in much the same phrases; courage, loyalty, labour: against the same nihilistic background of purposeless suffering. 'Mistah Kurtz—he dead.' These ideas are not enough for a reformer, but they have proved amply sufficient for an artist.

Whatever the worth of this not very serious comparison, it underlines something Greene found in Conrad, and this something, a quality of moral perception, a taking seriously of human behaviour, a recognition that choices have to be made and that people are responsible for them, implies a 'vertebrate' structure for the novels in which it is contained.

This is fairly obvious, but Greene takes it a little further. Conrad was concerned with 'the importance of the human act', and a conviction that human behaviour is purposeful, Greene holds, ultimately depends on 'the religious sense'. In an essay on Mauriac's *A Woman of the Pharisees* he argues that the religious sense has been lost to the novelist since the death of Henry James, and that the writer, 'unconsciously perhaps aware of his predicament', has created the subjective novel.

> It was as if he thought by mining into layers of personality hitherto untouched he could unearth the secret of 'importance', but in these mining operations he lost yet another dimension. The visible world for him ceased to exist as completely as the spiritual. Mrs. Dalloway walking down Regent Street was aware of the glitter of shop windows, the smooth passage of cars, the conversation of shoppers, but it was only a Regent Street seen by Mrs. Dalloway that was conveyed to the reader: a charming whimsical rather sentimental prose poem was what Regent Street had become.

These remarks by Greene are recent. Certainly in 1929 his understanding of Conrad was incomplete, but it contained an implicit approval of him on two important counts: first, Conrad did not make all experience equally luminous as exponents of the stream-of-consciousness technique have tended to do; second, Conrad's artistic success justified Greene in declaring himself for what I have called the 'vertebrate' novel. Greene, like Conrad, works with 'a few simple ideas'.

Conrad and Stevenson are literary influences: that is to say, they both supplied Greene with ideas and attitudes (or confirmed a bent towards a chosen way of registering experience) and at the same time helped him to organize his vision by teaching him how to construct his stories and in what language to tell them. There were other influences, some dating back to childhood, almost or quite as important, but not in this special sense literary at all. In the already quoted 'Heroes are Made in Childhood' Greene suggests that 'it is only in childhood that books have any deep influence on our lives'. If his journeys to Africa and his African books owe something, as he claims, to a reading in boyhood of Rider

Haggard's *King Solomon's Mines*, then it is reasonable to assume that the historical settings of *The Man Within* and *Rumour at Nightfall* (as well as that of an unpublished novel earlier than either) owe something to a confessed passion for Marjorie Bowen's *The Viper of Milan*.

> But when—perhaps I was fourteen at the time—I took Miss Marjorie Bowen's *The Viper of Milan* from the library shelf, the future for better or worse really struck. From that moment I began to write. . . . Imitation after imitation of Miss Bowen's magnificent novel went into exercise books—stories of sixteenth-century Italy or twelfth-century England marked with enormous brutality and a despairing romanticism. It was as if I had been supplied once and for all with a subject.

Similarly it is permissible to think of Anthony Hope in reading *The Name of Action*, since Greene has told us how he swallowed 'the clever, brittle sentiment' of *The Prisoner of Zenda* as a young adolescent, and how, much earlier, in 1911, one of the first films he saw was adapted from Hope's *Sophy of Kravonia*. 'I can hear still the rumble of the Queen's guns crossing the high Kravonian pass beaten hollowly out on a single piano.'

Marjorie Bowen, Anthony Hope, Robert Louis Stevenson, Conrad: what is common to this odd group of writers is some kind of romanticism. Greene's stories in school exercise-books were characterized by an 'enormous brutality and a despairing romanticism'. The schoolboy's love of Rider Haggard's Sir Henry Curtis 'perched upon a rock bleeding from a dozen wounds but fighting on . . . against the hordes of Twala' was modified by sophistication into a liking for authors who provided him with violence and romantic high principles preferably in an unusual setting, but at the same time exhibited a saving adult quality of observation in certain directions. The romantic courtship of Archie Weir and Kirstie in *Weir of Hermiston* is, as it were, 'authenticated' by the accuracy of Stevenson's description of the kirk where Archie first notices her with its box-pew and solid plaided congregation; and the brutality of the Elliott brothers avenging the death of their father is similarly made convincing. One of them, Hob, sees a wounded murderer lying in the darkness and crying for help. 'Damn you', he says as he catches the glint of the man's white teeth, 'ye hae your teeth, hae ye?' and he rides his horse to trample the dying man. Much of Conrad can be read in the same light. At the end of *Victory* there are 'more dead in this affair—more white people, I mean—than have been killed in many of the battles of the last Achin war', and not only the Jacobean death-roll but the strangeness of Lena's passion for Heyst and the sinister brutality of the criminal trio, Mr. Jones, Ricardo and Pedro, the sub-human alligator-hunter, must have greatly appealed to the younger Greene.[1] In *Under Western Eyes* the betrayal and expiation themes, always important in Greene's novels, and the horrible breaking of the drums of Razumov's ears would bid for his attention.

'The "taste" of the poet is, at bottom and so far as the poet in him prevails over everything else,' writes Henry James in the preface to *The Golden Bowl*, 'his active sense of life.' It is the active sense of life which is missing in Graham Greene's early books. He is too impatient at this stage of his development simply to underline certain elements of actual life, he must manhandle experience itself, distort it to serve his interests. Edwin Muir finds this manipulation even in the mature novels. 'Everything', he says, 'is shown up in a harsh light and casts fantastic shadows.' Perhaps this does less than justice to the subtlety of some of the later books, but it is unquestionably true of the three novels with which I am now dealing.

An obvious weakness, then, of *The Man Within*, *The Name of Action* and *Rumour at Nightfall* is that in them Greene is concerned with ideas at the expense of the visible world, and that the ideas—notably of the sex-relationship between men

[1] The mature Greene still brackets Conrad's *Victory* with *The Spoils of Poynton* by Henry James as two of the great novels of the last fifty years.

and women—unchecked by the continuous pressure of actuality, are too crudely obsessive. He is not yet a poet in James's sense, only a romantic versifier with streaks of poetry. *Stamboul Train* (1932), the book that follows *Rumour at Nightfall*, tends to go too far in the opposite direction. Its fidelity to everyday appearances is partly at the expense of the compulsion to embody ideas. *It's a Battlefield* (1934) is probably the first novel in which Greene does equal justice to ideas and appearances.

In the introductory chapter it was urged that the themes, obsessions or ruling ideas (as they have been called indifferently) of Greene's novels hold from first to last and are related to a key obsession or ground of obsessions defined as a 'terror of life'. To say so is not to deny that in the first three novels a theme may be given an emphasis peculiar to this stage of Greene's development, or that certain minor obsessions may occur recognizably only in them. Thus the themes of the double nature of man and of pity occur in the early novels and in the most recent, *The Power and the Glory* and *The Heart of the Matter*; but in the early novels the theme of man's double nature is dominant and that of pity recessive, while in the latest novels the opposite is true. Again, a variant of the theme of man's double nature occurs in *Rumour at Nightfall*, and more ambiguously in the other two early novels, and is peculiar to the early stage of Greene's development: in all three books different aspects of what may be thought of as a 'whole' single nature become separate characters. This is quite consciously worked out in *Rumour at Nightfall* where Chase, the newspaper correspondent, and his friend Crane are meant to be recognized as two sides of a single personality, but there is an approach to it in *The Name of Action* where the 'hero', the moneyed Oliver Chant, seems to stand uncertainly between Joseph Kapper, poet, sensualist and rebel, and Demassener the Puritan dictator.[1] In *The Man Within* the

[1] Charles Fenby, Mr. Greene tells me, said something like this in a review of *The Name of Action* and so suggested to Greene the trick of

theme of the divided mind is mainly expressed through the contending higher and lower natures of the young coward Andrews—like Archie in *Weir of Hermiston* he has had a brutal father and an ineffectual mother, and his double nature is explained in terms of this parentage; but it is not too forced to see Elizabeth, his sweetheart, and his friend Carlyon as personifications, at least in some respects, of the warring fractions of his nature, or to regard Elizabeth and Lucy, who sleeps with Andrews for a single night at Lewes, as representing his confusions about love and the conflicting claims, as they appear to him, of tenderness and desire. From this point of view a study of themes may serve to distinguish the early and late novels in spite of the fact that the main obsessions are common to the whole of Greene's fiction.

There is one more preliminary topic to be discussed before I turn to the examination of the early novels, and that is the important place given to sexuality in them. Some of the peculiarities of Green's attitude to sexual love are constant, it is true, for example, the remarkable polarity of attraction and repulsion that the sexual act ('the game') has for his characters and the fixity of the separation he makes between desire and affection. All the novels are shot through with sexuality. The difference between the treatment of the subject early and late seems to reside in the hectic quality of the attention paid to it in, say, *The Man Within.* There is an apparent lack of psychological distance, and as a result we have the feeling that the author is too personally involved. The early novels have various themes—the divided mind, escape, betrayal and so on—but these ruling ideas are contaminated by being associated with a young man's absorption in the 'otherness' of women, the strangeness of his feeling in front of them, and the paradoxes inherent in the sexual relationship.

---

dividing the main character in *Rumour at Nightfall.* It was not a very happy invention. Many of the reader's perplexities in the latter book are due to the attempt to think simultaneously of Crane and Chase as separate characters and as aspects of a single human being.

This is not hard to illustrate. Crane wonders to Eulelia Monti in *Rumour at Nightfall*:

> Whether I love anyone at all but myself. Whether I'd do anything for anyone to the injury of myself. Whether I love you or the peace from the world I think I can get from you. Do I know you enough to love you yourself? If you should lie to me, I ought to love your lies. If you have a deformity of body, I ought to know and love it. If you have a hidden foulness, I ought to love that too. Otherwise what do I love? Not you, but my idea of you. . . .

and his speech reminds us of Carlyon's words to Elizabeth in *The Man Within*:

> I think that you are lovely, good and full of pity, but that is only a dream. You know all about yourself, how you are greedy for this and that, afraid of insects, full of disgusting physical needs. You'll never find a man who will love you for anything but a bare, unfilled-in outline of yourself. A man will even forget his own details when he can, until he appears an epic hero, and it needs his woman to see that he's a fool. Only a woman can love a real person.

Both these voices are the voice of Greene the romantic theorist, so anxious to illustrate his ideas of the nature of human love and passion that he cannot see a woman for seeing her as an instrument of salvation or damnation, a St. Agnes or a Lady Castlemaine; cannot portray a woman with any actuality because to do so would interfere with her becoming a diagram to illustrate some Euclidean theorem about tenderness or desire—experiences to which only non-Euclidean geometries apply.

Thus in *The Man Within* Andrews sees a puff of smoke from Elizabeth's cottage-chimney dissolve into shreds which, caught by the sun, resemble a drift of birds.

> He found in the crevice of his mind, where childhood harboured, the faint memory of a pictured saint, a young girl with pale, set face, round whose head a flock of doves turned and twisted.

Here Elizabeth is being idealized. It is true that the process is taking place in Andrew's mind, but it can only be repeated that the author seems too much involved—the word 'harboured' has an awkward air of self-congratulation. In other situations the opposite tendency is at work, and it is interesting to watch the author set out to exaggerate the 'badness' of Lucy in *The Man Within*—she would be quite a neutral little tramp in his later work—or to humiliate Anne-Marie, the wife of the dictator in *The Name of Action*, when she fails to live up to the romantic expectations of Oliver Chant.

It is inaccurate to say, as I did above, that Greene at this time cannot see or portray a woman clearly; it would be fairer to qualify this and read 'a woman who can be made the subject of a sexual interest'. He can describe the minor women characters well enough, Mrs. Butler the servant in *The Man Within*, or the slatternly wife of Joseph Kapper the poet in *The Name of Action*, but only because they are too old or too browbeaten by life to call up the idea of pleasure. His line is not subtle, but he can put Mrs. Butler solidly before us in a near-Dickensian manner:

> She was a little stout old woman who gave the impression of being very tightly pulled together by a great number of buttons that strayed from their normal positions and peeped out from interstices and side turnings in her voluminous clothes. She had small eyes and very faint, almost indistinguishable eye-brows.

This is only the beginning of Mrs. Butler's description, and its wordiness is in notable contrast to the economy with which appearance is suggested in the later novels, but at least it gives us something of Mrs. Butler's 'look'.

Their physical appearance is the last thing we remember of Elizabeth, Anne-Marie or Eulelia Monti. We know that they are beautiful, if we drag our memories we recollect that they are dark, pale and self-possessed, but that is all or almost all. It does not help to be told at one moment that Elizabeth seemed 'a little like a slim upstrained candle-flame', or at another that 'a white flower upon a slender stem which trembled in the dusk was what he seemed to see'. All we are given is a series of shorthand signs for an Ideal Maid or a *femme fatale*, and the creator of these pale romantic heroines is more concerned with the impression they make on the mind than on the eye: Elizabeth, for whom the stock epithet is 'serene'; Anne-Marie who seems 'to wait a sword-thrust rather than a word' with her mysterious strain and bitterness; Eulelia, described by a soldier who sees her photograph as 'One of these good women. A spoilt nun'. Partly these heroines are mysterious because of their literary ancestry—a long one before Greene happened on their immediate forerunners in *The Arrow of Gold* and the romances of Stevenson and Anthony Hope; but more because he still found the relationship between a man and a woman baffling and mysterious in itself.

I have referred to the simultaneous attraction and repulsion that the sexual act, even the idea of sex, holds for the characters in many of the novels. In the three early novels, in accordance with the need to schematize experience at the expense of doing justice to the visible world, the simultaneous attraction and repulsion is associated with the concept of the divided mind and generates an antithesis between sacred and profane love. These aspects are thought of as mutually exclusive and are attributed either to separate persons or to the separate higher and lower natures in a single being—in *The Man Within*, for example, the respective instances are Elizabeth and Lucy, and the contradictory selves in Andrews. There was a difficulty here, because at least in theory Greene had to allow a sexual element in the 'purest' love, and we do find pairs of lovers (Andrews and Elizabeth, Crane and Eulelia Monti) whose love is of the sacred variety, looking forward to marriage. It is not much more than a bobbed curtsey to convention: in practice in the early novels sacred love is expressed in talk rather than lovemaking and ends in death (romantic love cannot think of modification without the idea of decline);

while the yielding to desire of profane love is always interpreted as a victory for the lower nature.

Sexuality also penetrates the imagery and is partly responsible for the selection of minor incident in the early novels. This cannot be taken wholly on trust, but demonstration must be restricted. A clear example of sexual symbolism occurs in *Rumour at Nightfall.* Two bats are seen by Chase and Crane outside the house of Eulelia Monti, and then later recalled by Chase at a significant moment when he is betraying his friend and is jealous in an obscure way of the love between Crane and Eulelia. On this second occasion the memory reflects a disgust which is a cover for envy, but here is the original passage, which the author allows to stand without direct or indirect comment:

> Two bats entered the realm of light. They were like dancers before the footlights in the act of performance as the curtain rises, arms extended, muscles taut, in the imitation of sexual ecstasy. But with the bats it was no imitation but the ecstasy itself. On a nuptial flight the square leather wings whispered and beat, the membranes shining, the long ears pricked. Slowly they flapped against each other, poking with rat noses, the coarse cobwebbed fur meeting and parting and meeting again, and so into the dark, oblivious in their dream of the attraction of light.

The whole image represents human love with its sacred element (the beauty of the dancers) contradicted by its profane element (the ugly physical description of the bats mating), and it contains a pointed reference to the danger of absorbing passion—'oblivious in their dream of the attraction of light'. Henry James tells us that Hawthorne was perpetually seeking images that would 'place themselves in picturesque correspondence with the facts', and he adds '. . . the search is of the very essence of poetry. But in such a process discretion is everything'. Greene is always aware of the need for discretion, but in these early books he sometimes allows his images to become 'importunate'.

Chase's disgust and envy when he recalls the flight of the

bats suggest a particular illustration of sexuality in Greene's choice of background incident. In *The Man Within* Andrews, alone at night in Lewes before the Assizes and full of self-pity, overhears two lovers.

> He passed on. Two voices speaking softly in a doorway made him pause. He could not see the speakers. 'Come tonight.' 'Shall I? I oughtn't to.' 'I love you, love you, love you.'
>
> Andrews, to his own surprise, smote the wall against which he stood with his fist and said aloud with a crazy fury, 'You damned lechers. . . .'

There is a similar moment in *Rumour at Nightfall* when Chase is watching the square of San Juan by night.

> The courting couple came directly below his window into the light of the inn door. He could see the man's lubricious face, the girl's stare of stupid ignorance. A word came up to him, spoken with excitement, cunning, hope, '*Mañana*'—tomorrow. That was what *mañana* meant to them—a closer meeting, the final embrace in the straw of a stable or against the wall in a dark street.

And it is not surprising that the incident is repeated once more in *Brighton Rock*, since that novel is remarkable among the later books for the emphasis laid on sexuality. Pinkie, slashed by razors at the Brighton races, escapes from the course to hide in a suburban garage till darkness falls.

> He sidled out of the garage. The new raw street cut in the chalk was empty except for a couple pressed against each other out of the lamplight by a wooden fence. The sight pricked him with nausea and cruelty.[1]

Naturally we cannot often trace the source of such recurrences —they are more frequent than a casual reading of the novels would suggest—but here a hint has been provided by Greene.

[1] Note that the description is of what Pinkie really sees and feels, not an author's pretence. After the fight on the race-course Pinkie naturally sees a 'raw street cut in the chalk' and is 'pricked' by the sight of the lovers.

In *Journey Without Maps* he recalls an Easter holiday in Paris in 1924 when he was nineteen. He went to see Mistinguette at the Casino and next day attended a Communist meeting in the slums.

> That night from the window of an hotel I saw a man and woman copulating; they stood against each other under a street lamp, like two people who are supporting and comforting each other in the pain of some sickness.

The detail lodged itself in a crevice of his mind to reappear as variously as I have shown.

II

What Greene means by the theme of the divided mind in his early novels is best understood by referring to an address he delivered to a Catholic conference at Brussels in 1947, when he appeared on a platform with François Mauriac to consider the question, 'Is Christian civilization in danger?' Greene began his speech by discussing the marks of a Christian civilization. If a Christian civilization implies a society or societies so organized that all their members can follow without hindrance the teachings of the Sermon of the Mount, then none has ever existed. Such a view, however, is false and springs from confusing 'the earthly and the heavenly city'. He went on:

> But if we surrender all idea of perfection—even of the struggle for perfection—what marks do we expect to find that separate the Christian from one of the pagan civilizations? Perhaps all we can really demand is the divided mind, the uneasy conscience, the sense of personal failure.

Great crimes can be committed in a Christian civilization, but, if there is sin, there is also contrition. 'We can admit to our enemies all our crimes because we can show all through history our repentance.' This uneasy conscience of Christendom is not unlike Gautier's skeleton—

> Le squelette était invisible
> Au temps heureux de l'art paien

—but Greene's literary reference is Sir Thomas Browne's, 'There's another man within me that's angry with me'.[1] Eighteen years earlier the same quotation had provided an epigraph for his first novel. *The Man Within* is the best of the early novels because in it these issues of the divided mind, sin and repentance are most simply and unambiguously expressed.

Superficially the novel cannot be faulted for its technique. This does not imply any advanced merit, but it does indicate the simplicity of the means devised for realizing the main themes and the unpretentiousness of the story's organization. The narrative moves forward chronologically: the past is not enacted and what we need to know of it is revealed in talk between the chief characters Andrews and Elizabeth, or in the musings and dreams of Andrews, through whose eyes the action is seen almost exclusively.[2] The plot is single and uncomplicated. The action falls into three massive sections, rather like the three acts of a 'well-made' play, and the interest is focused on a few important characters. The time, it has already been said, is the early nineteenth century.

The disposition of the action within the main sections of the story is also simple. The first and third of these sections are practically confined to the living-room of a cottage on the Sussex Downs. Here Andrews, who has betrayed his fellow-smugglers and in particular his friend and their leader, Carlyon, arrives exhausted and terrified. He finds a brief sanctuary with Elizabeth, whose guardian has just died. The second section takes place in Lewes during the Assizes where Andrews has

[1] Sir Thomas Browne's phrase is based on St. Paul's Epistle to the Romans, vii, 22–24.

'For I delight in the law of God after the inward man.

'But I see another law in my members, warring against the law of my mind, and bringing me into captivity to the law of sin which is in my members.

'O wretched man that I am! Who shall deliver me from the body of this death?'

[2] The main exception is the trial scene in Chapter 8, which is seen—apart from Andrews's evidence—from the viewpoint of an ideal spectator.

been persuaded to go by Elizabeth to prove to himself that the 'real' Andrews is not a coward, but 'the man within' who torments him for his cowardice and other weaknesses.

'Le cœur le plus serein en apparence', says Chateaubriand, 'ressemble au puits naturel de la Savane Alachua; le surface en parait calme et pur, mais quand vous regardez au fond du bassin, vous apercevez un large crocodile.' To show the crocodile under the calm surface, to distinguish the sinister ambiguities in the strength and goodness of a human being was beyond Greene's power in his first novel. The weakness of Andrews is apparent in all he does. On the other hand Elizabeth does not simply appear serene: she possesses an unbreakable serenity. Andrews is the more real of the pair because he can succumb to the 'good temptation' of his inner nature, when it is strengthened by the pleading of Elizabeth with whom he falls in love.

As a result of the information laid by Andrews the 'gaugers' have surprised the 'gentlemen', and one of the excisemen has been killed in the following scuffle. Most of the smugglers have been captured and they are to be tried at the Assizes. Their conviction is unlikely. It is conceivable that Andrews's evidence may mean the difference between the acquittal and conviction of the smugglers, and Elizabeth urges him to go to Lewes and give his evidence, not because she identifies the legal processes with justice, but because in this way the tormenting sense of inferiority which has turned him into an informer may be exorcized.

Courage is doubly required. The Sussex folk hate an informer and sympathize with the 'gentlemen', but a more serious danger to Andrew is the betrayed Carlyon, who is still at liberty with one or two of the other smugglers. Nevertheless, because Elizabeth has not feared or despised him, because she has called him her friend, and because 'she seemed to carry far behind her eyes . . . the promise of his two selves at one', he decides to go to Lewes; but he will make no promise about his appearance at the Assizes.

At Lewes he falls in with a Mr. Farne in a tavern and is taken to Sir Henry Merriman, the prosecuting counsel as a valuable witness for the Crown. Ironically, then, he is given a further opportunity to tread down his cowardice and fulfil more than the letter of his promise to Elizabeth. Another motive for staying is found in Lucy, Sir Henry's mistress. About Elizabeth, Andrews thinks, 'There was a kind of mystery . . . a kind of sanctity which blurred and obscured his desire with love', but Lucy is as simply Flesh as Elizabeth is Spirit, and she appeals to the habitual Francis Andrews as strongly as Elizabeth had appealed earlier to 'the man within'.

Neither woman can be thought of as much more than a symbol—they are the two ends of the see-saw of sacred and profane love—but Lucy as a hoyden is given a flash of more than abstract life by her odd defensive tenderness for her protector to whom, nevertheless, she is continually unfaithful. She offers herself to Andrews because Sir Henry is preoccupied and she is restless, but also because Sir Henry has set his heart on winning the smuggling case and she hopes to secure Andrews's evidence for him. If Andrews will stay in Lewes, she will sleep with him after he has given his evidence for the Crown. Andrews stays.

> He was doing for a wrong reason what he had refused to do for a right. He had turned a deaf ear to what his heart, supported by the critic within, had asked of him, but he had capitulated at the first hungry wail his dirty, lusting body had uttered.

His evidence is not enough to win the day for Sir Henry. But even before he goes into the witness box, he suffers a revulsion of feeling and rejects the lower motive for his action. He tells himself that he will not seek the promised reward from Lucy. From this decision, too, the sophistical cleverness of his lower nature later draws an argument for enjoying her. 'Didn't I, he thought, renounce this morning with perfect sincerity this very reward? I did what I did then for Elizabeth and why should I not take any small benefits which come after?'

Fear urges him too. His taking refuge with Elizabeth at the cottage has come out in cross-examination. Now that his former companions have been acquitted and Carlyon need no longer conceal himself, he knows that it will be dangerous to return there. He attempts to whip himself into unthinking lust for Lucy, but at first unsuccessfully. Ambiguous as his one act of courage has been, it has strengthened 'the man within'. He goes to Lucy's bedroom still undecided between his two selves, and it is only the sight of her naked on the covers that pushes him finally into her bed. Even at the last moment Elizabeth's face 'creased by fear till it was ugly, almost repulsive' nearly comes between him and his pleasure, and afterwards, the grey next morning, he feels the whole weight of his betrayal of 'the new life, in which he would learn courage and even self-forgetfulness'. Lucy cannot understand his disgust and despair, and guesses wrongly that he will not return to Elizabeth.

Andrews does return. Paradoxically it is his capitulation to the 'hungry wail' of his body that destroys fear in him temporarily, or rather his fear of pain and death is cast out by a greater fear—'a terror of life, of going on soiling himself and repenting and soiling himself again'. This terror has been established as the ground of all Greene's obsessions, linked equally to the nightmares of his childhood and to later religious desperations.[1] Temporarily blind to the lesser fear of painful death, Andrews goes back to the cottage, declares his love to Elizabeth and is forgiven for his betrayal of her with Lucy.

So far it has been possible to follow the book's argument

[1] In 'Heroes are Made in Childhood' Greene speaks of the witch who waited 'in dreams every night in the passage by the linen cupboard, near the nursery door' continuing to wait when the mind is sick or tired—'though now she is dressed in the theological garments of despair and speaks in Spenser's accents:

> The longer life, I wote the greater sin,
> The greater sin, the greater punishment'.

at the story-level and to comment incidentally on the antithetical 'two natures' as they are revealed in Andrews's relations with Elizabeth and Lucy. But it would be difficult to give any satisfactory account of the novel's climax without indicating other relationships which thicken the texture and other aspects of the conflict between the two selves of Andrews. After Andrews and Elizabeth the third important character in the book is Carlyon, now the leader of the smugglers and formerly lieutenant to Andrews's father. Carlyon only appears twice, but he is continually present to Andrews's consciousness. While Elizabeth can be identified simply with Andrews's conscience and Lucy with his weak habitual self, Carlyon's role suggests a further refinement. Ape-like in appearance, he possesses a very attractive voice, and it is his love of poetry, his sensitivity to beauty and his romantic attitude to the smuggling life which have attached Andrews to him. After the betrayal of the smugglers he is always a figure with a dual significance to Andrews; a friend who is loved and an enemy who is feared.

Carlyon is an important actor in Andrews's interior monologue because he is involved in the latter's understanding of himself. He represents what is least despicable in the lower self: the sentiment and romanticism. Early in the novel Andrews, analysing his own character, declares that he is made up of two persons, 'the sentimental, bullying, desiring child and another more stern critic'. He explains this:

> It's not a man's fault whether he's brave or cowardly. It's all in the way he's born. My mother and father made me. I didn't make myself.

Andrews's father had been domineering, brutal, insensitive; Andrews's mother had worshipped her husband with 'the serene faithfulness of a completely broken will'.[1]

[1] Information about Andrews's parents is given deviously throughout the course of the novel's action—for example, in the potting-shed, where he sleeps at the beginning of his flight, Andrews dreams that men are

The elder Andrews had been too devoid of imagination to dream. Carlyon resembles Francis Andrews in his addiction to daydreaming, but he is unlike him in lacking 'the inner critic'. His attitude to experience is entirely æsthetic. Moral issues present themselves to him as opportunities for romantic gestures. Thus the new life he opens to the younger Andrews after the deaths of the latter's parents—the poetry, the sunsets, the glorification of a smuggler's 'freedom'—is hopelessly flawed and can only provide a temporary escape. It is not an appeal to 'the man within', but to the sentimental, desiring elements in Andrews's lower nature. Andrews finds this out, learns to contrast the 'two musics' of Carlyon and Elizabeth, 'one alluring, unreal, touched with a thin romance and poetry, the other clear-cut, ringing, sane, a voice carved out of white marble'.

Andrews's lack of physical stamina has made his life at sea a misery. With nerves perpetually on edge he has been aware resentfully that the smugglers—with the exception of Carlyon—are always measuring him by the invisible standard of the 'real man' his father was. It is clear that one of his motives for treachery is the desire to lay the ghost of a tormenting memory by squaring accounts with his father. Treachery is still a following of his lower nature. By it he had intended to assert his importance, show cleverness and even a twisted sort of courage, but Elizabeth speaks with the voice of his 'inner critic' when she reminds him, 'You've made the whole pack of them... better men than you are'.

It is with all this in mind that we come to the mishandled climax of the book, the final scenes in and around the cottage

---

talking of his father's courage. This, incidentally, is the first example of Greene's use of dreams to convey information and deepen a sense of character. His course of psycho-analytic treatment mentioned in 'The Revolver in the Corner Cupboard' probably has something to do with his fondness for a device used very frequently; most boldly, perhaps, in Raven's dreams in *A Gun for Sale* and Arthur Rowe's in *The Ministry of Fear*.

on the Downs. Even in the simplified form in which I have presented the story it should be evident that Andrews's wish for peace, for a permanent reconciliation of his two selves, is a death-wish. Our dissatisfaction is bound up with this perception. The death-wish, it is true, is simply the final term of a series connected with the 'escape' obsession present in so many of Greene's novels. The climax of *The Man Within* is a failure not because it is there, but because at this crucial point the story, like an overloaded bridge, collapses under the weight of significance it is asked to bear. Greene, that is to say, has failed to communicate with enough concreteness through his fable the 'terror of life', so that firstly we do not see Andrews's predicament as genuinely symbolic of the human situation, an uncomfortable insight, and secondly we are only grudgingly convinced that he is in that predicament at all.

This is not to say that Andrews's death is unprepared or his death-wish unexplained. Early in the book Elizabeth asks him, 'Is there anything you care for or want?' and he replies unhesitatingly, 'To be null and void'. The state aspired to is described in terms of listening to music:

> When music plays, one does not see or think; one hardly hears. A bowl—and the music is poured in until there is no 'I', I am the music.

In *The Lawless Roads* Greene has written in similar terms of a peace experienced in childhood when, like Andrews, he escaped from school 'surreptitiously for an hour at a time' to the darkness of the croquet-lawn.

> It was an hour of release—and also an hour of prayer. One became aware of God with an intensity—time hung suspended—music lay on the air....

To Scobie in *The Heart of the Matter*, as to Andrews, peace is the only real object of desire. 'Peace seemed to him the most beautiful word in the language. . . . In the Mass he pressed his fingers against his eyes to keep the tears of longing in.' Like Andrews he thinks of peace as a state of nullity and achieves it by suicide. 'Once in sleep it had appeared to him as the great glowing shoulder of the moon heaving across his window like an iceberg, arctic and destructive in the moment before the world was struck.' That even so much of a parallel can be drawn between Andrews and Scobie is evidence of the genuine and obsessional nature of the experience on which *The Man Within* is based. Our dissatisfaction with the climax, then, derives from the fact that the characters and situations imagined do not provide an objective correlative for the *sehnsucht* for oblivion; and this weakness in conception is accompanied significantly by a temporary failure in technique.

The inner obsessional logic of the book makes Andrews's death necessary, but we have been convinced that he cannot silence his cowardly lower self and become 'the man within' except momentarily under the influence of Elizabeth. So, with our realization that Andrews can only obtain peace in one way, we also become aware that nothing but her death will be adequate to nerve him to a willing acceptance of his own. The logic of events, however, will not allow this conclusion to be produced naturally. Greene has therefore to force his story to the theatrical end necessary to deliver the predetermined emotional meaning. The forcing shows badly in the final narrative sequence.

'There must be sorrow if there can be love'—that is the mood of the final reckoning. Elizabeth is dead for no very good reason but the rounding-off of the book's emotional pattern, killed with Andrews's knife by one of the more louche smugglers who—also for no very good reason—has arrived at the cottage before Carlyon, who would have prevented the murder. Andrews returns—his disappearance from the cottage is another piece of patent contrivance—too late to save Elizabeth, but in time to regain Carlyon's friendship over Elizabeth's dead body and to dismiss his friend to safety while he waits for the officers. While he waits alone he realizes that his suddenly conceived plan of allowing himself to be taken for Elizabeth's murder and then committing suicide is not simply an expiatory act offered to Carlyon for the earlier betrayal, but a way of defeating his father. Once he knows this he can face with equanimity the hatred of the officers who find him with Elizabeth's body. As he is being taken into custody he smiles at the thought that his confession of guilt makes Carlyon safe. '. . . And yet it is true—I did kill her or my father in me. But, father, you too shall die.' An anticipatory peace is his as he leaves the cottage with the men.

> Regret had gone, even remembrance of the graceless body abandoned there. To his own surprise he felt happy and at peace, for his father was slain and yet a self remained, a self which knew neither lust, blasphemy nor cowardice, but only peace and curiosity for the dark, which deepened around him. . . . His father's had been a stubborn ghost, but it was laid at last, and he need no longer be torn in two between that spirit and the stern unresting critic which was wont to speak. I am that critic, he said with a sense of discovery and exhilaration.

In the last sentence of the book his hand moves out to steal his own knife from the belt of the officer in front of him in order to make his sense of happiness and peace permanent by killing himself.

III

The Name of Action begins and ends in a railway train. At the beginning of the book Oliver Chant, from whose viewpoint the story is seen, is making his way to Trier with the quixotic hope of using his money to upset the dictatorship there; at the end he is leaving Trier with the wounded dictator Paul Demassener beside him in the same carriage. The trains are 'contemporary', but what falls between the two journeys—Chant's plotting with Joseph Kapper, the revolutionary poet, and his friends, the smuggling of arms from Coblenz, the love-affair with Anne-Marie, Demassener's wife—belongs to a Ruritania of no particular date. According to Greene the book sprang from a visit to Trier in the early nineteen-twenties when there were rumours of French support for separatism—Anne-Marie is French so that Demassener is said to be in the pay of France; but this amount of actuality only provides a taking-off point for the author to soar in emulation of Anthony Hope. Naturally, since the novel is dated 1931, a latter-day Anthony Hope with cynical reserves about the heroics and a determined distrust of all 'pure' motives. Greene is determined to have his cake and eat it.

Rumour at Nightfall takes place in Spain in mid-Victorian times. Francis Chase is attached as a newspaper correspondent to the small force under Colonel Riego which is seeking to capture Ramôn Caveda, a guerrilla-leader who for unknown reasons continues the struggle after the defeat of the Carlists. Caveda is a 'faceless shadow' who carries on 'a losing duel among the mountains', but Chase discovers a postbag when some of Caveda's men are ambushed and in it a letter written by the guerrilla-leader, a pair of expensive gloves and the photograph of a woman. Colonel Riego does not think the finds important, but Chase decides to follow the clue of the photograph in San Juan. There he is joined by his friend Michael Crane. They find the woman, Eulelia Monti, and, after an abortive rising by Caveda's party in the town, the novel ends with Chase and Eulelia coming together over the dead body of Michael Crane. *Rumour at Nightfall* makes heavy going. There is not a great deal of action and what there is gets smothered under interminable analyses of what people think and mean. At the same time the author does away with chapter divisions. Like *The Man Within* and *The Name of Action* the book is divided into three parts, but inside these parts the movement is continuous. The action is seen from Chase's viewpoint in the first and third parts and from Crane's in the second. An atmosphere of mystery, intended to be felt as momentous, pervades the book and helps to antagonize the reader.

With these skeleton outlines of *The Name of Action* and

Rumour at Nightfall it should be possible to indicate what themes, situations and types of character the two novels have in common with their predecessor. The first theme is, of course, the divided mind. In *Rumour at Nightfall*, as in *The Man Within*, there is an explanation of coexisting higher and lower selves in terms of heredity. Eulelia Monti has the appearance of a fiercely good woman—a peasant comments on her photograph, 'You have only to look at the picture. . . . She cares for God, not for a man'—but out of curiosity, and as an obscure attack on her mercenary mother, who cares for her daughter's virtue only to raise its price in the marriage market, she has given herself once to the Carlist 'Liberal' Ramón Caveda. Her interest in Caveda puzzles Crane. 'There must be something bad in her after all', he says. 'How hopelessly weary one gets of that rottenness at the centre.' When Chase meets Eulelia's mother, Señora Monti, he is horrified:

> He had never met a woman who so combined an extreme emaciation with such an impression of the flesh. It was as if she had grown thin from the constant friction of indulgence. . . . Out of such a mother what a daughter it must be, he thought with revolt.

By way of contrast her father is a scholar and a recluse, intensely religious, a man of unbreakable rectitude with a distaste for the market-place. Eulelia explains herself to Crane as Andrews explains himself to Elizabeth.

> She asked him: 'What am I? I am my father and mother. If I have any virtue, it is my father's. He is a good man. . . . And if I have sinned, it is my mother's sin. . . . These are excuses. There should be something in me to resist my mother when she whispers of the lovers I might have. . . . Not the mother you have seen, but the one in me. But where am I, who should resist? Is there an I?'

The theme of the divided mind also appears in the early novels in the dressing-up of aspects of a single being as separate characters. I have already said that this is most obvious in *Rumour at Nightfall*, but I have not begun to hint at the complexities introduced by Greene. Francis Chase and Michael Crane are the two complementary fractions of a single nature: their quarrels and misunderstandings spring from the fact that they represent opposed sets of values, just as their intimacy expresses the need of each for a missing part of himself. Michael Crane is another Andrews, a physical coward, sensitive, romantic, with an added seismographic readiness to respond to the tremor of anything strange or mysterious. He has a gift for suffering and this capacity, he thinks, makes him human: '. . . if I had felt no pain, I should have been damned indeed. There would have been nothing human left in me. I should have lost even the desire for her [Eulelia], the friendship of Chase, and every alleviation in a life of fear—colour and sound, the taste of food, the desire for virtue and the admiration of courage'. Francis Chase is a Liberal, a believer in Darwin and progress, courageous, solid and dependable, rather obtuse in personal relations. To Crane his friend Chase 'was, in some sort, the modern world. He was a sceptic who was not even easy about his materialism'.

Chase hates the Spain in which he has to work for its refusal to separate the secular and the religious. He detests the fierceness of Spanish feuds and devotions, the quick drawing of knives, the outstretched arms of peasants in churches and at wayside Calvaries. He feels that Crane is betraying him when his friend is attracted by these things. He sympathizes with Caveda because the latter is a Liberal too, the one Spaniard—so Chase thinks—capable of humour and free of superstition. He confesses to Crane how Spain has irritated him.

> This country [is] affecting my nerves. The strange standards they have, the importance they put on death, the superstition. It's a dark atmosphere in the mountains, you know. Smoke and flames, the fear of hell, no gaiety, only small bitter songs about love betrayed and death, and all day long, as they believe, God

> being swallowed alive in their dismal churches.[1] That's why I sympathize with Caveda. He stands outside all that.

Crane cannot stand outside. He tells Chase:

> If hell means pain, fear, mistrust of oneself and everyone, then I believe in hell, and why should there not be heaven too? Heaven, I suppose, would be peace, and one has had that for long enough to know the lack of it.

Greene has written that in becoming a convert to Catholicism he accepted his new creed on intellectual grounds; but how his feelings predisposed him to entertain the case for Catholicism is clear if we relate Crane's remarks to Greene's confession in *The Lawless Roads*, 'One began to believe in heaven because one believed in hell, but for a long while it was only hell one could picture with a certain intimacy. . . .'[2]

That Chase and Crane stand for the contradictions in a single personality is gradually made clear to us by a succession of details. Riding to San Juan, for example, Chase wishes for company, immediately thinks of Crane and 'in the mirror of rain before him, where if there had been any reflection it should have been that of his own face, he saw the nervous attentive eyes and the lips parted to assert the wrong thing. Always the wrong thing, Chase thought, remembering with a slow pleasure how they had never agreed on any subject.' And again, when the two of them stand up after a meal in a courtyard at San Juan, the words used suggest their peculiar tie. 'Across the board his friend's body rose at the same time but slowly, like a retarded image of himself.'

This does not exhaust the treatment of the theme of the divided mind in *Rumour at Nightfall*. Numerous indications

[1] Greene's echo of Browning is, I think, unconscious. Cf. 'The Bishop's Orders his Tomb at St. Praxed's Church':

> And hear the blessed mutter of the mass
> And see God made and eaten all day long.

[2] This passage from *The Lawless Roads* is recalled in *Brighton Rock* in a conversation between Pinkie and Rose.

are given of Caveda's actuality to Chase, who has never seen the guerrilla-leader, and in one scene significance is found in the fact that Caveda's gloves fit Chase perfectly. At another point in the novel Crane mistakes Caveda for Chase. At a third an old woman, once Caveda's foster-mother, confuses Chase's voice with Caveda's. Obviously Chase and Caveda are identified by the author in some sense, and this notion becomes more acceptable when we turn to the other obsessions common to *Rumour at Nightfall* and the two preceding novels—betrayal, escape and the search for peace.

Chase is bent on discovering Caveda in order to have a good story to send to his newspaper, but as the book develops we find that this search takes on for him the emotional quality of treachery, and in the end he betrays his friend Crane to his death in order to save Caveda. On one level of meaning this is to save himself and the rational values that he represents. Crane has betrayed these values by turning to Eulelia. To Chase, as to Caveda, a love-affair is simply a love-affair, but Crane shares Eulelia's detestation for her act in giving herself to Caveda, and with her he is able to win a temporary peace that is a cessation of all his fears in the same way that Andrews finds peace with Elizabeth in *The Man Within*. The preoccupation with betrayal extends to Eulelia. At first she will not betray Caveda to Chase, but as soon as she finds herself in love with Crane she becomes prepared to betray her former 'lover' in repudiation of her own past, of her mother in her.

Like Andrews, Michael Crane is pursued by fear—'His life was taped out with terrors, and each new terror he could foresee. They were like a succession of peaks'; and like him, too, he longs for a peace that will be permanent. With Eulelia he does experience a peace that has the 'quality of timelessness', but only death can give him lastingly what he is seeking. Crane 'escapes' from life, and when Chase finds him, the body is crumpled by the murderers' bullets, but 'the face was at peace, if a complete lack of expression can be called peaceful, no mark retained of the terror, or the pain, or the disappointment'. With Crane's death Chase begins to alter. He gives entry to loneliness and fear, clumsily feeling his way into the world in which Crane had been at home. 'I am your lover too', he can say to Eulelia because Caveda had slept with her once, but now he recognizes what is mean and commonplace in the enemy he has preferred to his friend, and he contemplates union with Eulelia—a union never consummated in the hasty marriage between Crane and her—as a continuation of both their relationships with his friend. They are bound together by suffering. 'I suffer, therefore I am.'

In *The Name of Action* less emphasis is laid on the divided mind than in *The Man Within* or *Rumour at Nightfall*, and the most important theme is that of betrayal. To explain this we have to remember that the central character, Oliver Chant, goes to Trier not only to escape from the tedium of the London round, not only with a romantic desire to take part in a revolution, but also because he has been deeply attracted by a photograph of the dictator's wife, Anne-Marie Demassener, in an illustrated paper. His motives in electing to support the revolution are therefore as mixed as Andrew's motives for giving evidence at the Assizes. His feeling of intimacy with Anne-Marie, his 'enemy', recalls Chase's feelings about Caveda and Andrews's about Carlyon in the other early novels. Demassener is Chant's enemy too, both as dictator of Trier and as husband of Anne-Marie. The sensual poet Joseph Kapper and his revolutionary friends suspect betrayal in Chant's sudden friendship with the dictator's wife at Trier, and they are right in that he almost decides at one moment to return to London and take no further part in the underground struggle against Demassener. What keeps him in Trier, and what precipitates a revolution for which the conspirators are unprepared, is Anne-Marie's scorn when she finds that Chant thinks the revolutionary movement strong enough to shake her husband. But the real betrayals are Anne-Marie's revelation of her husband's impotence to Oliver Chant and his betrayal of her confidence to Joseph Kapper.

Greene's reversal of all the values of the conventional 'revolutionary' romance is evident both in his characters and in the ordering of his plot. There is something mean and egotistical about most of the conspirators: Joseph Kapper is more concerned with his reputation as a poet than with the freedom of Trier and hopes to get the Englishman's money to print and circulate his lampoons on the dictator; Peter Torner is known as an artist, but his art consists of caricatures of Anne-Marie offering 'her body, and with it black stockings and pink ribboned corsets, to a French officer'. Opposed to them is Demassener, the dictator. Instead of the usual man of blood and iron, Greene depicts an aging man, tired and courteous, who hates freedom because 'freedom means freedom for the animal in man', who would 'bind men in clean chains', who is impotent and unable to satisfy his wife.

Here is another version of the sacred and profane love antithesis of *The Man Within*. Demassener loves his wife, but his affection is divorced from physical desire. Kapper thinks of love only as the contact of bodies—'We all meet in the same place sooner or later. . . . I mean between the sheets.' One side of Chant is drawn towards Kapper because he is a young man eager to enjoy Anne-Marie, but another side sympathizes with the 'pure' affection of the dictator who has cleaned up the brothels of Trier and finds music dangerous in its power to stir the emotions. Chant is clearly the correct hero for this ironic political fiction. Between Kapper and Demassener, who represent the halves of his divided mind, he feels that he stands for nothing at all, that he has no personality.

The love-affair between Chant and Anne-Marie comes about by a kind of accident. Chant is almost run down by her car while he is keeping watch at night for the conspirators, who are unloading arms brought up the river from Coblenz. They take shelter in a *gasthaus* and Anne-Marie reveals her husband's secret to Chant. 'I've been faithful to him, faithful to nothing, for five years . . . you can have me if you want me. He doesn't want me.' She offers herself to him 'as a gesture illustrating her sad resignation to hunger'. This is all she can give him in return for his romantic passion.

Very soon after their night together Chant begins to realize that both his 'enterprises of great pith and moment', the revolutionary and the personal, are doomed to 'lose the name of action' because of the gap between his romantic expectations and the 'dinginess' of fact. As a secondary epigraph to his novel Greene uses a quotation from T. S. Eliot's *The Hollow Men*:

> Between the idea
> And the reality
> Between the motion
> And the act
> Falls the Shadow . . .

Anne-Marie speaks of a 'kind of faithfulness', and Chant adopts her phrase in a summing-up of everything that has happened.

> That, he thought, was the symbol of all his enterprise, nothing of his genuine desire, everything in a distant relationship to it—a kind of war, a kind of loyalty, a kind of love, and now a kind of faithfulness.

A parody of a Ruritanian fiction has been used to express a romantic bitterness at the nature of what we learn from experience.

The crowning irony in *The Name of Action* is that even the revolution succeeds for the wrong reasons. The revolutionaries are successful because Kapper's verses revealing that the dictator is impotent and that his wife has cuckolded him are being sung in the streets. It is not the passion for freedom that liberates Trier, not even the arms bought with Chant's money: the chains binding 'the animal in man' disappear in the gale of laughter following the revelation that Demassener is in the crudest sense less of a man than the humblest male citizen of Trier. By this time Chant's sympathies have swung to the dictator. He is disgusted with Joseph Kapper and even more with himself and Anne-Marie.

After his night in the *gasthaus* Chant at first has romantic hopes of taking Anne-Marie to England, but she quickly disillusions him. They meet in a church, and as she tells him that she does not and has not loved him, her voice contains 'no recognition of mystery and no trace of tenderness'. It is this betrayal of his love, for he thinks of it as a betrayal, that stings Chant into speaking too freely to Kapper. Greene leaves nothing to chance in this scene. Anne-Marie is carefully posed against a chorus of old women saying their rosaries, and the comparison is pointed by a verbal repetition: 'Soon they would be at the foot of the cross, raising eyes with an understanding of pain, tenderness, and mystery to the dim sacrifice above.' With this breaking of a butterfly on a wheel Greene shows that as yet he cannot, any more than Oliver Chant, accept 'the dinginess' that 'we can't escape from'.

This is a good opportunity to observe the part played by Catholicism in *The Name of Action* and *Rumour at Nightfall.*[1] Both books are set in Catholic countries—the Rhineland, Spain—so that Catholicism enters naturally into their backgrounds, but in neither does it furnish an essential element of the plot as in *Brighton Rock* or *The Heart of the Matter*. Catholicism, in fact, is conceived romantically. Catholics have, it is supposed, extraordinary inner resources to fall back on (Eulelia Monti), or they can achieve a happy normality forbidden the sensitive, self-conscious modern. An illustration of the latter point occurs in *The Name of Action* when Chant leaves the *gasthaus* and visits Frau Weber, the wife of one of the conspirators. She is undisturbed by the possibility of danger, content to leave everything to her husband and Providence. She has never been troubled by 'needs, question-

[1] Catholicism does not enter into *The Man Within*, but Elizabeth is a Christian, and her strength of character and her serenity are made to depend on her beliefs.

ings, doubts, analysis'. Chant feels that her happiness and the security of her married life are due to her religion.

> That, thought Chant, with some bitterness, was a haven to which neither he nor Anne-Marie Demassener could ever come. They were born in an age of doubt and to a class which wished to know too much. She would never make 'a good wife and a good Catholic' in that calm, tender, and unquestioning way, nor he 'a good husband'. They would speak to each other in double meanings, guard the heart with evasions, misunderstand the plainest speech, quarrel over clauses. And at the end—if they lived together so long—they would have no expectation but decay, no claim to any sentient eternity. . . . The compensation he supposed was rapture.

This is worlds away from Greene's insight in *The Heart of the Matter*, where the Catholic Scobie is having an affair with a girl, Helen Rolt, who cannot understand that he believes seriously in the existence of hell. If he does accept its existence, she asks, why does he commit adultery with her? Scobie reflects:

> How often . . . lack of faith helps one to see more clearly than faith. He said, 'You are right, of course: it ought to prevent all this. But the villagers on the slopes of Vesuvius go on . . .'

In his early novels, then, Greene is fascinated by Catholicism, but still sees it romantically, externally, as Horace Walpole saw his Gothic. In his mature work he knows that Catholics behave very much like everyone else, even if some of them have a profounder sense than the ordinary 'good pagan' of the meaning of their actions, and consequently a greater temptation to despair.

The Man Within ends theatrically with violence and unhappiness, and the endings of *The Name of Action* and *Rumour at Nightfall* conform to this pattern. All Greene's novels end sadly and violently, so that the three early books are only to be distinguished in a long line of similar endings by the stagy manner in which their curtains are run down.

Even in the entertainments, where Greene makes some concessions to the conventions of the popular thriller, the 'happy endings' are ironically conceived. Lovers are allowed to come together, but not to expect too much of life. Anne and Mather in *A Gun for Sale* are an apparent exception, but the remark is applicable to 'D' and Rose Cullen in *The Confidential Agent* and to Arthur Rowe and Anna Hilfe in *The Ministry of Fear*. The implications of the latter union are painstakingly exposed:

> They sat for a long time without moving and without speaking: they were on the edge of their ordeal, like two explorers who see at last from the summit of the range the enormous dangerous plain. . . .
>
> He tried tentatively a phrase: 'My dear, my dear I am so happy', and heard with infinite tenderness her prompt and guarded reply: 'Me too'. It seemed to him that after all one could exaggerate the value of happiness.

Of the early novels it is only in *Rumour at Nightfall* that two lovers (Francis Chase and Eulelia Monti) are united in the final chapter, and here too they are not so much left facing life as faced by it—the shift of words conveys the threat implied by having to endure, having to hang on.

IV

Arthur Rowe in *The Ministry of Fear*, wandering about bombed London, reflects that there is something almost domestic and cosy about a mere private killing in comparison with the violence of the blitz raging above him. 'The world has been remade by William Le Queux.' He knows that the Edwardian security of his childhood with its silver tea-pots and croquet-lawns has vanished: '. . . lady novelists describe it over and over again in "books of the month", but it's not there any more'. There is a sense in which Greene's obsession with violence and evil and his fondness for melodrama have seemed to become valid as the witlessness of modern civilization has revealed itself in the period between the end of the first world war and the present time. 'Today our world seems peculiarly susceptible to brutality', he wrote in *The Lawless Roads* before the second world war, and the remark is certainly not less true today. It is possible to imagine a writer with Greene's insight failing to make the same impression in a period of comparative optimism and security. Greene has been fortunate in that the most lumpish of his public must have seen things roughly from his viewpoint at times over the past twenty-five years. His obsessions gave him his vision of the world, but history has done its best to make it look like a neutral account of experience.

In the early novels the obsessions have a naked rawness. They are without the covering provided by the ugliness and violence of so many features in contemporary life, and they also lack the support of the developed insight into behaviour and the developed technical skill typical of Greene's later novels. Hence the early novels are melodramatic to their disadvantage—Lyceum melodrama—while we are able to swallow the much larger doses of melodrama in *Brighton Rock*, for example, without much misgiving.

A weakness continually felt in the first three books is the failure to dramatize. Characters are not realized through what happens to them or through their own dialogue: they explain each other directly in dialogue or they are explained in passages of reflective prose (including some that are nominally interior monologue). *Rumour at Nightfall* and *The Heart of the Matter* are at polar extremes in this respect: in the former a few insipid lines of dialogue are lost in labyrinthine explanations intended to give them significance; in the latter whole sections of the novel are in dialogue so sensitively organized that it both presents the characters—Scobie, Helen Rolt and Yusef particularly—and is simultaneously an oblique commentary by the author. This failure to realize characters through action and dialogue is also due to Greene's inability to see very far into human motives at this stage of his development.

This is as much as to say that the elements which enter into the composition of the early novels are chemically inert. Theme, character and action fail to coalesce, but remain distinct and easily separable. Similarly the set descriptions of background fail to support mood importantly. Today Greene is sparing of description. He slips it unobtrusively between sequences of dialogue, or breaks the action for a moment with it, to reinforce the effect of a conversation or to make what is happening more tense or immediate. The quick tempo of the later novels and the slow tempo of the early ones is vitally connected with this difference in method. The description of Andrews's walk over the Downs to Lewes in *The Man Within* occupies fourteen pages of the original edition, but we are left without the definite impression made in a fraction of the space by the dentist's room in *The Power and the Glory*, the church bazaar in *A Gun for Sale*, or the Orthotex Private Inquiry Bureau in *The Ministry of Fear*.

The images in a short passage from that description are reasonably representative of Greene's decorative use of metaphor and simile in the early novels. A coppice is like 'a band of soft brown fur fringing the hill'; the green of spring creeps 'cautiously, afraid still of an ambush from winter'; a scarlet cart on the road 'crawled like a ladybird along the rim of a leaf'. The images are sapless and conventional and fail to startle us into any new perception of the scene. On the other hand a comparison of the Surrey hills to 'an old nun's face' is certainly unusual, but affected and unconvincing. There are good images in all three novels, but the general effect is one of poverty of fancy. This uninventiveness is the more surprising because Greene's fertility of imagery is marked in the later novels and has become a stock point for parodists. Sometimes, indeed, he seems to parody himself.

In the later novels Greene has few unconscious literary echoes, so that when we read of 'the extreme decrepitude' of Elizabeth's dead body in the final scene of *The Man Within* and recall 'death's extreme decrepitude' in Wilfred Owen's poem, 'Greater Love', we are once more brought up against the question of the literary inspiration of the early books.[1] Every novelist, we are assured, 'creates a world'. In these three novels, then, Greene created a world, but he forgot too much of the real world when he did so. What did not derive from his obsessions was mainly supplied by literature, much of it romantic literature. The sensibility and intelligence revealed patchily by these novels might have been enough to constitute a poet—a young man can write remarkable poetry. But a young man cannot be a remarkable novelist: he can only show promise of becoming one. The world exists and he must know something about it. He must learn in his own person, as Auden puts it, 'to suffer dully all the wrongs of Man'. What Greene's three early novels reveal is the obsessed creative artist desperately trying to make bricks with very little straw; and sounding therefore at times like a writer for the glossier women's magazines. The intelligence is present, but not the active sense of life; the gift, but not yet the world of experience on which it has to feed.

[1] There are similar unconscious echoes in *The Name of Action* and *Rumour at Nightfall*. An example from *Rumour at Nightfall* has been given earlier. See p. 64 and footnote.

CHAPTER THREE

THE FALLEN WORLD: I

Stamboul Train (1932)
It's a Battlefield (1934)
England Made Me (1935)

Why, this is Hell, nor are we out of it.
Dr. Faustus, MARLOWE

What theme had Homer but original sin?
Vacillation, W. B. YEATS

I

No two books by Graham Greene are more different than *Rumour at Nightfall* and *Stamboul Train*, both published in 1932. In the former Greene's special early obsession with the divided mind is tortuously examined in a story without much intrinsic interest and lacking in variety. There are few characters and these stand about in shadowy symbolic attitudes. There is an almost total lack of concreteness. In the latter the theme of the divided mind has disappeared, and even the obsessional ideas common to all Greene's fiction are not easy to discern. The several interrelated stories are filled with a lavish variety of human types presented from direct observation with a plethora of visual detail. *Rumour at Nightfall* is set in the eighteen-seventies and *Stamboul Train* in the present. It was bound to occur to Greene sooner or later that he was getting deeper into a blind alley and starving himself as a novelist by his neglect of the contemporary scene. Once he had realized this a startling difference between two successive books was to be expected, and critical self-dissatisfaction cannot be ruled out as a cause of the change that did take place. There was another more active trigger-cause. Greene has told me that what shocked him out of the cultivation of his hysteria—a brief, unkind but not unfair description of the early novels—was a scathing, salutary review by a well-known novelist and reviewer.[1] At the time Greene was living by his writing and the review seemed a serious matter. In reply he decided to write a book with a contemporary subject as rapidly as possible—by contrast *Rumour at Nightfall* had been very slowly elaborated. It would not be a serious book[2]—it would be written too rapidly for that—so he would call it an 'entertainment'; but it would show the reviewer of *Rumour at Nightfall*, other reviewers and the public that he could tell a contemporary story with all the slickness required. He began *Stamboul Train* in this mood. Then, as he developed his plot and added to his characters, I think he surprised himself. He found that the story came with unexpected fluency, that his setting released accumulated stores of observation necessarily excluded by the settings of the earlier novels. Before *Stamboul Train* was finished he had forgotten his resentment of the reviewer's standpoint and had ventured further into radical self-criticism. He had finally rejected the idea of an historical background for his serious novels and determined to express himself through stories set in the present and fed by daily observation.

The need to evoke contemporary atmospheres with exactness had at first the result of checking and controlling the expression of Greene's obsessional ideas. *Stamboul Train* is in intention, if not altogether in effect, a pot-boiler, and it was not to be expected that the serious themes would emerge

[1] Frank Swinnerton.

[2] Cf. *Journey Without Maps*, Part I, Chapter 2, 'Ballyhoo':

'One had never really taken the book seriously; it had been written hurriedly because one had desperately needed the money...'

strongly in it. But *It's a Battlefield* and *England Made Me*, the two novels of the second phase of Greene's work, are also less haunted not only than, for example, *The Man Within*, but than later work again such as *Brighton Rock* and *The Power and the Glory*. The two novels following *Stamboul Train* show that Greene's attention had turned pointedly from the self-unravelling of his early novels to the solution of technical problems which became pressing in dealing with the contemporary scene. Paradoxically, this temporary lessening of interest in his obsessions led him to develop a technique for the first time adequate to project his vision of life.

There is room here for a misunderstanding. It must not be thought that Greene's view of life, which has always remained essentially unchanged, is weak in *It's a Battlefield* or *England Made Me*: it is there powerfully, but spread over the whole range of experience portrayed, 'distanced' by the new kind of interest in technique, and supported by fewer of the obsessional ideas discoverable in the early and the late novels. Some of these ideas do occur with considerable importance—betrayal, the loss of integrity in childhood and so on—but they do not provide the main subjects of the books in which they appear, and may be developed chiefly through the situation of some minor character.

Greene's eagerness to master the technical problems set him by dealing with the contemporary scene is evident in the literary influences to be detected in the books of this new phase. Literature is no longer a substitute for experience as in the early novels, but, in rendering his own observation of life, he is glad to take lessons from other writers who have faced the same or similar problems in their treatment of the modern world. The minor influences of James Joyce and Virginia Woolf can be seen in the style of certain passages of description or interior monologue, though at the time of writing this was nearly common form. The two major influences are Conrad and Henry James. From James he learnt how to give interest and subtlety to story-telling by the employment of the shifting 'point of view' and by an imaginative rather than fanciful use of imagery. The influence of Conrad is instructive because Greene had studied him (as he had not studied James) while writing his early books. Yet inevitably in the first phase Conrad's influence had been comparatively superficial. Now he could learn from Conrad's use of irony as a technique of presentation—the close relationship between *It's a Battlefield* and *The Secret Agent* shows how much.

It has been suggested that 'the terror of life' in this phase of Greene's work is no longer projected mainly through the self-torture of a single character, such as Michael Crane in *Rumour at Nightfall*, but is spread to create a general picture of a fallen world. The first signs of Greene's preoccupation with the seedy and squalid appear in the subsidiary elements of *Stamboul Train*. In the two novels seediness goes beyond the cruelties of material poverty, even beyond the 'spiritual bankruptcy' of modern life, until it stands for a permanent truth about the human situation. *It's a Battlefield* and *England Made Me* both depict the chaotic desolation and cut-throat values of the contemporary 'waste land'. In *England Made Me* Krogh, Kate and Anthony stand for rootlessness and meaninglessness—'What are the roots that clutch, what branches grow out of this stony rubbish?' *It's a Battlefield* shows that justice is no longer the 'keystone of the arch': whether human or divine, it seems equally incomprehensible. A horrified sensitiveness to the universality of pain produces the characterization of grotesques like Conder and Minty and devises the predicament of Milly Drover, the condemned man's wife in *It's a Battlefield*. Greene's world is already that of Newman's 'aboriginal calamity'.

In the later periods of Greene's development this vision of life takes hold of all his fiction, novel and entertainment alike. The most recent entertainment, *The Ministry of Fear*, is no less serious in theme than the most recent novel, *The Heart of the Matter*. In general the entertainment has to be distinguished from the novel by the comparative lack of development in the characters, by the wilful use of interesting background for its own sake, and, more particularly perhaps, by the freedom Greene allows himself in linking up the various sections of his narrative by coincidences and improbabilities. After *Stamboul Train* the pattern of the entertainments may be as subtle as that of the novels, but it is more easily achieved.

In *Journey Without Maps* Greene describes seeing in a cinema at Teneriffe the film made from *Stamboul Train*. He did not enjoy it.

> It was a bad film, one of the worst I have ever seen; the direction was incompetent, the photography undistinguished, the story sentimental. If there was any truth in the original it had been carefully altered, if anything was left unchanged it was because it was untrue. By what was unchanged I could judge and condemn my own novel: I could see clearly what was cheap and banal enough to fit the cheap banal film.

There are elements in *Stamboul Train* to appeal to the weekly film-goer and the 'C'-class novel reader, but even the strictest and stuffiest critic should find something to enjoy. There is an obviousness about the use of the 'closed setting', the Orient Express, with the opportunity it gives to present heterogeneous groups thrown together by chance, the ironical interaction and interdependence of ill-assorted people, the quickened tempo of thoughts and emotions under abnormal hot-house conditions. Yet, given this obviousness, Greene manages to introduce enough originality into his treatment of character and situation to raise the book above the level of the ordinary thriller.

Myatt, the Jewish business man, more self-conscious than his fellow-passengers, is aware of the seclusion of the setting, but not of its dramatic possibilities. His interior monologue at the outset of the journey is therefore an instance of irony:

> In the train, however fast it travelled, the passengers were

> compulsorily at rest; useless between the walls of glass to feel emotion, useless to try to follow any activity except of the mind; and that activity could be followed without fear of interruption. The world was beating now on Eckman and Stein, telegrams were arriving, men were interrupting the thread of their thought with speech, women were holding dinner-parties. But in the rushing reverberating express noise was so regular that it was the equivalent of silence, movement was so continuous that after a while the mind accepted it as stillness. Only outside the train was violence of action possible, and the train would contain him safely with his plans for three days. . . .

'Between the walls of glass' emotions will be felt, the course of lives be changed: at each stopping-place the violence of the outside world will break in on the passengers and its effect travel with them to their new destinations. Greene's story is unpretentious, yet the selection of characters and the railway-train setting imply an attempt to represent a fairly extensive cross-section view of life. And the train becomes, for one of the characters at least, a symbol of existence. As Czinner lies dying in a hut in Subotica he sees that to succeed one must be able at once to control and to exploit the movement of the express, 'leaning this way and leaning that, altering the balance now in this direction, now in that. One had to be very alive, very flexible, very opportunist.'

Of the dozen or so passengers whom we are told about in some detail four are most important. There is the shrewd young Jewish merchant Carleton Myatt (with a pocket full of currants like T. S. Eliot's Mr. Eugenides) whose uneasy sensitivity responds to the pathos of the chorus-girl Coral Musker, although she lacks altogether the sophisticated, expensive air that he likes his women to have. Myatt and Coral Musker are both on their way to Constantinople, he to conclude a business deal and she to join a dancing-troupe. Then there is Paul Czinner, political leader and refugee, returning to Belgrade to take part in a doomed rising, and Mabel Warren, an aggressive masculine woman who joins the train at Cologne on a sudden impulse because she has seen Czinner and scents a story. Other characters are grouped round these and acquire some significance from their position. Others again are not much more than picturesque movable properties in the background. One character, Joseph Grünlich, a thief eluding the police after a particularly cynical and sordid job in Vienna, does not fall readily into either of these classes. Though of no interest in himself, he is important in the action: it is through his behaviour that Czinner and Coral come to grief when they attempt to break away from a military guard at Subotica. Even the characters described as movable properties are given some sharp individual or 'specific' characteristics, from the cricket-playing English chaplain returning to Buda ('I'm trying—oh, so hard—to get up two elevens at the Embassy') to the rakia-drinking, card-playing station-clerks at Subotica.

In the foreground of the action is the rapidly developed, swiftly broken union between Myatt and Coral, a love-affair based on emotions like tenderness and pity entirely unknown in Czinner's world of violence and in the world of material comfort to which Janet Pardoe, another passenger and temporarily Mabel Warren's 'friend', calculatingly aspires. Coral presents a complete contrast to the beautiful, stupid, egotistical Janet. She comes from the same mould as Anne in a later entertainment, *A Gun for Sale*. Like Anne, she works in a chorus. Like her, she is used to 'the innumerable necessary evils'—the long waits in an agent's office, the dreary journeys to fulfil provincial engagements, the knowing how far to let men go—but cherishes a secret dream of security, even of love. Greene always romanticizes these girls, stressing their pathos and courage, the special appeal to him of their thinness and cheerfulness. Coral is shown as quick, matter-of-fact, capable of generous emotion; Myatt as immediately responsive to her frank easy friendliness. When she faints in the corridor of the train from cold and discomfort, Myatt gives up his first-class sleeper to her. Myatt's complex Jewish nature is admirably suggested, though with an occasional touch of glibness. For example, when he makes this gesture, Greene comments (in a passage that has dated since 1932):

> Forty years in the wilderness, away from the flesh-pots of Egypt, had entailed harsh habits, the counted date and the hoarded water, nor had a thousand years in the wilderness of a Christian world, where only the secret treasure was safe, encouraged display; but the world was altering, the desert was flourishing; in stray corners here and there, in Western Europe, the Jew could show that other quality he shared with the Arab, the quality of the princely host, who would wash the feet of beggars and feed them from his own dish....

Myatt continues his 'princely' hospitality the following morning. After spending an uncomfortable night in the corridor while Coral sleeps in his compartment, he buys her a ticket for a sleeping-berth. Coral's reactions—she too has had her dream, corresponding to Myatt's, of receiving gifts in the style of a great courtesan—are a confused mêlée of the warnings of older women, her own pride and a sense of the vulgarity of her suspicions. But a feeling of companionship develops in both of them and out of gratitude Coral that night becomes Myatt's mistress. He is deeply moved when he discovers that he has been her first lover. His proposal that they should live together in Constantinople opens up a new world to the girl. She derives from it the same excitement, gratitude and feeling of amazing luck that she would have known if Myatt had asked her to be his wife. The handling of the pathos of their short-lived relationship achieves a good balance between sympathy and detachment, a balance not always so happily struck even in the serious novels.

Into the uncovenanted idyll break the violence of Czinner's political world and Josef Grünlich's criminality. Czinner's whereabouts have been discovered by the government authorities, and he is arrested when the train stops at Subotica. Coral is alone on the platform when it happens. Because Czinner, as the military guard arrives, hands her some papers to post in Istanbul, she is arrested as an accomplice. Later Grünlich is thrust into the waiting-room and locked in with them because his gun has been discovered during the customs inspection. In spite of bewilderment Coral keeps up her spirits through the loss of the train and Czinner's immediate court-martial in the belief that Myatt will discover her absence and come back for her. Myatt makes his effort: he leaves the train at the next stop and hires a car to take him back to Subotica as quickly as possible. Czinner has been condemned to death. Now through one of the guards he learns that a car —Myatt's—has arrived near the station. Josef Grünlich picks the lock of the waiting-room door and all three manage to break away. But before they can reach Myatt's car Czinner is shot, Coral turns back to help him, and Grünlich, racing on ahead, jumps in and saves his own neck by telling Myatt that there is no one with him and that they must drive on at once to escape pursuit by the military police. Myatt is the more eager to believe Grünlich because here in eastern Europe he finds his money cannot save him from contemptuous snubs on account of his race.

Coral and Czinner shelter at night in a hut, concealed behind some sacks—a situation anticipating in some ways Raven's and Anne's in *A Gun for Sale*. Czinner dies in the small hours. By the morning Myatt has rejoined the train and soothed his conscience with the reflection that he has done everything possible to find Coral. Already he is beginning to take notice of the overtures of a Janet Pardoe intolerably bored with Mabel Warren's jealous possessiveness. Back in Subotica the military guard find Czinner's body, and Coral staggers to the door of the hut to fall into the arms of Mabel Warren, who has returned to pick up the trail of the Czinner story. This decides Coral's fate. Her role will be to fill the vacant place left by the exotic Janet in Mabel Warren's carefully decorated flat in Cologne.

The chief impression that remains after reading *Stamboul Train*, exclusive of the sense of irony and pathos injected into the story by Greene, is of the vast amount of information we seem to have acquired about the lives and background, not only of the principal figures, but of everyone who makes even a fleeting appearance in the action. This effect is obtained partly by following interior monologues, partly by the use of the appropriate image, partly by means of the packed station interludes, and partly by the exact disposition of broken fragments of dialogue in which Greene reveals his excellent ear for characteristic inflections and turns of phrase. Obviously the story he has to tell lends itself to most of the now familiar technical devices of the modern novel, and, though these appear to greater advantage in Greene's later work, they are used here unamateurishly and with discretion. Further, like all the entertainments, *Stamboul Train* is cinematic. In the opening scenes, as in the gas-practice of *A Gun for Sale*, it is impossible not to see the action in terms of tracking-shot, panning, close-up and fade-out. The camera-eye wanders from one compartment to another, resting now on the smug features of the insensitive clergyman, now on Coral's cheap white mackintosh, Czinner's weary face, or Myatt's expensive overcoat with its fur collar. Conscientiously a visible world is created: the blaze of the furnaces, the tables in the restaurant car, even the bizarre reflections in the dark glass of the window, where the transparent likeness of a hand, 'floating like a fish through which water and weeds shine', is carried gleaming through the night. It is interesting to compare the total impression made by this visual method with that of a novel of the same period. The setting of *It's a Battlefield* is London, but all the exteriors and interiors are pictorially less sharp than those of *Stamboul Train*. In the novel, mood blurs the edges of visual impressions in a manner sometimes reminiscent of Virginia Woolf's *Mrs. Dalloway*.

It has been said that hints of Greene's fallen world already appear in *Stamboul Train*. We have creations like the dreary, selfish Mrs. Peters with her plaintive burden about her digestion:

> Get me a sandwich. . . . I'm so empty I can hear my stomach. . . . No, I won't have any more of this foreign beer. My stomach won't stand it. Ask them haven't they got a Guinness. I'd just fancy a Guinness.

We have, too, the commercial Lesbian relationship between Mabel Warren and the vapid 'lovely' Janet Pardoe. Each of them thinks only of herself. We have the self-congratulation of the popular writer Savory, blown-up with the sense of his own importance. The fallen world is the world of the ruthless ego. 'No brotherhood in our boat', as Kate says in *England Made Me*. 'Only who can cut the biggest dash and who can swim.'

II

It's a Battlefield is a good example of the extent to which form and substance may assist each other in a novel. The book gains inner coherence partly through the skilful use of certain phrases in the manner of the leitmotiv, but more through the subtle management of the relationship between structure and theme.

The novel describes the reactions and the destinies of certain people connected in different ways with a London bus-driver sentenced to death for killing a policeman at a Communist meeting. Among these are his brother, his wife, his sister in law and the Police Commissioner. Early in the book the Police Commissioner visits Beale, private secretary to the Home Secretary, and overhears fashionable women chattering aimlessly:

> 'My dear it was divine. They tied the pram on the top of a taxi and Michael——'

The foolish image stays in the Commissioner's mind. Later, walking on the threshold of Piccadilly, he wonders about it.

> 'What were they saying?' he asked, 'about a pram on a taxi?'

> The Secretary laughed. 'A pram on a taxi—they are always up to something, those two. I expect it was Michael. A pram—on a taxi—and who was in the pram?' He laughed so loudly that two shop-girls turned small vivid faces towards him; a clerk in dark clothes carrying an attaché case, halted suddenly and stared at them. 'A pram—on a taxi', the phrase had lodged for a moment on the Commissioner's mind, and now spun like a teasing fly into other brains. . . . And the clerk flushed with anger, watching the two men turn the corner, rolling the phrase over on his tongue: 'A pram—on a taxi', convinced that he would never forget the meaningless joke which had set the man laughing.

The repeated phrase suggests the numerous disparate elements in the city, the different sections of the 'battlefield'; it also serves as a connecting-link to draw a central character into the action. The clerk who overhears the Commissioner and the Secretary is Conrad Drover, brother of the condemned man. In the section of the book which gives his 'point of view' we learn why 'he would never forget the meaningless joke'. He has recognized the Police Commissioner:

> After his brother's trial, in Piccadilly, on the steps of the Berkeley, he had heard the thin man with the jaundiced face say: 'A pram on top of a taxi' and laugh. . . . On the same day as his brother's fate was decided, the Commissioner could laugh at a stupid joke. His brother was just one of many men strung up for justice.

The phrase has sown a hatred which grows into an impulse to kill and ends with Conrad Drover's own death in an attempt to destroy the man he holds responsible.

This is only one example of the way in which the book is 'stitched together internally'—to use Mr. E. M. Forster's phrase. The many chance meetings, the intersecting pathways of people who, unknown to each other, are yet implicated in the life or death of the bus-driver Jim Drover, help to reinforce the theme stated in the title of the book. The words 'It's a battlefield', uttered unthinkingly by the Secretary, become another motif, often associated with the ex-colonial Police Commissioner for whom, after the simplicities of justice in eastern forests, the punctilio of Scotland Yard is bewildering. The novel's epigraph from Kinglake describes the conditions of a battlefield where separate groups fought their individual battles in ignorance of the general state of the action, 'nay even very often in ignorance of the fact that any great conflict was raging'. The battlefield as it appeared to 'the bare eye-sight of men':

> . . . had no entirety, no length, no breadth, no depth, no size, no shape, and was made up of nothing except small numberless circlets commensurate with such ranges of vision as the mist might allow at each spot. . . .

An impression of such 'small numberless circlets' is given by the glimpses we have of the novel's action as we move from the Commissioner's office to a match-box factory, from a condemned man's cell to his deserted house, from the condemned man himself to his wife, and see these places and people from different 'points of view' through mists of incomprehension, indifference or despair.

The fact of Greene's debt in this book to Conrad's *The Secret Agent* has been mentioned. In the first part of the novel the likeness between Greene's Police Commissioner and Conrad's Assistant Commissioner is striking. They have led the same kind of life, they have held similar posts under Colonial Administration; both are attempting, when they come under our scrutiny, to adjust themselves to the unfamiliar environment of home, and both encounter hostility on the part of their subordinates. They are troubled, conscience-stricken and tired, feeling out of touch with younger men and constantly travelling back in memory to the simpler ways of justice in the tropics. Either of the following passages from Conrad's *The Secret Agent* might apply to Greene's Commissioners in *It's a Battlefield*:

> His career had begun in a tropical colony. He had liked his

> work there. It was police work. He had been very successful. . . . But he did not like the work he had to do now.

Or again, with the 'battlefield' notion appearing:

> The Assistant Commissioner did not like his work at home. The police work he had been engaged on in a distant part of the globe had the saving character of an irregular sort of warfare or at least the risk and excitement of open-air sport.

Greene's Commissioner, walking through London, thinks that the administration of justice at home conflicts with his sympathies. He tries to reassure himself by seeing it in familiar terms of warfare:

> It was something to realize that the defence of this city was in his hands; it was easy to imagine for a moment that its enemies were all outside, that evil did not belong in this peace. . . . But the war which he fought was a civil war; his enemies were not only the brutal and the depraved, but the very men he pitied, the men he wanted to help. . . . It often occurred to him that he was less the general in control than the private soldier fighting in a fog like the men at Inkerman, in a fury of self-preservation.

The treatment of the interior monologue keeps us informed of the progress of the Commissioner's thoughts and of his journey at one and the same time:

> By the time he reached the courtyard he had decided that he did not care for politics. In Northumberland-avenue he said to himself that justice was not his business.

This inward comment not only provides us with a key to the Commissioner's special problem, but refers as well to an important idea running through the novel. The Commissioner constantly seeks to shelve his conscience-stricken preoccupation with justice by the idea of loyalty to the system which he serves:

> I've got nothing to do with justice, he thought, . . . One left justice to magistrates, to judges and juries, to members of Parliament, to the Home Secretary.

He relies as much for a sense of security on the knowledge that he belongs to an organization as Mather, the detective, does in *A Gun for Sale*. Mather says:

> . . . it's the routine which counts. . . . It doesn't matter to me if there's a war. When it's over I shall still be going on with this job. It's the organization I like. I always want to be on the side that organizes.

There is more bitterness and passion in the Commissioner's vision than in Mather's: *A Gun for Sale* is, after all, an 'entertainment'. The Commissioner is overwhelmed by the conflict between his view of humanity and his own need to be 'on the side that organizes'. By the end of the book it is clear that his strongest emotion is 'the sense of great waste, of useless expenditure of lives'. In a sense the book's main subject is the workings of what passes for justice in the world. The action is bounded on one side by the vain initial attempt on the part of the Commissioner to persuade himself that justice is not his business, and on the other by the closing incident, the resignation of the prison chaplain who can no longer stand its arbitrariness and incomprehensibility.

The quality of Greene's irony in this book is again reminiscent of the Conrad of *Victory* or *The Secret Agent*. Justice in *It's a Battlefield* demands Jim Drover's life in return for that of the policeman he killed: and yet justice, after taking certain mitigating factors into account, ordains that Drover's sentence be commuted to penal servitude for 'life'. On his release he will be long past middle-age and his wife, who is deeply in love with him, will be forty-five. A passage in the earlier book, *Stamboul Train*, foreshadows the tragic situation faced by the Drovers. Dr. Czinner, reading about the deaths of revolutionaries during the recent uprising, remembers a man 'who had a wife scarred and blinded in a factory accident, whom he loved and to whom he was sadly and unwillingly faithless'. Milly Drover, the condemned man's wife, faces an existence similar to that of the revolutionary. Because he knows that while he lives she will never be free, her husband tries to commit suicide by flinging himself from the top floor on his way back from the condemned cell to another part of the prison. That is why the prison chaplain resigns. There is further irony in the fact that from the beginning no one has wanted Drover to die. Even Beale, the suave young Ministerial secretary whom the Commissioner is preparing to meet at the beginning of the book, admits this:

> 'But the Minister, you know, doesn't want the poor devil's blood. Nobody does. It was a political meeting. Everyone was excited. Drover thought the bobby was going to hit his wife. He had the knife in his pocket. That, of course, is the snag. Why did he carry the knife?'
>
> 'They all do,' the Commissioner said. 'Helps to scrape away oil, mud. Cut up bread and—er—cheese.'

No one wants Drover's blood, not even the wife of the policeman he killed. Greene's study of this woman is an instance of his success in reproducing the vitality of a character fitted briefly into the dramatic pattern. Milly Drover visits her in order to secure if possible her signature to the usual petition. Mrs. Coney is fussy, frightened, kind and incompetent, 'a woman who drives the dust from one room to settle in another, who buys Danish eggs for economy and leaves the gas burning'. We are seeing now from Milly's point of view and the terms of reference are those she would use. Mrs. Coney has 'a commonplace kindliness', but what is felt most strongly is her particular blend of ignorance, fear, hatred and submissiveness. She will not add her name to the petition at first because she has a terror of signing anything:

> 'I don't like to *sign* anything without asking Arthur's brother. But you can tell them that I don't want him hung.'
>
> 'That's not enough. Please, Mrs. Coney', but she realized too late that begging would get nothing from the meek suspicious woman. Mrs. Coney for the first time in her life was tasting power. Though submission had always satisfied her, there was something in the novel taste which thinned her lips.

In the end it is only by blackmail that she can be persuaded to sign the petition. She gives in because she is too frightened and weak to deal with an eccentric newspaperman, Conder, and she can buy Milly's help with her signature. Conder turns on Milly with a bitter attack on people who say 'All I want is justice':

> 'As if justice were a pound of tea, as if it existed anywhere, as if——'
>
> 'I don't want justice,' Milly said, 'I've seen enough of it. I was in Court every day.'

It is not only the working out of this kind of justice which provides the larger ironies of the book. When, in the concluding pages, the prison chaplain tells the Commissioner that he is about to resign and makes his comment on the incomprehensibility of human justice, the Commissioner replies:

> 'I don't mean, of course, to be blasphemous, but isn't that very like, that is to say, isn't divine justice much the same?'
>
> 'Perhaps. But one can't hand in a resignation to God.'[1]

In effect, while the overt theme is obviously concerned with human justice, an underlying theme demonstrates the even greater mystery of another kind of justice and another kind of sentence. At the beginning of the book, when the Commissioner and the Secretary peer into the condemned cell to watch the gentle, apathetic figure of the bus-driver, the Commissioner knows that Drover's is not the worst kind of pain. He thinks of the effect on the man's wife:

> . . . the gossip in the fish-and-chip shops, the kind neighbours and the pain on Monday mornings with the washing for one hung out in the back garden, and the voices calling to and fro over the wooden fences.

[1] There would appear to be an echo here of Ivan in *The Brothers Karamazov*. 'Too high a price is asked for harmony. . . . And so I hasten to give back my entrance ticket. . . . It is not that I don't accept God, only I most respectfully return Him the ticket.'

Somewhere at the back of his mind a memory stirs of Dante's circles of hell, and, as the searchlight swoops over the prison buildings, over the graded blocks A, B and C, he knows that what he is watching now is 'only the outer circle'. This Dantesque symbol recurs. The section closes with a description of London at night: buskers entertaining theatre queues, prostitutes 'moving west', the match-factory turning out its last ten thousand boxes, the headlines in late editions screaming the latest case of rape and murder, the failure of a disarmament conference and the football news. The last words of the section are:

> At each station on the Outer Circle a train stopped every two minutes.

A recurrence of this notion may be taken as an example of Greene's use of symbol, in this case to reinforce the overt theme of the arbitrary nature of human justice. From the opening stages of the novel we know that some of the passengers on the 'Outer Circle' will be girls from the Battersea match-box factory, among them Kay Rimmer, Milly's sister. The parallel between Drover's prison and the factory in which Kay spends her working day seems over-contrived unless one takes into account the larger symbolism of which it is a part. The system of promotion in the factory is explained in terms identical with the description of the progress for good conduct in the prison: Block A for beginners, Block B for those who have shown signs of improvement, Block C where 'everyone is a skilled employee. Any serious mistake and they are moved back to Block B'. The authorities point out the excellence of the canteen and the hospital. Meanwhile, inside the factory,

> . . . between death and disfigurement, unemployment and the streets, between the cog-wheels and the shaftings, the girls stood, as the hands of the clock moved round from eight in the morning until one (milk and biscuit at eleven) and then the long drag to six.

The comparison between the factory and the prison requires an obvious emphasis in order that the underlying theme may be brought out. Because the horror is imposed on them by human authority, judicial or economic, the prisoners and the factory girls belong only to the Outer Circle of hell. Some of them even manage to escape the worst effects of standardization and loss of liberty. Kay, for example, fights against conformity. She attends Communist meetings not out of political interest, but because she knows that at these gatherings there will be 'fifty men to every woman' and that she will be better off than Greta at the cinema with one boy or Norma 'at a church meeting with a few pale men from a choir'. But there are others whose misery lies deeper—Conder, Jules Briton, even Mr. Surrogate and Caroline Bury. Worse off than any of these is Conrad Drover, condemned first to isolation from his kind, then to hopeless love, then to unwilling betrayal of his brother, and finally to attempted murder and suicide and a lonely, agonizing death.

Conrad Drover is the centre-pin of the action and, if plot and story could be dissociated from theme, *It's a Battlefield* would be largely his story and Milly's. We see him waiting for Kay at the end of her day at the factory. Through Kay's eyes we note his white face and twitching nerves:

> Pale, shabby, tightly strung, he had advanced from post to post in his insurance office with the bearing of a man waiting to be discharged . . . she considered the dark coat, the stiff collar, the old-young face, with pride and contempt, as much as to say, it's not everyone who could be like you and it's not everyone who'd want to be, 'you've got brains'.

Conrad Drover is Greene's first serious treatment of a recurrent type, the man who is isolated from the group to which he might belong because some ability or oddity or heightened sensibility sets him apart. In Conrad's case the isolating factor is his intelligence. It has brought him through examinations and finally earned him a well-paid job as a chief clerk while his brother has had to sit in a high glass cage and drive a bus. But he pays for it with his isolation and lack of love. He tells Kay that she ought to be glad there is someone on hand now with brains enough to help:

> She could not have told from his voice how he longed that it might be someone else. Brains had only meant that he must work harder in the elementary school and suffer more in the secondary school than those born free of them. At night he could still hear the malicious chorus telling him that he was a favourite of the masters, mocking him for the pretentious name that his parents had fastened on him, like a badge of brains, since birth. Brains like a fierce heat had turned the world to a desert round him, and across the sands in the occasional mirage he saw the stupid crowds, playing, laughing and without thought enjoying the tenderness, the compassion, the companionship of love.

It's a Battlefield is the novel in which this anguish first makes itself intensely felt. As long as they were secure Milly and Jim, the only two people in the world whom Conrad loves, had no need of him. Now, ironically, when the catastrophe occurs, he is the only man to whom they can turn, the only man who really cares what becomes of his brother. He sets out doggedly to do what he can:

> Conrad Drover, attaché case in hand, walked all the way to Battersea. He could not bring himself to spend any pence on bus or tube that might be spent on his brother's petition.[1] His brother was the only man he loved in the world, and his brother for the first time in his life needed him; strength for the first time needed brains.

[1] For ironic contrast compare this passage with the malicious description, in an earlier section, of the repulsive rentier and fake Socialist, Mr. Surrogate, practising his speech for the political meeting under the 'insolent Tartar eyes of Lenin in the plaster bust':

> 'Sacrifice, Mr. Surrogate thought, as he stared from the window of his bare and tasteful room into the wide blue pool of the Bloomsbury square . . . sacrifice. . . . Comrades, one man must die for the people. We accept Comrade Drover's sacrifice. . . .'

Here Greene uses the same devices he employs in the sections showing the Commissioner's point of view. As Conrad walks through the city towards Milly's house, streets and localities carry relevant associations. Battersea Bridge, the Battersea Polytechnic, bring memories of his own and his brother's childhood, their subsequent lives, his own secret love for Milly.

Milly is as typical a Greene character. She is another edition of Coral Musker in *Stamboul Train*, thin, pale, not clever, but sensitive, generous and impulsive. Coral, we remember, was 'plain and piquant, her manner daring and depressed'; Lucia Davidge in *England Made Me* has the same lack of taste and style, the same desperation:

> There was an amateurish look about her whole face, the too-pronounced lipstick, the dry flakes of powder on her neck. Her manner had the unconvincing swagger of a new boy at a boarding-school who has something to hide.

Anna Hilfe in *The Ministry of Fear* is 'very small and thin'. and looks 'too young for all the things she must have seen'. Greene's treatment of these women characters reflects his obsession with childhood. Their suffering resembles that of children who suffer without clearly understanding why. The emotions they arouse in their men-folk are more than anything the tenderness and pity felt for what is young and helpless, intensified by compassionate knowledge of inevitable guilt and pain. Paul Rostenne, a recent French critic of Greene, sees his female characters primarily as vessels of salvation and redemption, a view which can find some support in the treatment of Rose in *Brighton Rock*, the first novel in which the Catholic theme is overt. But to say further, as this critic does, that Greene's women can only be fully understood in the light of their special mission, is not only to treat the evidence of the novels in a disrespectful fashion; it is to ignore some of Greene's most fixed obsessions: the nostalgia for the lost innocence of childhood, the usual terror at what life can do to the young.

In *It's a Battlefield* Conrad's doomed relationship with

Milly is the focal point of the theme of betrayal. Because of Conrad's love for her, and Milly's bitter knowledge that she will one day be unfaithful to her husband, their betrayal of the man they both love becomes inevitable. Equally inevitable is their unhappiness. Conrad thinks as he lies awake:

> . . . it was not their fault. They had been driven to it, and holding her body close to him with painful tenderness, it was hate he chiefly felt, hate of Jim . . . of two men laughing in Piccadilly. When he awoke in the night she was crying, and nothing that he could do would stop her tears.

Counterpointing this part of the story is the experience of Milly's sister Kay. The treatment here of the love-and-lust opposition is a measure of the distance travelled since *The Man Within*. Kay is simply after enjoyment; she escapes from the day's fears and perplexities into sensuality, 'she never felt more at home than in a bed or a man's arms'. In love with a young Frenchman, Jules Briton, she takes up with Mr. Surrogate, whom she also encounters at a Communist meeting, and relaxes in the comfort of his exquisite flat and the luxury of his rose-coloured semi-circular bed. The theme of betrayal reappears here too in Surrogate's constant infidelity to the memory of his beautiful and talented wife, who had known him only too well. Back in her room next to where Conrad and Milly lie together in their misery, Kay falls deeply and happily asleep. Conrad thinks bitterly of her contentment:

> . . . lust, he thought, they call that lust and this is love. He meant the hate and the pain and the sense of guilt and the sound of crying in the greying room and sleeplessness and the walls shaking as the early morning lorries drove out of London.

Since injustice is 'as much a part of the body as age and inevitable disease', Conrad becomes the man who takes the law into his own hands. He buys a gun, pursues the Commissioner half-way across London, and tries to shoot him from the middle of the road as his quarry stands on the doorstep of a house he has just visited. A car attempts to brake quickly to avoid him, skids over the surface and knocks him down. All this is told in the stream-of-consciousness manner, a mingling of actuality and fantasy in which one idea is incessant—Conrad's belief that with one shot he will have freed himself from hatred, jealousy and lust. We follow his thoughts and sensations from the moment of raising the gun, through the time when he lies on the edge of the pavement watching his own blood and feeling pain struggle like a bird for freedom, to the end in the hospital ward, when in spite of his broken jaw he screams aloud and dies, his brain recording in a last flash of consciousness the other patients, the nurse reading by a lamp, 'and nobody beside his bed'.

To the world, to the little groups skirmishing in other parts of the battlefield, Conrad's behaviour is meaningless. Only two characters in the book are really concerned to understand the nature of the general war. One of these is Caroline Bury, the wealthy aging friend of both Surrogate and the Commissioner; the other is the Commissioner himself. Nobody else will recognize a general responsibility. Some are too stupid: others are too selfish. Surrogate, for example, has almost buried a half-awareness in luxury, in sex, in compensatory abstractions like Comradeship, Ideology, the New Order. Caroline Bury is wholly disinterested. A shrewd, sincere and wise woman who had befriended Surrogate's disappointed artist wife, who has known poets, painters, novelists and politicians, she is a survivor from the shipwreck of a more gracious era. She thinks with compassion of Jim Drover and summons Surrogate, the political dabbler, to the sitting-room where, we are told:

> Henry James had constructed his sentences like Chinese boxes which held at the centre a tiny colloquialism; Meredith had unloosed a torrent of epigrams; Hardy had wondered what it was all about. . . .

She learns the facts from him, then invites the Commissioner to dinner:

> 'I wanted you to come early,' Caroline Bury said, 'to ask you about Drover. People say he's going to be hanged. It's absurd.'

She knows there are wheels within wheels. She is aware, for example, that the Commissioner has been asked for a report on the possible reactions in certain areas to Drover's hanging. But she is also sensitive enough to realize, in the midst of her appeal for the Commissioner's help, that since Drover has a wife perhaps she ought after all to be urging the Commissioner to see that he is hanged. Her delicacy and unselfishness prove quite useless. Alone, aging, and perhaps about to die as a result of an operation she fears but will endure without complaint, she is as incapable as anyone else of affecting the strategy of the general war.

Everything we need to know about the meeting-plane of these two 'survivors', about the Commissioner and Caroline, is revealed in a few short passages of conversation between them. They dine tête-à-tête to the Commissioner's surprise:

> 'Are we alone, Caroline'? he asked with astonishment.
>
> 'Yes,' she croaked at him, 'alone,' and trailed before him to the door in her absurd, her expensive, her timeless dress. She might have added that they were alone as far as she knew in not caring for their own troubles, for not fighting their own battle in ignorance of the general war.

Over dinner they talk of faith: Caroline feels it would be maddening to die now, 'with the world in the state it is', if one had not faith. Not Christianity but the feeling that things make sense:

> 'Well,' he said, 'of course one—er—hopes . . .'
>
> 'What do you hope?'

But as he sits crumbling his bread the Commissioner has no real hope at all:

> 'Well,' he said, 'one lives and then, that is, one dies.' It was the nearest he could come to conveying his sense of a great waste, a useless expenditure of lives.

In his mind are the images of Caroline in the operating theatre, Drover on the scaffold, the girl in a new case who was raped and murdered on Streatham Common: 'It was impossible to believe in a directing purpose, for these were not spare parts which could be matched again.'

For a critic who wants to prove the existence in Greene of a lively social concern about the 'death throes of the old society', *It's a Battlefield* provides the necessary ammunition. It is a real part of a book which belongs indisputably to the political 'thirties. A critic could point to the privileged few who, at their best, are troubled with the sense of their own weakness and impotence: Caroline; the Commissioner; perhaps even the effete Surrogate playing at revolution, and Beale, the public-school man who as private secretary to the Home Secretary has no special qualifications beyond 'charm' for the job. He could find passages in conversations between Caroline and the Commissioner where the social problem is explicitly stated:

> 'Do you believe in the way the country is organized? Do you believe that wages should run from thirty shillings a week to fifteen thousand a year, that a manual labourer should be paid less than a man who works with his brains? They are both indispensable, they both work the same hours, they are both dog-tired at the end of their day. Do you think I've the right to leave two hundred thousand pounds to anyone I like?'
>
> 'No.'
>
> 'But you support it. You support it more than any other single man. Without the police force such a state of affairs couldn't last a year.'

The political aspect is certainly discernible, but it does not require to be recognized 'with the last fineness'. The total impression made by the book is, in Newman's words, that of a 'heart-piercing' and 'reason-bewildering' mystery. One of Greene's short stories, 'The Lottery Ticket', concludes with the despair of the principal character, Mr. Thriplow: 'it was the whole condition of human life that he had begun to hate'. This is closer to the truth underlying the action in *It's a Battlefield.* The waste and error and pain are nearly unendurable. A catastrophe has occurred and man suffers permanently as a result. Edwin Muir once suggested that the modern novelist had ceased to interest himself in man as a being capable of salvation or damnation and now saw him only as a creature whose happiness might be compassed by social engineering. Greene would agree with him. *It's a Battlefield* is an attempt to juxtapose 'political' and existential anguish, seeing the lesser in terms of the greater, by means of an elaborate technique of irony.

It is an immature book and, consequently, not a wholly successful one. At times successive influences can be traced as the style alters from section to section. Most of these influences—hints and half-hints of Woolf, Joyce, even Auden—are unimportant and can be ignored, but the irony is Conrad's irony and part of the book's pattern is owed to *The Secret Agent.* Apart from the likeness between the Police Commissioner and Conrad's Assistant-Commissioner, there are other parallels to be found. Greene borrows no more ideas for character, but he has sometimes hit, perhaps unconsciously, on relationships similar to those in Conrad's novel. For example, the relationship between Conrad's Assistant-Commissioner and Inspector Heat is echoed; and Surrogate stands to Caroline Bury somewhat as Michaelis, the ticket-of-leave apostle of humanitarian hopes, stands to his 'great lady'. Conrad's technique of ironic presentation strengthened Greene's hand enormously in this first novel of his that needs to be taken seriously. But Greene's own tragic and ironic vision was not yet fully capable of integrating the various elements over which it is seen to play.

III

Greene himself places *England Made Me* third after *The Heart of the Matter* and *The Power and the Glory* in order of achievement among his novels. Taut construction, a more than usually arresting and worked-over style and the sharp, distinct realization of character may account for its being also one of the most generally praised of his books. Technically it is extremely skilful, though it lacks the structural complexities of *It's a Battlefield*. If it still shows quite definite traces of outside literary influences, these are less disturbing to unity of tone than in the preceding novel.

Notions of exile, isolation and estrangement are heavy in the atmosphere of the book. These are combined with the old theme of betrayal in a setting of High Finance, more exotic for its situation in Stockholm. (Krogh, it has been said, was inspired by Kreuger.) Against this background there is a curious emphasis on the relationship between a twin brother and sister, Anthony and Kate Farrant, which is almost incestuous in its special intensity. The angle of vision from which the characters are seen displays their loneliness, cynicism and frustration. One of the principal characters, Kate Farrant, says:

> We're all thieves. . . . Stealing a livelihood here and there and everywhere, giving nothing back. . . . No brotherhood in our boat. Only who can cut the biggest dash and who can swim.

The most notable technical achievement in *England Made Me* is Greene's use of the shifting 'point of view'. This reaches a more sophisticated level than in *It's a Battlefield* and is reinforced by a special use of imagery only occasionally anticipated in the earlier book. Each of the seven parts belongs primarily to one of the main characters, but at the same time takes up and develops relationships introduced in other sections. Greene uses a method, which he was again to employ consistently in *Brighton Rock*, of subdividing these parts into sections which can 'cut' to a number of different 'points of view'.

Part II, for example, is mainly concerned with the financier Krogh whose name is associated with everything that money can buy—in Sweden, in England, on the Continent:

> Krogh like God Almighty in every home; impossible in the smallest cottage to do without Krogh; Krogh in England, in Europe, in Asia, but Krogh, like Almighty God, only a bloody man.

As with the Police Commissioner in *It's a Battlefield*, Greene follows Krogh's thoughts through the activities of an afternoon and evening to reveal his obsessions and anxieties. Occasionally there is an interpolated passage of description:

> His high bald face, like a roll of newspaper, showed at a distance only bold headlines; the smaller type, the little subtleties, obscure fears, were invisible.

Gradually we discover facts about Krogh's life: the obscure penurious childhood in Chicago, the struggles of his youth in Barcelona, the new cutter which brought him his fortune, his fatalism:

> He did not believe in God, but he believed implicitly in the lines on his hand. . . . If the company failed he would never hesitate to kill himself. Kreuger lying shot in the Paris hotel was his model. He questioned his courage for the final act as little as he questioned his honesty.

Outside his business world his position is symbolized by the 'wilderness of his own contriving' which surrounds him each night at the opera—'He was Krogh; his taste in music had to be displayed in Stockholm'—and which at once advertises his presence and guards his ignorance. Krogh invariably books the surrounding seats to ensure that nobody will talk to him. The things his money can buy bring him no pleasure; the nearest he gets to any real relationship is in watching the enormous initials of his own name flashing at him in electric lights over every doorway in the vast Krogh office-building, 'like the lights of a semaphore carrying a message over the vast distances which separate him from other men'. So it is significant that during the course of his day at Krogh's and at the British Embassy among fashionable women, there should be no mention of his secretary and mistress, Kate Farrant, whose point of view is given with a marked change of manner and style in the last section of this part of the book.

Subjective commentaries in Greene's novels usually demonstrate his control over the freedom with which we are allowed to follow the thoughts and feelings experienced by his characters: like James he avoids the 'terrible fluidity of self-revelation' by checking and restricting the material. In this phase of his work, however, he sometimes introduces variations which recall Dorothy Richardson, or even Joyce's Molly Bloom—Kate Farrant's thoughts, for example, blurring and confusing and mingling in half-sleep as she lies beside Krogh. She has just returned from England with her scapegrace brother Anthony, whom she intends to place at Krogh's. Their relationship has already been defined in Part I, which describes their London meeting and opens with Kate waiting for Anthony at a railway station with the words 'She might have been waiting for a lover'. With great rapidity this scene sketches in outline Anthony's weak, shifty nature, his humour and charm, and goes on to suggest Kate's jealous devotion. Now memories of their childhood, Anthony's accident with a knife, his long series of seedy disreputable adventures, her present plans, the difficult but successful negotiation with Krogh, return at the end of her day:

> I awake and Erik sleeping and his cold hand on my side. All settled. . . . So tired he was. Never seen so tired now asleep so cold his hand. Anthony asleep now, the scar below the eye, the knife slipping upwards suddenly through the rabbit's fur, the scream, he went on screaming, no control, the matron said. I woke in the middle of the night hearing him fifty miles away. Knew he was in pain. Father ill. They wouldn't let me go. The French exam all that day long, the irregular verbs and twice the supervisor went out with me to the lavatory. . . . Awake sleeping hand cold all settled.

The final passages of this section with their fragmentary images, merging associations and puns are thoroughly Joycean. Krogh, unexpectedly amused, has given Anthony a job as his bodyguard after hearing that he has won a toy tiger at a shooting-gallery. The scenes at the fair mingle in Kate's mind with her relief and her sense that she may yet save Anthony and keep him with her:

> Tiger burning bright in Tivoli, immortal eye, the hand against my side, feet touching mine; even there the women watched him . . . what shoulder, and what art, to see the rockets throwing down their spears. . . .
>
> Don't be afraid. Don't hesitate. No cause of fear. No bulls on this exchange. The tiger bright. The forests. Sleep. Our bond. The new redemption. And we rise, we rise. And God Who made the lamb made Whitaker, made Loewenstein. . . . 'Krogh's safe. Whatever comes or goes people will always everywhere have to buy Krogh's.' The market steady. . . . Sleep. The new redemption. No bulls, the tiger and the lamb. The bears. The forests. Sleep. The stock is sound. Sleep. The closing price. We rise.

This section balances Anthony's section of first-person narration in Part I, which opens without preamble in the stream-of-consciousness manner and recounts, unchronologically, events and emotions characteristic of Anthony's life. Recurrent images of the book are worked in: the knife slipping upwards through the rabbit's fur, the cracked bell ringing in school (Greene's symbol for an unhappy childhood). Certain themes also emerge: Anthony's grudge against the world for not trusting him, and his sense of exile, the feeling that he never belongs. A similar method is used in introducing another exile, the newspaperman Minty, who is the first of Greene's full-length grotesques. Minty's main source of livelihood is Krogh, who is always 'news'. Momentarily seen in the second part of the book when he makes a deal with Anthony, Minty in his turn is put on the slide later for close inspection.

The various points of view so far are subtly interconnected: the characters are related to each other not only through the plot but by exemplifying different aspects of similar themes. An exception occurs with the introduction late in the story of a young worker named Andersen. A threatened crisis comes to a head when Krogh finds it necessary to manipulate, not altogether legally, the finances of subsidiary companies in order to preserve the parent company's reputation for unshakable security—'Value's confidence. As long as we receive money, we're valuable.' At the same time there is trouble at one of Krogh's factories out of town, where the outcome of a strike involves the dismissal of an old Socialist workman, Andersen's father. The son—a Conservative, who believes in paternalism in industry and thinks there has been a mistake—travels up to the city: he imagines that he has only to see Krogh for the injustice to be put right. Greene follows Andersen all the way to Stockholm, revealing his thoughts and sketching in small incidents to show us Andersen's youth, inexperience and stubborn earnestness. This is to ensure that the brutal outcome of his journey shall make its full effect. The closely worked drama of these sequences and our anticipation of an ironic climax prevent us from finding the break in continuity disconcerting.

As Andersen travels up from the country a Dutch plane is bringing Fred Hall, Krogh's staunch bitter little henchman, from Amsterdam. Hall has the dangerous loyalty that sticks at nothing. Greene shows him smoking an illicit cigarette in the lavatory of the plane, 'endangering the lives of twelve passengers, a pilot, a wireless operator, and several thousand pounds of property', but not giving a damn:

> . . . his flat narrow skull had no room for anything but obedience to the man who paid him, fidelity to the man he admired, and the satisfaction of certain physical needs: cigarettes, a monthly drunk, and what he always called 'blowing off steam' . . . he didn't trust anyone near Krogh except himself, he wanted to blow off steam, there was nothing he would like so much at the moment as to beat someone up.

When he arrives he finds more than one person 'near Krogh'. He has become used to Kate, without ever growing to trust her: now he has to put up with her brother and, at sight, is jealous and distrustful. He finds brother and sister together with Krogh in the midst of a celebration dinner. Unknown to Hall, Kate has agreed in this time of crisis to marry Krogh as a precautionary measure. They have even arranged if necessary to leave Sweden for England, where a wife need not give evidence against her husband. Hall's arrival at the hotel restaurant coincides with that of young Andersen.

The dinner-party is one of the book's central scenes, drawing together most of the characters and indicating with the aid of technical subtleties the substrata of relationship and emotion. Krogh's celebration coincides with that of the eccentric Professor Hammersten, whose life-long ambition to produce *Pericles* is to be realized with Krogh's financial backing—Krogh's gesture is the kind of extravagance which is expected of him from time to time. The two groups converge: Krogh and his dependants; the Professor and his company of twelve theatre folk chattering in French, Swedish, and Anglo-American. The scene is presented almost entirely in the form of dialogue, in which misunderstandings and gossip mingle with Shakespearean quotations in a gradually thickening drunken haze. We hear Professor Hammersten reciting snatches of *Pericles*—'What a wet play. . . . The sea. And ooze', says Anthony. The theme of death by drowning and the comments it provokes, especially Anthony's 'the easiest death', are ironical when we remember the end of the book. Anthony's quotation, 'And her to incest did . . .', is used to underline the renewal of an old intimacy felt by Kate and him. The words are on Anthony's lips when he takes an actress from Hammersten's party into the gardens and finds young Andersen, soaking wet in the rain, looking for Krogh. Out of a sense of fair play Anthony does his best to help by bringing him indoors and returning to tell Krogh. Fred Hall arrives in the middle of Anthony's unsuccessful attempts to persuade Krogh to see Andersen. Without hesitation he fits on his knuckle-dusters, walks to the entrance hall, and brutally puts

Andersen out of action. As he retraces his steps, thinking bitterly that no one besides himself is disinterested enough to help Krogh, he leaves Andersen, half-blinded with his own blood, saying: 'I don't understand . . . don't understand.'

Almost all these widely different characters have one thing in common: the loneliness they feel in their isolation. For a time Kate thinks Krogh is self-sufficient and immune from ordinary human weakness, and it is important to her understanding of her own predicament when she realizes that in some matters he can feel hesitant and insecure. On the way to the celebration at Saltsjöbaden, Krogh, already a little drunk, makes Anthony stop the car so that he can have a word with some men at work on a new railway bridge. 'I worked on a bridge myself once', he says, and, as if to stress this fact, one of the workmen has his own Christian name. As Kate watches Krogh standing on the track, 'interested in spite of himself . . . without words to explain what he wanted', she thinks:

> He's one of us, fighting for his own security like one of us, he's not the future, he's not self-sufficient, just one of us, out of his proper place . . .

and her genuine disenchanted sympathy goes out to him. Unconsciously she describes the fate of the uprooted and the exiled everywhere:

> . . . poor devil, what a long and tiring way he's come and they wouldn't take any notice of him, wouldn't recognize that he was once of their own kind. . . .

She puts her arm round his shoulder:

> . . . a family party, one might as well be kind: three of us now climbing together, honour among thieves.

The main themes of the book are the loneliness of the displaced person (and we are all displaced if not so obviously as the expatriate like Minty or the declassé like Krogh); and the consequent nostalgia for something representing 'home'. The latter entails secret loyalties to half-forgotten traditions in the past. When Krogh tries to think of some way of putting his men at their ease he can only think of one joke. It comes to him 'out of a secret past' and carries with it 'the pathos and beauty that attach to something from an unhappy youth that has never been quite forgotten'. He is saddened and ashamed that even this story must be used for the sake of his career. Minty remembers his years at Harrow with hatred, but there is still the feeling of an unbreakable tie:

> He hated and he loved. The school and he were joined by a painful reluctant coition, a passionless coition that leaves everything to regret, nothing to love, everything to hate, but cannot destroy the idea: we are one body.

Anthony's 'depraved innocence'—he is an instance of what E. M. Forster has called 'the undeveloped heart'—has its roots in his 'Berkhamsted' schooldays. All he remembers of that time is his misery:

> Feet on the stone stairs, running, scrambling, pushing, up to the dormitory. . . . Not a moment of quiet even at night, for always someone talks in his sleep the other side of the wooden partition. I lay sweating, unable to sleep . . . waiting for the thrown sponge . . . the hand plucking at my bed-clothes, the giggles, the slap of bare feet on wooden boards.

He had been prevented from running away only by Kate's persuasions. Their meeting in a barn half-way between the two schools is a recurrent memory in the book. Kate's efforts to help Anthony now—the job at Krogh's, the settlement she exacts in return for her agreement to marry Krogh—are attempts to repair the damage done then:

> I've undone the damage I did when I sent him back, back from the barn to conform, to pick up the conventions, the manners of all the rest. . . . Now I've discovered a way out for him.

But Anthony, like Minty, still proclaims allegiance to a system he has hated. He even promotes himself from his minor public school with an Old Harrovian tie that arouses

Minty's indignation. Anthony and Minty are akin and Anthony knows it:

> . . . he saw himself and Minty clearly as one person; the exile from his country and his class . . . the refuse of a changing world. If Minty was to be envied at all, it was that he had chosen his dump and stayed there.

The 'changing world' has no place to offer Anthony, Minty or even Kate:

> They were not fresh enough, optimistic enough to believe in peace, co-operation, the dignity of labour, or if they believed in them, they were not young enough to work for them. They were neither one thing nor the other.

Of Anthony and herself Kate thinks:

> Good Looks and Conscience . . . the fine flowers of our class. We're done, we're broke, we belong to the past, we haven't the character or the energy to do more than hang on to something new for what we can make of it.

Yet, natural rolling stone that he is, Anthony rejects Krogh's and breaks with Kate for the sake of something he thinks of as 'home'. Home is represented by the pathetic charm of Lucia Davidge with her suburban talk about the freedom of women, her love-affairs—'Once in Coventry . . . and once at Wotton-under-Edge'—and her background of Lyons, Woolworth's and the Moroccan café in the High Street at home. Anthony meets her while she is on holiday in Sweden with her parents. When he sees her off at the station he suddenly succumbs to the fear of losing her flattery of his vanity—Kate tells him too many unpleasant home-truths—and arranges to meet 'Loo' in England at the end of the week.

Of all the book's exiles Minty is perhaps the most pitiable. Earning a little extra money in a squalid job, he is a being constantly on the edge of despair. His perversions of mind and spirit cast a distorted reflection of some still glimpsed personal ideal of human behaviour. To this type belongs Conder the newspaper man in *It's a Battlefield*. Conder has not Minty's religious consolation—Minty is an Anglo-Catholic—but he shores up his existence with fantasies against the knowledge of failure and of the real Conder living alone in a bedsitting-room: fantasies of being a powerful business magnate, a revolutionary, a successful journalist and, most frequently and most inventively, a family man. Where there is faith, in Greene, there is the profounder sense of evil and the more hopeless degeneration. Thus Acky the unfrocked clergyman in *A Gun for Sale* is much closer to Minty. Acky's marriage to the aged 'Madam' symbolizes the union of madness and wickedness: between them is 'the complete belief, the awe and mutual suffering of a great love'. Minty's fanatical hatred of the human body shows the same distorted idealism that lies behind Acky's perverted sense of injustice. Minty's bitterness goes back to the steel nibs dug into his calf on account of his piety and his incense-cones, his smallness and his ridiculous clothes. Now, immune from ridicule but still the outsider, he tries, like the book's other English characters, to make 'a home from home'. In his dingy room are the Harrow photograph, the religious missal in the cupboard, the one cracked cup, the cigarette stub waiting in the soap-dish, the spider trapped under the tooth-glass. Outside in the alien world bitterness and malice colour his behaviour, but in his room the urge to tease and torment is worked off on the spider. In bed at night after his prayers, no longer 'blown out to meet contempt', he himself lies 'humbly tempting God to lift the glass'.

The loneliness and misery of exile is brought out with special emphasis in a scene where Anthony takes Lucy to Minty's room. He takes her there because there is nowhere else for them to go. Minty is surprised into believing that he is being visited as a friend. He becomes an excited host, offering his one spoon, his opened tin of condensed milk. When he realizes it is his bed that is wanted he sets off, laughing, a perfect Pandarus, to the newspaper office, but nothing can conceal his bitter disappointment. Even when they are alone

Anthony and Lucy feel the contagion of Minty's unhappiness. The thin smell from his incense cones attaches itself to Anthony's fingers 'like misery'. Close beside Lucia, Anthony's careful optimism vanishes:

> 'Poor devil,' he said. Their bodies touched and suddenly they were together again in their hunger, their sense of time passing. 'It's a dreary world.'

But for the moment she will not have it so:

> 'No,' Loo said, 'no. It's good. There's always this.' 'This' was their kiss, the closer embrace, the half-reluctant effort which drove them to the bed.

The relationship between Lucia and Anthony is in many ways a characteristic Greene affair. It involves the idea of a betrayal—'the recurring itch of the flesh' is stronger than 'thirty years in common' and wrecks the intimacy between Kate and Anthony. The girl is plain and pathetic, yet desirable. The man feels mostly tenderness and pity for his new mistress. Less usual however is the light-hearted treatment of their early morning meeting before calling on Minty. 'Loo' has a kind of teen-age charm with her scruples and her simplicities about avoiding sentimentality and being frank about sex. Her emancipated prattle provokes Anthony to say, 'I don't believe you've ever had a man. . . . I believe you're a virgin', and she slaps his face for saying 'such a beastly thing'. But, as in the Saltsjöbaden scenes, this light-heartedness has tragic overtones.

Anthony never meets Lucia in the Moroccan café 'in the High Street'. He never gets home at all. 'I haven't a future', he tells Kate early in the story and, unreliable, 'deceitful in small ways, hopeless with money' as he is, he has this amount of self-knowledge. Before he can leave Stockholm he is killed by Fred Hall, who thinks that Farrant knows too much and fears he will betray Krogh. After all this is the only logical outcome for Anthony: he has to die because there is nowhere else for him to go. Kate, sensing Hall's suspicions, tries to explain that Anthony is only leaving to join Lucia, but he refuses to believe her. Hall both hates and respects Kate:

> They had the same ideas, neither had cared a hang what happened to Andersen; the only difference was that they did not work for the same man.

He tells her that he will try to take all Anthony's money off him in a poker-game that evening to prevent his sailing, but Anthony buys his tickets and with the last hand of the evening wins back all he has lost and more in one coup. His straight flush is his death-warrant. Hall and he leave Krogh's apartments within a moment or two of each other. There is dense fog outside, and when his body is recovered from the lake next day no one is held responsible.

In 'Heroes Are Made in Childhood' Greene mentions his early reading of a boy's adventure story about a young subaltern captured in the Sahara by a Yankee pirate:

> He was captured and watched his enemies dig his grave. He was to be shot at dawn, and to pass the time and keep his mind from uncomfortable thoughts, the amiable Yankee pirate played cards with him—the mild nursery game of Kuhn Kan. The memory of that nocturnal game on the edge of life haunted me for years until I set it to rest at last in one of my own novels with a game of poker played in remotely similar circumstances.

In *England Made Me* the scene of Anthony's last game of poker is written with great skill in dialogue which suggests all the hidden cross-currents of the situation. Hall bids quickly, then withdraws interest from his cards and sits in patient, suspicious silence, staring at Krogh. Krogh silent almost throughout the scene, knowing Hall's determination to win. Kate does not play but watches Anthony, trying to fix the scene in her memory. She is filled with anguish thinking of his departure in the morning:

> I love no one, nothing but him; therefore give him me, let me keep him; never mind what he wants, save me . . . from pain;

> do I call it pain, agony, parting here . . . the wires down, no more thoughts in common.

She looks out of the window, seeing the lights turned off one by one in houses across the lake, the mist driven up from the water to a man's height by the wind. On the radio a voice singing of love from Paris:

> Aimer à loisir,
> Aimer et mourir,
> Au pays qui te ressemble,[1]

reminds us of Lucia Davidge waiting at home in England. Most remarks possess an ironic force. Kate refuses to play any more with 'I'm out of this. . . . I've lost enough.' When Gullie, the blunt witted military attaché at the British Embassy, is childishly boisterous, she says, 'There'll be tears before night'. Gullie alone is outside the situation, his running-fire of facetious comment increasing the tension of the others. The climax of the game is reached when Anthony, himself always quite happy and 'beaming at nothing, or everything', gets his straight flush. Kate thinks:

> He's beaten them after all. . . . Tony happy, the mist rising . . . in his hand a straight flush. . . . He'll remember this . . . year after year he'll talk about tonight, playing poker with Krogh, drawing five cards, drawing a straight flush. The story going round the world, in how many clubs, always unbelieved.

After Anthony's departure it is characteristic of the style and manner of the scene that we should realize, without being told in so many words, when it is that Krogh is suddenly aware of what is going to happen. Without comment he walks to the bathroom to take some aspirin, and when Kate notices that the bottle is empty and asks him what is wrong, he replies briefly, 'A headache'. Krogh's affection for Anthony is real and the outcome of the poker game is a tragedy for more

[1] These lines are, of course, from the first stanza of Baudelaire's *L'Invitation au Voyage*.

than one of those taking part. Even Hall, returning out of the fog to fetch his abandoned wallet, gives Kate the impression of 'some great pain hopelessly demanding sympathy'.

The allusive economy of Greene's method in *England Made Me* is increased by his use of images. He makes them serve the twofold purpose of reinforcing his themes and revealing character. Whether or not the influence of Joyce is conscious in passages of first person narration or interior monologue, Greene is ready to admit a deliberate imitation of Henry James, especially in his opening pages. In general James's influence is 'probably indetectible', but there are occasions in *It's a Battlefield* and *England Made Me* when Greene employs images, like James, to achieve 'deep-breathing economy and organic form'. To the Commissioner in *It's a Battlefield*, driving past Clapham Junction into the Victorian suburb and looking sadly out at the streets:

> Candahar-road, Khyber-terrace, Kabul-street, the Victorian villas wavered in the mist like a shaking of shakos in old imperial wars.

This is pure James in its way of revealing something about the person to whom the image occurs as well as about the objects it describes.[1] There may be instances in *England Made Me* of the merely clever decorative comparison—'his tenderness welled from him like an ectoplasm in the darkness of the hall', 'worry which sat his face uneasily like a recruit at a riding-school'—but there are many passages in which metaphorical language is used in the Jamesian manner.

For example, in a passage describing Anthony Farrant, Greene writes:

> Congratulate me, he seemed to be saying, and his humorous, friendly shifty eyes raked her like the headlamps of a second-hand car which have been painted and polished to deceive.

[1] It is Jamesian even in grammatical form—the characteristic use of the indefinite article and verbal noun at the beginning of a simile.

With this we may compare James's description of Owen Gereth in *The Spoils of Poynton*—a book which Greene greatly admires:

> 'You don't think I'm rough or hard do you?' he asked of Fleda, his impatience shining in his idle eyes as the dining-hour shines in club windows.

The two images suggest Gereth's vacant, gentlemanly days, Farrant's makeshifts, deceptions and seediness. Farrant has the gentlemanly appearance and charm of an Owen Gereth—they are his stock-in-trade—but at the same time he shares the characteristics of James's plausible twister, Horton Vint, in *The Ivory Tower*. The following quotation might serve for 'Horty' and his 'beautiful mitigating smile':

> When Anthony turned his smile explained everything; he carried it always with him as a leper carried his bell; it was a perpetual warning that he was not to be trusted.

Images occurring in passages about Krogh's world of sterile efficiency and speculative high finance are often drawn from mechanical things and may carry the further implication of collapse and breakdown. When Krogh remembers the wild duck his father shot in childhood, he links it now, in his mechanically ordered present, with the idea of an abandoned, half-submerged aeroplane. He hears voices muffled by the mist and thinks of 'the human heat damped down like the engines of a liner flooded and floundering'. It is apt then at the time of Krogh's crisis for Kate to recall a runaway tram:

> . . . glass and steel and the face of the driver with his hand pressed on a lever and the current running through and sparking behind the glass. It rocked by her in the dark and she could tell by the flicker of light that something was wrong.[1]

She thinks of this again when Anthony tries for a moment to persuade her to blackmail Krogh:

[1] Greene has a similar memory. Cf. *The Lawless Roads*, Chapter 4, 'Journey Downhill'.

> It almost seemed as if there was nothing he wouldn't do, but she knew that somewhere on that straight steel track down which his brain now so quickly drove there burned a permanent red light; somewhere he would stop, waver, make a hash of things.

Imagery is also used to tell us about the old Kate–Anthony relationship. Watching him in her office, she thinks it happiness to have him there, making for himself 'a home from home'. Everything about him pulls at her heart, but with her intellect she belongs to the efficient Krogh world: 'she was like a dark tunnel connecting two landscapes'. It is her tragedy that this is untrue. Through working with Krogh and identifying herself with his schemes she has lost her old power to understand her brother sympathetically: a failure made clear by their mutual loss of telepathic rapport. This is not the only time that Greene attributes this peculiar kind of communication to twins. In a short story, 'The End of the Party', he describes the sympathetic tie between twin brothers, Peter and Francis, of whom Peter is the elder by a few minutes:

> . . . that brief interval of light, while his brother struggled in pain and darkness, had given him self-reliance and an instinct of protection towards the other.

Peter's brain 'beats' with his brother's thoughts and fears. Kate Farrant, older than Anthony by half an hour, for thirty years shares his thoughts and feels 'his fears beat in her own body.' The power wanes. Early in the story Anthony says, 'I think we were happy knowing what the other thought, feeling what the other felt. This is the curse. The ceasing to know.' Without real understanding Kate makes a last attempt to compete with 'home' and with Lucia, and she breaks into tears when she fails:

> His bonhomie infuriated her. . . . She said . . . 'Everything I've done was to help you, and now because a little bitch——' She despised her own tears; they were too cheap an appeal. . . .

She turns away with a final 'Go to hell', and that is the end.

They are so completely pulled apart now by divergent loyalties that not even the faintest premonition reaches her of Anthony's death the same night.

After Anthony's death Kate decides to leave. At the cremation when Minty asks her whether she is returning to England she replies, 'No . . . I'm simply moving on. Like Anthony'. This last conversation is tinged with the bitterness of total loss. Minty's pain makes him feel 'like a dumb man for whom another acts as interpreter and falsifies his meaning'; the few friends he has had are dead—'There wouldn't be many more'. Kate's unhappiness is increased because she knows that even before his death Anthony had deserted her. She leaves Sweden for any destination. The job in Copenhagen is not the beginning of a new life: she is simply moving on to an exile that has lost all its redeeming features. She leaves behind her Krogh and Hall bound together in a terrible isolation:

> They had nothing to say to each other; what lay between them, held them apart, left them lonely as they drove away together, was nothing so simple as death, it was as complicated as the love between a man and a woman.

She leaves Minty hugging his loneliness in his attic room with only the Harrow photographs, 'the missal in the cupboard, the Madonna, the spider withering under the glass' for company in his 'home from home'. The sense of desolation and exile is complete.

CHAPTER FOUR

THE FALLEN WORLD: II

A Gun for Sale (1936)
Brighton Rock (1938)
The Confidential Agent (1939)

> So far as we are human what we do must be either evil or good; so far as we do evil or good, we are human; and it is better, in a paradoxical way, to do evil than to do nothing: at least we exist. It is true to say that the glory of man is his capacity for salvation: it is also true to say that his glory is his capacity for damnation.
>
> *Baudelaire*, T. S. ELIOT

I

In the three years from 1936 to 1939 Greene wrote two 'entertainments', *A Gun for Sale* (1936) and *The Confidential Agent* (1939), one novel, *Brighton Rock* (1936), and two travel-books, *Journey Without Maps* (1936) and *The Lawless Roads* (1939). He began another novel, based on the African experiences recounted in *Journey Without Maps*, but gave it up after a few thousand words, because, he tells us, 'another book, *Brighton Rock* was more insistent to be written and because I realized that I had already dealt with the main character in a story called *England Made Me*. Hands, I realized, had the same origin as Anthony Farrant in that novel'. Passages from this fragment, 'The Other Side of the Border', are incorporated almost word for word in *The Lawless Roads*.[1]

[1] 'The Other Side of the Border' is included in *Nineteen Stories*, where with the author's note (from which the quotation is taken) it occupies thirty-five pages.

The connection between the fiction and non-fiction of this period needs stressing, especially since the travel-books are exploratory in more senses than one. In earlier books Greene had been interested in the importance of childhood to an understanding of what goes on in the present (Minty and Anthony Farrant are explained in terms of their schooldays), but now this idea becomes at once both more powerfully significant to him and of wider application. *Brighton Rock* has the theme of salvation and damnation, but it is studied in the light of the assumption that what happens to us in our early years largely governs what we become. The increased interest in childhood is reflected in the fabric of Greene's fiction by the much more frequent use of places, events and memories important in his personal experience. Many of these references may be traced to passages of self revelation interspersed in the travel-books—childhood reminiscences, definitions of attitude, statements of belief. The epigraph to *The Lawless Roads* has already been quoted in the introductory chapter: it ends, we may remember, with the statement that '*if* there be a God, *since* there is a God, the human race is implicated in some terrible aboriginal calamity'. A passage in *Journey Without Maps*, on which too much stress could be laid, seems to relate this idea of a fallen world in a curious personal way to civilization's perilous development of the cerebral at the expense of the instinctive; at the same time it sheds a light on Greene's preoccupation with cruel violence:

> Today our world seems peculiarly susceptible to brutality. There is a touch of nostalgia in the pleasure we take in gangster novels, in characters who have so agreeably simplified their emotions that they have begun living again at a level below the cerebral. . . . It is not, of course, that one wishes to stay at that level, but when one sees to what peril of extinction centuries of cerebration have brought us, one sometimes has a curiosity to discover if one can from what we have come, to recall at which point we went astray.

This desire drew Greene to Liberia, which attracted him

by its remoteness, its proffered opportunity for discovering 'one's place in time, based on a knowledge not only of one's present but of the past from which one has emerged'. Through its terrors and virginity ('the graves not opened yet for gold, the mines not broken with sledges'), Liberia gave him an intenser pity for what humanity has done with itself since it went beyond the digging-stick and travelled at the same time, Greene hints, further and further from innocence. Liberia also revealed an atavistic element in the appeal of the seedy—its advantage over 'the smart, the new, the chic, the cerebral' in 'being nearer to the beginning'.

It has been held that in childhood we recapitulate the stages of human history. Greene does not go as far as this in *Journey Without Maps*, but he senses a parallel between human development away from the primitive and the individual loss of innocence in childhood. Certainly he investigates together, as if the collocation were significant, the personal and the human beginnings. For both the evidence is scrappy and perplexing. He chooses the epigraph for this book from Oliver Wendell Holmes, who describes the nature of an individual's life in terms of a child's dissected map:

> Many of these pieces seem fragmentary, but would in time show themselves as essential parts of the whole. What strikes very forcibly is the arbitrary and as it were accidental way in which the lines of junction appear to run irregularly among the fragments. With every decade I find some new pieces coming into place. . . . If I could look back on the whole, as we look back on the child's map when it is put together, I feel that I should have my whole life intelligently laid out before me.

'If I could look back on the whole . . .' writes Holmes, but he knows that none of us can—we forget and remember new things every year: it is an act of faith, though a reasonable one. Meanwhile we are left to make what we can of the fragments.

The principal ideas Greene examines in the course of his

two travel-books—for *The Lawless Roads*, though to a lesser extent, is like *Journey Without Maps* an attempt to piece together some of these fragments—appear also, restated and transposed in the three intervening works of fiction. The novels and entertainments of this period probe Greene's idea of a fallen world with a special pity for a doomed innocence and the too quickly acquired knowledge of brutality and evil. In *The Confidential Agent* 'D' is haunted by the spoilt youth of Rose and Else. In *Brighton Rock* and *A Gun for Sale* Greene traces the perversions, despair and violent death resulting from early corruption. These things are related for the first time specifically to Catholic dogma in *Brighton Rock* through the use of central characters who are themselves Catholic.

It is through the altering forms of his private symbols of good and evil that, in *Journey Without Maps*, Greene traces his development up to the time of his conversion to Catholicism. Even his earliest dreams suggested some power prowling outside which had somehow to get in. Soon there came the intrusion into actual life, as well as into dreams, of the sense of evil. In dreams evil might be 'the man with gold teeth and rubber surgical gloves; the old woman with ringworm; the man with his throat cut dragging himself across the carpet to the bed'. In life the primary symbols of evil were the brutalities read about or observed in his native town and more directly encountered in school. There was the man running into an almshouse to commit suicide, 'having no hope and without God in the world'; there were two children who killed themselves on a railway line:

> They had lain down together with their necks on the rails. She was expecting a child—her second. Her first had been born when she was thirteen, and though that wasn't mentioned at the inquest, her parents had been unable to fix responsibility . . . among fourteen youths.

At school Greene's sense of evil was so strong that he was

driven into isolation—'One began to believe in heaven because one believed in hell':

> . . . appalling cruelties could be practised without a second thought; one met for the first time characters adult and adolescent, who bore about them the genuine quality of evil. There was Collifax, who practised torments with dividers. . . . Parlow, whose desk was filled with minute photographs—advertisements of art-photos.

And so as a young man in Nottingham:

> . . . riding on trams in winter past the Gothic hotel, the super-cinema, the sooty newspaper office, where one worked at night, passing the single professional prostitute trying to keep the circulation going under the blue and powdered skin, one began slowly, painfully, reluctantly, to populate heaven.

Instead of the brass eagle on the Anglican lectern there was the Virgin Mary, and in place of isolation and a shapeless undogmatic faith, a faint conception of the mystery of the divine love: 'the Curé d'Ars admitting to his mind all the impurity of a province, Péguy challenging God in the cause of the damned'. But the primary forms of evil remain unchanged. As before they represent a ravaged world. Greene quotes Rilke to extend his inventory of the misery, violence and despair with which this 'mystery of divine love' is associated:

> . . . all the torments and agonies wrought on scaffolds, in torture chambers, mad-houses, operating theatres, underneath vaults of bridges in late autumn. . . .

Even here there is a reminder of a personal symbol of evil—the metal bridge by the railway station, 'a place without law'.

With their original force undiminished Greene's early symbols of evil and violence reappear in the fiction of this period to deepen the scars of his fallen world. Both Pinkie and Raven exemplify a childhood in which, from the beginning, the spirit has been set towards evil. His own early reaction against squalor and brutality may be measured by Pinkie's revulsion against Nelson Place in *Brighton Rock*: Greene gives him his own images of violence to remember. On his wedding-morning Pinkie thinks of a girl who was at school with him:

> She put her head on the line . . . up towards Hassocks. She had to wait ten minutes for the seven-five. Fog made it late from Victoria. Cut off her head. She was fifteen. She was going to have a baby and she knew what it was like. She'd had one two years before, and they could 'ave pinned it on twelve boys.

Raven's memories of childhood in *A Gun for Sale* are shaped from his father's execution, his mother's brutal suicide—'the kitchen table, the carving-knife on the linoleum, the blood all over his mother's dress'—and the Christmases spent in the institution. Pinkie's disgust with sexuality is another aspect of Greene's obsession with early corruption. In *The Lawless Roads* Greene tells us of seeing the groups of youths at Berkhamsted greeting the servant girls:

> . . . with careless roughness. There were so many fish in the sea . . . sexual experience had come to them too early and too easily.

The ceaseless wail of sexy music in the Brighton air acts on Pinkie as a constant reminder of the frightening exercise he had watched every Saturday night from the cot in his parents' bedroom. His enemy, Ida Arnold, is always ready for 'fun' ('. . . it's only human nature'), but the typical result of sexuality for him is the girl's brutal death in despair on the railway line.

As the Catholic element emerges in the novels, symbols of evil begin to be associated with the 'mysteries of divine love'. The sense of 'something outside that has got to come in' pervades the last hours of Pinkie's life; the scapegoat self-defilement of the Curé d'Ars, the challenge made by Péguy, reappear in the selfless, defiant passion of a down-at-heel little waitress ready to forgo salvation because her lover must be damned. In *A Gun for Sale* the 'Nottwich' setting is Nottingham, the 'midland city' where Greene 'began slowly, painfully, reluctantly, to populate heaven': it has the same rainfilled square, the same solitary tart, blue and cold under her umbrella, waiting while the business men smoke a last cigar in the hall of 'the vast Gothic Hotel'. There is even an emergent religious theme in ideas suggested to Raven by the Christmas background to his misery. Cribs in the Catholic repositories remind him of the story he was taught in the institution and arouse his horrified tenderness for 'the little bastard' double-crossed by Judas.

Raven's explanation of the Christian story reminds us again of Greene's obsessional interest in betrayal. Treachery, one of the features of the fallen world, brings the three books of this period into close relationship with each other, and the group they make into relationship with the rest of Greene's fiction. *The Confidential Agent* is pervaded by notions of distrust and betrayal; Raven in *A Gun for Sale*, conditioned to treachery, is destroyed by the first breach in his protective armour of suspicion. The characters in *Brighton Rock*, the most pessimistic of all Greene's novels, are betrayed by life: *Brighton Rock*, with its weight of disillusion, seems to suggest a heightened sense of pity for what human beings have managed to make of themselves, and a feeling that, whether they are damned hereafter or not, they may certainly be damned here.

II

A Gun for Sale and *The Confidential Agent* make their appeal to popular taste by their highlights of exciting melodrama and their speed of telling. Their concessions to the happy ending are more apparent than real, but, alongside certain other features, help to explain why these books are entertainments rather than novels. Anne and Mather, for example, in *A Gun for Sale* are an amiable, normal pair—driven apart and involved in a series of violent events for the sake of the plot, they come together at the end with a prospect of wedding-bells. But it is still true that their relationship is not of the first importance, and the part of the story which is important—everything concerning the hired murderer and dupe, Raven—is coloured by Greene's familiar grim obsessions. In *The Confidential Agent*, the later of the two books, where the relationship between the agent 'D' and the girl Rose Cullen is a necessary part of the theme, the prevailing tone is sombre, even though the principal characters are brought together at the end. Their relationship grows out of and survives not only external violence and danger, but despair, inner conflict and complicated emotional entanglements.

Yet the gloom which hangs over this entertainment and over great sections of *A Gun for Sale* does not suggest the spiritual despondency discoverable in *Brighton Rock*. In both entertainments attention is frequently led away from the miseries of the involved characters by virtuosity in handling plot and action, and by the dexterity with which the story is told and events are made to follow each other arrestingly and with an appearance of logic. It is noticeable that Greene is more explicit in this form than he is in the novel. It is also interesting to find that in the most serious, that is to say, the least 'entertaining' passages of his thrillers, he abandons the explanatory method and reverts to the direct presentation of a situation. For example, in the long railway-shed scene in *A Gun for Sale* between Anne and Raven, he ceases to define Raven and allows him to speak for himself. Raven merely talks or dreams or performs certain actions, and through these events we come to our own conclusions concerning his loneliness, fear and frustrated sense of pity.

Greene's style in his entertainments is usually racy and economical. *The Confidential Agent*, perhaps because of the speed at which it was written, sometimes suffers from being almost too terse in manner. Even so, a passage like the following with its jerky, disjointed sentences makes its effect well enough in the context. The situation is a desperate attempt to escape capture; 'D' plunges down some steps into an area and finds himself looking into the window of a basement flat:

> There wasn't a light on. That alone was dangerous: they wouldn't expect to find him in an occupied basement. He peered through the window: he couldn't see much: the corner of what looked like a divan. It was probably a basement flat. There was a notice on the door: 'No milk till Monday'; he tore it down: a little brass plate beside the bell: Glover. He tried the door: hopeless: bolted and double-locked. The footsteps came nearer: very slowly. They must be searching thoroughly. There was only one chance: people were careless. He took out a knife and slipped it under the window: levered it: the pane slid up. He scrambled through and fell—silently—on the divan. He could hear somebody working up the square the other way; he felt weak and out of breath, but he daren't rest yet. He closed the window and turned on the light.

In the descriptive passages you feel the same immediacy. Here, from *A Gun for Sale*, is an account of early morning in Nottwich:

> There was no dawn that day in Nottwich. Fog lay over the city like a night sky with no stars. The air in the streets was clear. You only had to imagine that it was night. The first tram crawled out of its shed and took the steel track down towards the market. An old piece of newspaper blew up against the door of the Royal Theatre and flattened out. In the streets on the outskirts of Nottwich nearest the pit an old man plodded by with a pole, tapping at the windows. The stationer's window in the High Street was full of Prayer Books and Bibles: a printed card remained among them, a relic of Armistice Day, like the old drab wreath of Haig Poppies by the War Memorial: 'Look up, and swear by the slain of the war that you'll never forget'. Along the line a signal lamp winked green in the dark day and the lit carriages drew slowly in past the cemetery, the glue factory, over the wide tidy, cement-lined river. A bell began to ring from the Roman Catholic cathedral. A whistle blew.
>
> The packed train moved slowly into another morning: smuts were thick on all the faces. . . .

Ultimately, the most important difference between Greene's entertainments and the ordinary thriller—besides the quality of the style—lies in the fact that, though so much of the action and the violence depend on a series of ironical coincidences, the element of irony is a natural growth from the underlying serious view of life. Other determining forces of the action are found in idiosyncrasies of character and the complicated motives and attitudes of the people involved.

In *A Gun for Sale* there is irony in the similar origins of the principal characters: the millionaire armament manufacturer, Sir Marcus,[1] has spent his childhood in the same institution as the man he hires Raven to kill, and Raven himself has been familiar with the same kind of institution in his own youth. The situation underlines Raven's special sensitivity about betraying one's own kind. The other entertainment of this period centres on the ironical situation of a confidential agent in whom no one has any confidence, and who in turn finds it impossible to trust either himself or anyone else. He even questions the beliefs for which he is willing to risk his life:

> You could trust nobody but yourself, and sometimes you were uncertain whether after all you could trust yourself. *They* didn't trust you, any more than they had trusted the friend with the holy medal; they were right then, and who was to say whether they were not right now? You—you were a prejudiced party; the ideology was a complex affair: heresies crept in. . . . He wasn't certain that he wasn't watched at this moment. He wasn't certain that it wasn't right for him to be watched. After all there were aspects of economic materialism which, if he searched his heart, he did not accept. . . . And the watcher—was he watched? He was haunted for a moment by the vision of an endless mistrust.

An example in *A Gun for Sale* of the way in which character determines the action, hastening or slowing down the course of events, is Mather's behaviour on his arrival in Nottwich. As the detective on the Raven case Mather comes to the town

[1] Sir Marcus has the same connection with the real 'mystery-man' Sir Basil Zaharoff as Krogh in *England Made Me* with Kreuger.

where his girl has a Christmas engagement in a pantomime chorus. Unaware that she is in danger, he wastes valuable time because he is the kind of man who is by nature undemonstrative. Though capable of feeling tenderness he is always a little afraid of looking a fool. He likes organization—the connection with the Commissioner's attitude in *It's a Battlefield* has been pointed out earlier—and he wants his love organized too:

> . . . he wanted love stamped and sealed and signed and the licence paid for. He was filled with a dumb tenderness he would never be able to express outside marriage. He wasn't a lover: he was already like a married man, but a married man with years of happiness and confidence to be grateful for.

It is the extreme of eccentricity to go as he does late at night to look at the outside of Anne's lodgings. More than that he is somehow unable to do, even though he longs to see her and comfort her in the unfamiliar town. As a result Anne's disappearance is not discovered until much later. In the same way Anne's furious pity, aroused by the sight of people suffering from war-nerves, puts her against the Big Battalions of authority and sends her to face danger in partnership with Raven. The one weak strain of disinterestedness in the Chief Constable's character is enough to frustrate Sir Marcus. The cowardice which invariably confines the gross, self-indulgent Davis to half-measures prevents him from killing Anne. The most obvious of such instances in *A Gun for Sale* is Raven's obsession with betrayal, perhaps the most important single determining force in the action.

In *The Confidential Agent*, where the texture is less rich, there are fewer 'round' characters. 'D' himself is fully realized: we know more about him than about anyone else because the action is seen almost exclusively from his point of view. Otherwise, with few exceptions, the people are either sketched with just enough detail for us to accept their presence and function, or else make a brief vivid appearance and are seen no more. The situation in *The Confidential Agent* involving as it does danger and the violent carrying of 'war' into a neutral country, has the excitement of any spy story which is not dependent on character for the unfolding of plot. Yet here again the elements which lend interest are to be found in the personality of the confidential agent, in his sense of isolation, his memories and his lack of self-confidence. This lasts only until the brutal death of the child who befriends him; then in an access of bitterness he reverses the situation and becomes the hunter instead of the hunted. Here 'D' arouses the same kind of interest as Raven. In each case a preoccupation with treachery and a deep emotional upset at an encounter with unselfishness and decency forces the man into the role of avenging angel. Raven's first simple intention to get his own back on the man who double-crossed him is complicated by his encounter with Anne, who bewilders him by her frankness and friendliness. As a result he goes after Davis and Sir Marcus and kills them both; as a result, too, he meets his own death, stricken into perplexity at the crucial moment by the knowledge that even Anne has betrayed him. Raven's inspired actions, after parting with Anne on the day of the gas practice, are paralleled by 'D's' unprecedented and desperate swiftness in getting away from the police when he learns of Else's death, and by the ruthlessness of his dealings with the terror-stricken 'K'.

Again, in both cases, an awareness of 'the inseparableness of us from the past' establishes an affinity between Raven and 'D' and the rest of Greene's characters in his entertainments and novels. For Raven the brutality of his childhood colours everything in the present. 'D' does not look so far back, but, like Arthur Rowe in *The Ministry of Fear*, he is a man haunted by the memory of his dead wife. In addition 'D' is hag-ridden by the memory of an air-raid which destroyed his home and left him half-buried under débris with a dead cat over his face, its fur filling his mouth. The fear and the sensation of being suffocated are revived at moments of crisis, the cat and its fur constituting one of the book's leitmotivs. So in Raven's dreams the evil symbols of his childhood keep the past constantly before his eyes and the reader's. In both books anguish at the loss of some quality like innocence, and the faint memory of an irrecoverable feeling akin to happiness, relate these entertainments to *Brighton Rock*, the serious novel of the period.

A Gun for Sale, richer in texture and more complicated in plot than *The Confidential Agent*, is also much more highly organized and patterned than the first entertainment, *Stamboul Train*. It is true that in *A Gun for Sale* Greene does not have to solve the problem of working into an adventure story the subtle study of an emotional relationship as he does in *The Confidential Agent* and *The Ministry of Fear*, but he has problems comparable in difficulty to surmount. He has for example to keep the reader informed of what is happening in the simultaneous worlds of the pursuer and the pursued, an obligation he meets with the utmost skill in the see-saw between Raven and Mather.

The situation in *A Gun for Sale* rises out of the attempt of the aged millionaire armament-maker, Sir Marcus, to make secure his vast business concern, Midland Steel, which is financially endangered. A war-scare must be manufactured, and the best way of bringing this about is to have an amiable pacific Minister for War in Middle Europe assassinated. Sir Marcus sets one of his business associates, Davis, to hire a murderer for this purpose but advises him for security's sake somehow to dispose of him afterwards. Davis hires Raven, a man with a hare-lip and a grudge against life, and then lays a trap for him by paying him in stolen bank-notes—with numbers known to the police. Raven, discovering that he has been double-crossed and with the further bitterness of betrayal by his landlord and a hunchback girl, manages to escape from the police and sets off, almost penniless, to find Davis and enjoy his revenge.

The entertainment *A Gun for Sale* tells the story of the pursuit but only gradually reveals all the details behind the murder. The real motive and the prime mover are not disclosed till more than half-way through the book. Consequently, since we know nothing about Sir Marcus till then, we encounter an instance of narrative clumsiness at one point when we are introduced to an entirely new set of people and switched suddenly to a different milieu so that Sir Marcus may make his entrance. Other more adroit transitions are constantly being made. Although the main thread of the story is Raven's pursuit of Davis, we have also to keep track of Detective-Sergeant Mather, called in to trace the man with the stolen bank-notes, and of his girl, Anne, who becomes involved in Raven's life and death.

In the first section Raven is seen committing the murder. In the second section we are back in London with Anne and Mather after one of their hastily snatched evenings together. As Anne walks away from Mather, anxious in her happiness ('let me get some money quick, let *this* go on *this* time'), Raven passes her, cold, miserable, pulling up his black overcoat but not enough to hide his hare-lip. Anne has a moment of pity for the wretched-looking stranger, then forgets him as she goes up to her room in her lodgings and plays a record on the gramophone. Raven, still walking about in a vain attempt to keep warm, hears the tune:

> . . . like Kay in *The Snow Queen* he bore the cold within him as he walked. The flakes went on falling, melting into slush on the pavement, the words of a song dropped from the lit room on the third floor, the scrape of a used needle.
>
> 'They say that's a snowflower
> A man brought from Greenland
> I say it's the lightness, the coolness, the whiteness
> Of your hand.'
>
> The man hardly paused; he went on down the street, walking fast; he felt no pain from the chip of ice in his breast.

Later this incident is seen as part of a design, its poetic overtones fixing it as a memory ready for recall when Greene develops the curious relationship between Anne and Raven and draws together some of the threads of his plot.

To 'D' in *The Confidential Agent* it seems that people are united only by their vices, but Raven, like Kate in *England Made Me*, learns there is no honour even among thieves. After the first betrayal at his lodgings he seeks help from a disreputable surgeon, hoping that plastic surgery will remove the danger of recognition by his hare-lip. But the doctor and his nurse accomplice call the police and again Raven escapes in the nick of time:

> He was touched by something he had never felt before. . . . These people were of his own kind . . . for the second time in one day he had been betrayed by the lawless. He had always been alone but never so alone as this.

He manages to trace Davis through a poste restante—a squalid little shop similar to that which holds Pinkie's attention on his wedding-morning and a remote descendant of the Verloc establishment in Conrad's *The Secret Agent*. He shadows him to the Nottwich train and boards it at the last moment to avoid buying a ticket. He has only a few loose coins in his pocket besides the wad of marked bank-notes. As well as Davis, going north to rejoin Sir Marcus and Midland Steel, the Nottwich train carries Anne to her new job in the Christmas pantomime. Ironical chance brings even Mather to the scene. He tries without success to wave goodbye to Anne, but the huge bulk of Davis blocks the carriage window.

The pity that characterizes Greene's treatment of the isolated individual, however brutalized, and his instinct for the chink in the armour of defensive hatred, now reappear in the treatment of the hunted man. Raven in Nottwich is shown in unfamiliar real contact with a fellow human-being. In an empty house on a new housing-estate to which he has forced Anne at the point of his gun, Raven becomes confused at her friendly refusal to be rattled. To keep up her spirits she sings the refrain of the song she had played on her gramophone:

> He said 'I've heard that tune'. He couldn't remember where: he remembered a dark night and a cold wind and hunger and the scratch of a needle. It was as if something sharp and cold were breaking in his heart with great pain. He sat there under the sink with the automatic and began to cry.

The scene is important, not only as an example of the way in which Greene links different sections of the book, but also because Raven thaws enough to take Anne partly into his confidence. He tells her the half-truth that it is Davis (known to him as Cholmondeley) who is responsible for the Minister's death. This decides Anne. 'There won't be a war at all if you find Cholmondeley', she says. She escapes to join the rest of the chorus at the Royal Theatre, but it is not long before she decides to pursue Davis on her own account. She recognizes him from Raven's description as one of the backers of the show and picks him up. From this moment her isolation is as complete as Raven's. Her zeal lands her in the top room of a 'short-time' house, owned by the unfrocked clergyman Acky and his evil old wife, with a pillow across her face and the pressure on her throat of Davis's plump, sweet-sticky hands.

The same night, unaware that Anne is fighting for her life, Raven walks the icy streets astonished that she has not betrayed him yet:

> He wasn't used to any taste that wasn't bitter on the tongue. He had been made by hatred; it had constructed him into this thin smoky murderous figure in the rain. . . . He had a sudden terrified conviction that he must be himself now as never before, if he was to escape. It was not tenderness that made you quick on the draw.

He tries to persuade himself that Anne will betray him if she is given time and attempts 'to freeze again as hard and safe as ever the icy fragment'.

A feature of the Greene entertainment is the selection, in

what we have learnt from the cinema to regard as the Hitchcock manner, of some harmless festive gathering as the setting for crime. We have a charity-fair in *The Ministry of Fear* and the 'Entrenationo' tea-fight in *The Confidential Agent*: in *A Gun for Sale* there is a jumble-sale. The sale is the contrivance by which Greene brings pursuer and pursued together, unknown to each other, in a common desire for revenge.

Mather traces his man to Nottwich to discover, shortly after his arrival, that a girl seen with Raven at the station must have been Anne and that she too has disappeared. He hopes for a clue from the star of Anne's show, a Miss Maydew, and waits patiently to question her at the St. Luke's parish jumble-sale, which she is to open that afternoon. This is a lively scene—local colour is laid on thickly in the bright curate whose idea it was to get Miss Maydew 'as a draw'; in the perky woman, probably the vicar's wife ('Henry . . . you *must* interfere. Mrs. Penny has priced that very good hat Lady Conifer sent at eighteenpence and bought it herself'); in the vicar himself, miserable over the non-appearance of St. Luke's Boy Scouts (who should have turned up with autograph books to please Miss Maydew). In the midst of them Mather tries to remain imperturbable, but thinks:

> 'Your damned jumble is of no importance. My girl's in danger. She may be dead.' He wanted to do things to people, but he stood there heavy, immobile, patient, even his private passion and fear subdued by his training.

Standing among the stalls and watching people drift 'in an air thick with their own deaths and sicknesses and loves', he is brought to a standstill by seeing Anne's handbag in the hands of a hideous old woman. He receives a second shock when he catches sight of the man he is looking for also gazing at the handbag. Raven has slipped into the crowd in an effort to remain inconspicuous, and, unconscious of Mather's scrutiny, he too recognizes Anne's property. The confrontation is the high-point in this scene of Greene's play of irony and suspense.

The subsequent follow-my-leader, with Mather shadowing Raven who is shadowing the old woman, brings us to Khyber Avenue and the 'short-time' house, from which, still trailed by Mather, Raven manages to rescue Anne.

The treatment of Acky and the old woman, the evil creatures who own the house and are bound together by genuine mutual love, suggests that here Greene's rioting in the grotesque is for the sheer pleasure of his own inventiveness. The characterization of Chief Constable Calkin, on the other hand, a figure important in Mather's world of law and organization, is essential to the plot. The reader might well wonder on his first appearance why he is given so much attention, but the book's outcome depends to a great extent on Calkin's behaviour, and Greene is at pains to persuade us that his motives are plausible. We have to understand at what precise point Sir Marcus, in trying to bribe him, misjudges this weak place-hunting bully, who prides himself on having been a terror to pacifists during the war. In peace-time Calkin makes up for his hen-pecked home-life and a wife who despises him by weak attempts to drink 'with the boys'.

Calkin might be developed into a character for a novel; here he is adroitly but lightly sketched, like most of the subsidiary figures in an entertainment. The same skill goes into the much fuller representation of Raven, particularly in the night-sequences describing his broken conversations with Anne in the shack of the railway marshalling-yard. In these scenes, where Raven's need to confess can finally only result in alienating Anne's sympathy, the atmosphere of nightmare is intensified by his feverish dreams. Pain, fear and icy cold throw up dreams of warmth, escape and expiation. Greene recounts his own dreams frequently in his travel-books; in the novels more especially he reflects in them two worlds, one in which peace may be attained, another in which the violence of the actual world emerges with a heightened sense of evil. Raven's private symbols of evil appear in his dreams, but these alter after his conversations with Anne on the subject of dreaming and on the subject of the murdered Minister for War.

Goaded by wonder at her friendly attitude, he tests it as far as he dares—even telling her that he had intended to murder her. He holds lighted matches up to his face so that she may see his disfigured lip, and lets the flame burn down to his fingers:

> . . . the pain was like joy. But he rejected it; it had come too late; he sat in the dark feeling tears like heavy weights behind his eyes, but he couldn't weep.

They discuss the ethics of killing. Anne argues that a man like Davis ought to be killed for trying to bring about a war. Raven, still concealing his deadliest secrets, stubbornly maintains that the poor are better off dead and that he has no time for the rich. He follows a familiar mental track—his terrible childhood, the selfishness and irresponsibility of human beings ('Three minutes in bed or against a wall, and then a lifetime for the one that's born'), the inhumanity of the Institution, the only 'home' he has ever known. Anne talks to him about the dead Minister—'He wasn't one of the rich. He wouldn't have gone to war. That's why they shot him'. His father had been a thief, his mother had committed suicide. The shock to Raven is profound. For a moment he has an impulse to go out to the police, waiting there in the dark, and let them take him. Then this feeling is replaced by the renewed intensity of his desire to get Davis, and not only Davis but the man behind him. Suddenly he falls asleep from exhaustion and dreams:

> . . . the old Minister was coming towards him saying: 'Shoot me. Shoot me in the eyes', and Raven was a child with a catapult in his hands. He wept and wouldn't shoot and the old Minister said: 'Shoot, dear child. We'll go home together. Shoot'.

On awaking he is impelled to tell Anne everything about himself. Pretending to recount bad dreams, he runs through all the horrors including the murder. Again, exhausted, he sleeps:

> He dreamed that he was building a great bonfire on Guy Fawkes day. He threw in everything he could find: a saw-edged knife, a lot of racing-cards, the leg of a table. It burned warmly, deeply, beautifully. A lot of fireworks were going off all round him and again the old War Minister appeared on the other side of the fire. He said: 'It's a good fire', stepping into it himself. Raven ran to the fire to pull him out, but the old man said: 'Let me be. It's warm here', and then he sagged like a Guy Fawkes in the flames.

The significance of these dreams is interesting. In the first there is obviously an association of the figure of the Minister with that of 'the little bastard' who'd consented to his own death ('Shoot, dear child. We'll go home together. Shoot'), as well as a wish-fulfilment element—the heat of the fire and pity for the intended victim ('He wept and wouldn't shoot'). In the second dream the process of unburdening conscience and memory, which closed with the pitiful comment 'It feels good to trust someone with everything', is re-enacted in images. Fuel for the fire consists of the weapon with which his mother had killed herself, the leg of the table on which she fell, the racing-cards which represent his time with a race-course gang.[1] Again there is the desire to save the man he killed. Both dreams also suggest the wish for peace, synonomous here, as in other books, with annihilation. The full pathos and irony of the situation in this sequence is only revealed when one realizes that the price of Raven's impulse to trust someone is his betrayal to the police by Anne. The next morning she helps him to elude the police by acting as a decoy, but once in their hands she tells them everything.

In the outside world, to which we are now returned, war seems very near. Raven escapes from the shack into the fog-ridden morning of Nottwich's gas practice, an exercise

[1] Raven tells Anne that he took part in the razor-killing of the gangster Kite. It is Kite's old gang that Pinkie commands in *Brighton Rock*.

regarded by medical students at the hospital as an excellent opportunity for a rag. Anyone not wearing a mask will be patriotically snatched from the streets and held prisoner. This new scene gives us another neat thumb-nail sketch of a minor character. Buddy Ferguson, who sees himself as a leader of men, takes charge feeling powerful and resourceful, conquering for once the memory of secret fears and shames. We meet him at his worst, leading a gang of hooligans to wreck the room of a student, his social and intellectual superior, who refuses to take part in the rag:

> Buddy suddenly saw him as he was . . . marked from birth for distinction, for success, and hated him. . . . What was the good of talking about free will? Only war and death could save Buddy from the confinements, the provincial practice, the one dull wife, and the bridge parties.

So he pours ink over a valuable folio and swaggers into the street where he encounters Raven without a mask. Blundering away from his friends after this defaulter, Buddy is forced at the point of a gun into a garage and made to strip. From this moment everything is changed for him:

> . . . he was stripped of more than his gas-mask, his white coat, his green tweed suit. . . . It was no good hoping for a war to prove him a leader of men. He was just a stout flushed frightened young man shivering in his pants in the cold garage . . . it was a dreadful thought that he had been keeping fit for this: to stand shivering and silent in a pair of holey pants while the mean thin undernourished city rat, whose arm he could have snapped with a single twist, put on his clothes, his white coat and last of all his gas-mask.

This is Greene's ingenious and effective method of bringing Raven across Nottwich undetected, so that he may reach Midland Steel and kill both Davis and Sir Marcus before dying himself.

The treatment of Raven's death is reminiscent of that of Conrad Drover in *It's a Battlefield.* There is the same drowning-man's view of past life, the final emergence of certain symbols, and an overwhelming sense of despair. Raven dies knowing that he is betrayed by the one person he had trusted. For Conrad Drover agony is something beating against the bars of a cage seeking to escape. As for Raven:

> Death came to him in the form of unbearable pain. It was as if he had to deliver this pain as a woman delivers a child, and he sobbed and moaned in the effort. At last it came out of him and he followed his only child into a vast desolation.

This is the true ending of the story. Raven's death completes the meaning of the book and puts him finally into the same class as Conrad Drover in the earlier novel and as Pinkie in the later *Brighton Rock*.

To round off his entertainment Greene uses a favourite device, visiting each set of characters in turn and discovering them in some characteristic situation. Acky, for example, is seen writing yet another letter to the Bishop on the subject of his unjust treatment and the ease with which one may succumb to carnal temptation ('Even you, my lord bishop, have in your time no doubt sported among the haycocks'). Anne, in the London train with Mather, has a moment of self-reproach and doubt thinking about the man who trusted her and whom she has betrayed. Then she puts it from her as they draw near home and face a reasonable chance of security and happiness. The threat of war has been averted.

A Gun for Sale is an 'entertainment' and therefore may be expected to be eminently readable, but it also has shape, pattern and, in the figure of Raven, something of the novel's dimension of depth.

The action in *The Confidential Agent* is seen almost exclusively from the point of view of one man, so that the incidents which follow each other in swift succession are all coloured by his special outlook on life. This central figure is known as 'D' because Greene wishes to avoid indicating his nationality, but the circumstances of the story make it sufficiently obvious, especially when we take into account the date of publication (1939). 'D' is employed on a mission to England by one side in a country torn by civil war. Suspicion and distrust, he feels, surround him wherever he goes, and on arrival at Dover he notes with envy the different atmosphere, and even imagines 'a certain sense of trust at the passport control'. One remembers how in *Under Western Eyes* Conrad is at great pains to explain the state of fear and suspicion familiar to Razumov under a repressive régime. The England of the nineteen-thirties needed no such explanation. Greene is concerned with something else. 'D's' temporary high spirits are not allowed to last:

> He had imagined that the suspicion, which was the atmosphere of his own life, was due to civil war, but he began to believe that it existed everywhere: it was part of human life. . . . It was as if the whole world lay in the shadow of abandonment.

In other words suspicion, distrust, treachery and fear are universal signs of the 'great aboriginal calamity'.

To reinforce this theme of betrayal Greene uses the 'Song of Roland'. Before the war 'D' had been a lecturer in the Romance languages and had edited a rare version of the tale in which praise went not to the flashy courage of Roland, but to the humanity and common sense of Oliver. Greene suggests the universality and inevitability of betrayal by frequent references to Ganelon, another character in that story. When 'D' is asked about Ganelon his reply—'He was the traitor'—is an assumption that whatever the situation treachery is always to be expected. The traitor, moreover, may be anyone:

> He had seen many people shot on both sides of the line for treachery: he knew you couldn't recognise them by their manners or faces: there was no Ganelon type.

'D' is also haunted by the 'knowingness' of the young: even in a country at peace they meet evil and disillusionment too soon:

> You learned too much in these days before you came of age. His own people knew death before they could walk: they got used to desire early—but this savage knowledge, that ought to come slowly, the gradual fruit of experience. . . . In a happy life the final disillusionment with human nature coincided with death. Nowadays they seemed to have a whole lifetime to get through somehow after it. . . .

Out of this compassion grows a sense of responsibility. 'D' foreshadows characters in the Catholic novels who carry responsibility to the point where they are prepared to risk damnation, but at this stage it is the guilt-feeling accompanying the sense of responsibility that matters. 'D', coming from the hatred and suspicion of civil war, thinks: 'I shall infect everything. I ought to wear a bell like the old lepers'. His guilt is further complicated by a passion for his dead wife, which makes any fresh 'willingness to love' a sign of treachery.

This man, thrust out of academic life, now finds himself engaged on a semi-secret mission. He is to obtain from an English peer an exclusive trade agreement to buy coal for his own side, the Have-Nots, before the opposing party, the Haves, are able to do so. As might be expected he is not very successful, but he does manage to prevent his rival from gaining the concession.

The suspense and excitement of the story are largely due to the fact that the reader sees no further than 'D' himself; since the story is told from inside 'D's' brain, we share his perplexity and at moments of crisis his sense of nightmare bewilderment. Appearance and reality are confused to such a degree that on one or two occasions this affects the working-out of the plot. Certain points are never cleared up—for example the real nature of Currie and the theft of 'D's' credentials.

The first part of the book is called 'The Hunted'. Arriving in England by the same boat as 'L', the rival agent, 'D' is held up by passport control and misses the London train. His situation is symbolized at the outset by the mists through which he dimly makes out the figure of 'L' leaning over the rails as the ship moves into port. The same shadowiness seems at first to blur the outlines of Rose Cullen, daughter of Lord Benditch—the man he has come to see. Like 'D' she has missed the train. They hire a car together to drive to London, but Rose pulls up not far out of Dover at a road-house owned by a suave military-type of gentleman called Currie. Within the space of an hour several attempts have been made to put 'D' out of action, the casual but deliberate provocativeness of 'L's' chauffeur especially emphasizing 'D's' feeling of isolation and helplessness. Since Rose is drunk and capriciously refuses to leave, 'D' decides to drive on alone. On the high road he is held up by Currie and 'L's' chauffeur (Rose is in the back of Currie's car), who beat him up on the pretext that he has driven off with Rose's jewellery. Battered and limping, without his wallet but with his credentials still safely hidden in his sock, 'D' finally gets a lift on a night lorry to London.

Within twenty-four hours he meets Rose again. She has traced him to the Bloomsbury hotel to which he has been directed by 'the Party', and on this occasion 'D' succeeds in convincing her of the reality of his danger. He has been attacked again, barely escaping with his life, and he shows her the evidence—a bullet-mark in the wall of a side-alley. Two of 'D's' obsessions already mentioned are brought out by this meeting. At the end of their evening together Rose admits that she has fallen in love with him. 'D' remembers his wife, shot as a hostage in the civil war in mistake for someone else, but tries very hard nevertheless to feel something besides fear of intimacy and a little pity. The attempt is enough: yet turning away into his seedy hotel, he discovers in himself with disgust the willingness to betray.

During their evening 'D' also learns about Rose's life, spent in the corrupt world of her father's mistresses and business associates. He thinks it 'immeasurably sad that one so young should have seen so much fraud'. His pity is aroused in the same way by the little hotel skivvy, Else, who responds to his kindliness with passionate devotion. Her combination of innocence and worldly knowledge fills 'D' with horror—'fourteen was a dreadfully early age at which to know so much and be so powerless'. Else's experiences give him:

> ... a glimpse of the guilt which clings to us all without knowing it. None of us knows how much innocence we have betrayed.

It is Else's death later through her association with him that transforms him into a savage hunter in search of revenge. This comes about through the suspicious vigilance of his Party. 'D's' profound distrust is well-founded in the case of 'K', a fellow-agent who, along with the brutal manageress of the hotel, has been told to keep an eye on him. 'K' is a teacher in Entrenationo, an enterprise to further peace and international friendship by means of a universal language. 'D' feels that even in this absurd, well-meaning group 'there wasn't much trust', and sees in the eyes of the underpaid teacher 'secrets of greed and envy':

> What could you expect on that salary? How much treachery is always nourished in little overworked centres of other people's idealism.

After his evening with Rose 'D' has to face an inquisition by 'K' and the manageress from which he is saved at a crucial moment by Else. This is one of the sequences in which obsessive images from 'D's' past emerge in a nightmare way to blur the focus of the actual scene while emphasizing its horror. 'K' and Marie, the manageress, become for a moment symbols of pure evil. In return for her aid and out of pity 'D' promises to take Else away as soon as his business with Benditch is finished. He makes the mistake of letting Marie know his intention. The conference with Benditch is a failure, however, because at the point where he has only to show his credentials to close the affair he reaches in his pocket and finds that they have been stolen. At the Embassy where Rose takes him in the hope of establishing his identity—she is still faintly suspicious in spite of being in love with him—not only is 'D' accused of being an impostor: he is also said to be wanted by the English police for the murder of a child in a Bloomsbury hotel. 'D' realizes that Else has been killed, probably by 'K' and the manageress, and in a sudden frenzied scramble manages to get away.

The second part of the book is entitled 'Hunter' and describes 'D's' pursuit of 'K' from an empty flat to the hotel room where Else's body lies; thence to a tea-party at Entrenationo and a chase down a London thoroughfare; and finally back again to the empty flat where 'K' dies and Rose again appears.

In the third part, 'The Last Shot', the tone and the scene are changed. 'D' has settled his own feud and now decides to warn the people of the mining-town of Benditch that their coal is to be used in his country against the interests of people of their own class and kind. Benditch reminds us of the picture of Nelson Place in *Brighton Rock*—Greene uses the image of bombardment with similar reference in both books. Here it occurs to 'D' that bombardment is a waste of time since 'you could attain your ruined world as easily by letting it go'.

'The Last Shot' demonstrates how deeply 'D's' recent experiences have affected him; the love of Rose and the death of Else have brought him a new load of pain. He is in the world of Rose's childhood: the porter at the station, her old nurse in the town, help to keep her in his mind. Then as he pursues his inquiries for the local union leader he is shocked to find one door opened 'by Else':

> Of course it wasn't Else. It was only somebody out of the same mould of injustice and bad food.

Much has to happen yet in this section and in the final one, 'The End', before 'D' at last escapes from England. There are obvious signs in the book of the speed at which it was written, particularly in these two final sections. The

Benditch scenes might, in a more thorough revision, have been filled out with greater neatness, and the last stages of 'D's' adventures would almost certainly have been expanded. On the other hand these faults happen to emphasize the urgency of 'D's' predicament. No one could deny the legerdemain of the section 'The End' where, in a matter of thirty pages, we follow 'D' through a trial scene, a cross-country drive, a stay in a fantastic seaside hotel, a second arrest, and a quick get-away by boat to join a dingy Dutch coaster for the voyage to his own country. Here Greene resorts to every trick of melodramatic effect including the last-moment appearance, in the middle of the night and on the high seas, of the 'heroine' herself.

What is missing in these sequences is the more detailed commentary by 'D' which accompanies events in the earlier part of the book. But the pity and the pain are clearly implied and become explicit in the last scene of 'D's' and Rose's wry but permanent reunion. Whatever the flaws of writing in the final stages, the book is held together by the projection of 'D's' unhappy vision of life. Its inner coherence is aided by Greene's communication of 'D's' constant sense of the past through obsessive images like the dead cat's fur which filled his mouth when he regained consciousness after the air-raid that destroyed his home. At moments of crisis or violent attack this image returns with accompanying sensations of suffocation, fear and disgust. It comes back to him when he is knocked down by Currie and 'L's' chauffeur on the Dover road:

> . . . for a moment he believed he was at home, buried in the cellar with the rubble and a dead cat.

It recurs during the inquisition by 'K' and the landlady in a room heavy, it seems to 'D', with the traces of hysteria. Exhausted and sensing defeat, 'D' experiences a curious moment of paralysis and remembers the dead tomcat close to his face:

> . . . he couldn't move: he just lay there with the fur almost on his mouth.

The next morning on the way to Benditch's he notices, as he goes down in the lift to the Underground, a woman 'with a bit of fur round a scrawny neck', and this, combined with his phobia of going below the surface of a street, again recalls the experience. There are other recurrent images and motifs: the references to the Roland and Oliver story; certain memories of London which remind 'D' of happiness with his wife. There is also an occasional careful use of extended metaphor in a single passage to evoke a special atmosphere—as in the opening paragraph with its multiple images of death.

Greene's peculiar talent for combining the grotesque and the pathetic finds opportunity for expression. It appears, half-concealed by the play of irony, in his account of the film which Rose and 'D' see together:

> . . . a musical play full of curious sacrifices and sufferings: a starving producer and a blonde girl who had made good. . . . There was a lot of suffering—gelatine tears poured down the big blonde features. . . . It was curious and pathetic: everybody behaved nobly and made a lot of money. It was as if some code of faith and morality had been lost for centuries, and the world was trying to reconstruct it from the unreliable evidence of folk memories and subconscious desires—and perhaps some hieroglyphics upon stone.

It appears again at its best in the treatment of the equally 'curious and pathetic' Entrenationo enterprise. The headquarters are in Oxford Street 'over a bead shop, an insurance company, and the offices of a magazine called *Mental Health*'. The secretary, a middle-aged woman in a blue woollen jumper with scarlet bobbles, has 'a wizened idealist's face and ragged hair'. The head of the concern is little Dr. Bellows with 'smooth white hair and an air of timid hope', whose gestures and voice are more grandiloquent than his face 'which seemed to shrink from curious rebuffs'. His first words to 'D' are 'Me tray joyass', because the first words of Entrenationo must always be welcoming. Greene is a past-master in the art of conveying by means of epithet and gesture the anguish and futility of a whole existence. Through Dr. Bellows's 'little wretched sigh' and his way of saying 'la hora sonas' with 'a frightened smile' we sense the extreme pathos and foolishness of his idealism:

> He had dreamt of universal peace—and he had two floors on the south side of Oxford Street. There was something of a saint about him but saints are successful.

Perhaps the most revealing phrase in the book occurs during the scene of 'D's' attempt to murder 'K' (whose constant refrain 'No hope at all' anticipates the melodrama of Cost's suicide in *The Ministry of Fear*). 'D's' own misery and despair are equally acute: the hand holding the gun trembles with repulsion because he is 'damned like a creative writer to sympathy'.

III

The intense absorption with obsessional ideas in *Brighton Rock*, the one novel of this period, makes it less to the taste of some than the quieter novel preceding it, *England Made Me*. It is as though Greene's distress at the plight of the young in his fallen world had led him to probe its worst evils. *Corruptio optimi est pessima*, and the two adolescents who grow up with evil in the back streets of Brighton's underworld are both Catholics: 'a Catholic is more capable of evil than anyone', says a priest in the book.

In certain respects *Brighton Rock* shows a considerable technical development. There is an attempt to deal with day-to-day existence in a special environment—by contrast in the entertainments the succession of events calls for rapid movement from place to place. There are also signs of the interplay and development of character. As the relationship between Pinkie and Rose unfolds and the themes emerge, *Brighton*

Rock loses the characteristically racy manner of an entertainment—which Greene in writing his first chapter intended his story to be—and acquires the overtones of the serious novels. Where it differs from these is in Greene's attempt to create for once almost a pure figure of evil. He endows this brutal, undersized, seventeen-year-old criminal with the capacity to choose evil, to parody his Creed ('Credo in unum satanum') and to take a bitter pride in the prospect of his own damnation. This is difficult to swallow. Pinkie is not a Rimbaud. He is not even educated beyond the Board School level. Yet, for all his improbability, Pinkie is as vividly drawn as his girl Rose, the helpless pathetic member of his own religious world of good and evil; and as his enemy, Ida Arnold, a sort of Wife of Bath, the large blowsy jolly representative of the secular world of right and wrong.[1] Vitality of characterization springs in great measure from the dexterous treatment of the 'point of view' that enables us to follow events through the eyes of each of these principal characters.

The most important fact about this novel is its conscious handling of a specifically Catholic theme, which relates it to *The Power and the Glory* and *The Heart of the Matter*. Catholicism in Greene is usually seen in relation to a universe of pain and brutality and *Brighton Rock* gives special emphasis to this connection. The intensity with which pain and violence are felt colours the style throughout with images of hatred and disgust.

The first part of the narrative belongs to Fred Hale, a typical Greene 'outlaw', neurotic, isolated and in danger. Betrayer of Kite, the former leader of a gang which Pinkie has taken over, Hale knows from the moment the boy recognizes him that his number is up. Greene traps him in an inescapable situation by making him his newspaper's seaside mystery-man. As 'Mr. Kolly Kibber', Hale has to spend a

[1] See T. S. Eliot, *Baudelaire*:

. . . the knowledge of Good and Evil (of *moral* Good and Evil which are not natural Good and Bad or Puritan Right and Wrong).

certain time in the town leaving cards at various places for visitors to find—there is a small prize attached to each card. He has also to be ready to reward with a larger prize the correct challenge from anyone carrying his newspaper. The background of Hale's pursuit and death—the sunny seaside, the band playing, the holiday crowds—suggests James's 'the horrible and sinister embroidered on the very type of the normal and easy': an antithesis repeated in the opposition of Ida and Pinkie seen for the first time through the eyes of Fred Hale. In the public bar where Hale seeks momentary refuge he finds Ida Arnold, a little drunk 'in a friendly accommodating way' and confidently aware of her blown charms. She represents security and warmth, she is 'life itself in the public bar', but looking towards the door Hale catches sight of the thin boy with his shabby 'smart' suit and his expression of 'starved intensity, a kind of hideous and unnatural pride'. Hale reflects Greene's obsession with the idea of escape and peace: 'from childhood he had loved secrecy, a hiding-place, the dark'. Ida is 'like darkness to him', she can lead him 'back to the womb'. Pinkie shows him another channel of escape: the razor-cut and life going out with the blood in pain. Hale's narrative ends at the point where Ida, who has allowed him to pick her up, spends a few minutes in the 'Ladies'. Moved by Hale's apparent ardour and his anxiety that she should not leave him, she makes haste only to find on her return that he has disappeared.

In the following section the 'Boy' is the central figure, and his conversation with the three members of his gang reveals the fact that Hale has been killed. Spicer, Cubitt and Dallow are uneasy and nervous, Pinkie's cold-blooded ruthlessness making them sit 'like children before his ageless eyes'. To establish an alibi they have used the cards which Hale was to have deposited along his route. Pinkie's fury is aroused by the carelessness of Spicer, who has risked leaving one of these cards under a table-cloth at Snow's restaurant: a waitress might have noticed that the man who left the card was not the man photographed in the newspaper as 'Kolly Kibber'. Since the others are panicky, Pinkie decides to retrieve the card himself and meets Rose the new waitress at Snow's. She is pathetically enthusiastic about her job, especially since her discovery under the table-cloth of one of the prize-winning cards. From the moment that Rose notices Pinkie's hand groping under the cloth for the card which is no longer there and guilelessly comments on the appearance of the man who left it, she is lost. The story of her gradual subjugation opens with the Boy's elaborately casual, 'I'll be seeing you. . . . You and me have things in common'. The phrase is heavy with irony.

Rose would not have been dangerous. Pinkie's biggest mistake is to disregard Ida, whom the gang know to have been with Fred. 'She don't matter. . . . She's just a buer', he says, unaware that life is so important to her that 'she was prepared to cause any amount of unhappiness to anyone in order to defend the only thing she believed in'. Ida's is the third angle of vision from which events are seen—later we have those of Rose and Spicer—and the third section of Part I is devoted to establishing her character and consequently her motives for taking up the cause of Fred Hale. Ida, who recalls Greene's description in an early film review of Mae West, is 'on the right side' in the secular everyday world:

> She was cheery, she was healthy, she could get a bit lit with the best of them. She liked a good time, her big breasts bore their carnality frankly down the Old Steyne, but you had only to look at her to know you could rely on her. She wouldn't tell tales to your wife, she wouldn't remind you next morning of what you wanted to forget, she was honest, she was kindly, she belonged to the great middle law-abiding class, her amusements were their amusements, her superstitions their superstitions . . . she had no more love for anyone than they had.

The men she befriends, Phil Corkery, Hale and the rest, belong to the same bowler-hatted tribe that Greene visualizes lined up behind Mae West in the homely rowdy world of smoke-filled bars and Guinness advertisements. The big vague abstractions, which are anathema to Greene, provide Ida with all the spiritual sustenance she needs. She identifies Hale from the newspaper reports of 'Kolly Kibber's' death, attends his cremation and is moved to easy tears by the oration —itself a nice specimen of Greene's malicious satire. Ida is genuinely shocked by death:

> She didn't believe in heaven or hell, only ghosts, ouija boards tables that rapped. . . . Let Papists treat death with flippancy: life wasn't so important perhaps to them as what came after; but to her death was the end of everything.

The miserable chance acquaintance made on holiday in Brighton, who had clung to her for dear life and then disappeared, remains in her memory as a supreme figure of pathos. She weeps again outside the crematorium:

> . . . the twin towers above her head fumed the very last of Fred. . . . Fred dropped in indistinguishable grey ash on the pink blossoms: he became part of the smoke nuisance over London, and Ida wept.

The strength of her passionate belief in life and her 'eye-for-an-eye' philosophy render her a formidable adversary.

From Part II onwards the book is an account on the one hand of Ida's investigations and on the other of Pinkie's attempts to cover his tracks and also hold his own in open competition with Colleoni, a racketeer so successful that he is a respected member of society staying at the best hotels. One of Greene's technical achievements is to interweave these two parts of the story so that when we view events from Pinkie's angle of vision we are conscious, sometimes more often than he is, of Ida's dogged persistence. On the way to the races where Pinkie has arranged for a razor attack to be made on Spicer, whom he no longer trusts, a woman's voice can be heard singing in the car behind them and we recognize Ida's song. When Pinkie is hiding in a cellar under Snow's, bleeding from the slashing he had intended only for Spicer, he hears coming down from the teacups and cakes Ida's laugh 'full of beer and good fellowship and no regrets'. Later, when he thinks he has reached comparative safety, her laughter comes to him across a crowded room 'like defeat' and drives him to the final act of destruction.

With equal deftness Greene develops the relationship between Rose, Pinkie and Ida in order to stress the opposition between the secular and the religious views of life. Though Pinkie conceals the fact, he comes like Rose from the slum of Nelson Place. Rose, already resentful of 'that woman asking questions', says '*She's* never lived there':

> 'We were all Romans in Nelson Place. You believe in things. Like Hell. But you can see she doesn't believe a thing'. She said bitterly: 'You can tell the world's all dandy with her'.

Because of his perverted attitude to sexuality and his contemptuous dislike for Rose's immaturity and weakness Pinkie endures hours of misery in her company. But when Ida unsuccessfully tackles Rose—'I'm going to work on that kid every hour of the day until I get something'—Pinkie realizes that he and Rose complete each other:

> She was good, he'd discovered that, and he was damned; they were made for each other.

They have 'things in common' and Ida is the alien:

> It was as if she were in a strange country: the typical Englishwoman abroad. She hadn't even got a phrase book. She was as far from either of them as she was from Hell—or Heaven. God and evil lived in the same country, spoke the same language, came together like old friends, feeling the same completion.

Rose's contempt for Ida is always unqualified:

> Right and wrong. That's what she talks about. I've heard her at the table. Right and wrong. As if she knew.

Pinkie has unwittingly tapped a source of fierce loyalty and devotion: we remember Else in *The Confidential Agent*. Ida may try to save Rose, but her arguments and the language she uses—'He doesn't love you. . . . I'm not a Puritan, mind. I've done a thing or two in my time. . . . You'll have plenty of boys. . . . All you want is a bit of experience'—are irrelevant and incomprehensible:

> The Nelson Place eyes stared back at her without understanding; driven to her hole the small animal peered out at the bright breezy world: in the hole were murder, copulation, extreme poverty, fidelity and the love and fear of God; but the small animal had not the knowledge to deny that only in the glare and open world outside was something which people called experience.

Neither trusting nor even understanding her capacity for devotion and self-sacrifice, Pinkie does not yield to the good temptation Rose unconsciously offers; hating her, in spite of his momentary sense of affinity, he marries her so that she will not have to give evidence against him, and ultimately drives her to the point where she is ready to commit suicide for his sake. In theory Pinkie's schemes for establishing his security and for ridding himself of an incubus suggest ingenuity. But part of the book's irony is the gulf between his grandiose ambitions and his achievement. His misjudgment of Ida and Rose is only one instance of inadequacy. He sets himself up as a mob leader, but two of his gang are scared aging men, the third loyal but slow-witted. He attempts to rid himself of one of them and is nearly killed. He involves himself in further crimes to cover a murder he need not have committed. He tries to outwit the rival who will not even recognize his existence as a rival, and is easily double-crossed. Greene's gift for selecting the revealing detail makes even Pinkie pitiable as he presses his one suit before visiting Colleoni at the luxury hotel. Shabby and down-at-heel, he tries to bully the wealthy Jew:

> 'You are wasting your time, my child,' Mr. Colleoni said. 'You can't do me any harm' . . . the hand with the cigar moved

> expansively, mapping out the world as Mr. Colleoni visualized it: lots of little electric clocks controlled by Greenwich, buttons on a desk, a good suite on the first floor, accounts audited, reports from agents, silver, cutlery, glass. . . . There wasn't a point, he seemed to be indicating, fingering his gold lighter, at which their worlds touched.

Pinkie's Board School cunning meets with failure time after time, but his pride reasserts itself and drives him on. The images with which Greene describes his moments of rage, pain and humiliation suggest that it is not blood but venom that runs in his veins: poison 'twists' in him when he is unnoticed in restaurants; it 'oozes' out of him when he looks at Rose; it is 'stirred' when the police try to warn him. Pride again is an important element in his perverted attitude to sex. In the relationship with Rose he is struck at through one of his major obsessions, the disgust and loathing aroused in him by every aspect of sex. When we first see him he is shaken with fury by a song of Ida's about bridal robes and orange blossoms. 'Christ won't anybody stop that buer's mouth', he says and in a vicious spurt of hatred smashes a glass. His feelings are exacerbated by his inexperience. He watches couples dancing on the pier with contemptuous disgust:

> He eyed the slow movement of the two-backed beasts: pleasure he thought, they call it pleasure: he was shaken by a sense of loneliness, an awful lack of understanding.

Even his most contemptible associates know more about 'the game' than he does, but when he tries to remedy the situation with an experienced girl—Spicer's mistress—he only brings further humiliation on himself. It disgusts him that he should have to make love to Rose; there is not even the compensation that she is anything to look at:

> He hated her as he had hated Spicer and it made him circumspect; he pressed her breasts awkwardly under his palms, with a grim opportunist pretence of another man's passion, and thought: it wouldn't be so bad if she was more dolled up, a bit of paint and

henna, but this—the cheapest youngest, least experienced skirt in all Brighton—to have *me* in her power. 'Oh, God', she said, 'You're sweet to me Pinkie. I love you.'

The marriage of Pinkie and Rose is the central incident in the book. It symbolizes their fundamental 'sympathy' and isolates their Catholic view of the world from the 'common-sense' view of Ida or the crooked lawyer Drewitt—for him contriving a marriage between a boy and girl both under age is a simple matter. Pinkie and Rose are aware of their mortal sin: they even take a kind of pride in their abjection. The twenty-four hours from their marriage to the next morning, when Rose attempts to take on the duties of a married woman in a broken-down house where people eat out of tins and the stove is never lit, is a sustained account of misery shot through with this mournful pride in abandonment. It opens with Pinkie waiting for Rose near the registry office, remembering his Catholic childhood and saying with a kind of horror, 'When I was a kid, I swore I'd be a priest', and ends with Pinkie, who has 'graduated now in the knowledge of the last human weakness', escaping into the early morning streets and the cool air with a deceptive sense of freedom. As he walks through the empty town he comes on an old woman sitting on the ground:

> . . . he could just see the rotting and discoloured face: it was like the sight of damnation. Then he heard the whisper: 'Blessed art thou among women', saw the grey fingers fumbling at the beads. This was not one of the damned he watched with horrified fascination. This was one of the saved.

In the intervening hours lie the events, squalid and pathetic, of the wedding day and night: the perfunctory ceremony at the registry office with the bride tricked out in her small finery of the new mackintosh, the cheap lipstick; the purposeless wandering afterwards; the humiliating experience at the luxury hotel, entered in a moment of bravado; the making of a wedding-gift unlike any other (the sixpenny disc on which Pinkie records his terrible message); Rose's foolhardy claim,

'Nothing can spoil today'; the Hollywood film during which Pinkie suddenly gives way to uncontrollable weeping; the return at last to Pinkie's room with the final brutality between one jangling of the front-door bell and another.

Along with Pinkie's sense of sin goes his contempt for the child by his side, undernourished, half-grown, abject, but lumped together in his mind with every other 'poloney' who 'has her eyes on the bed'. Yet the fact of their kinship is inescapable, sometimes showing itself in Pinkie's involuntary tenderness:

> . . . again he was touched by the faintest sense of communion between himself and Rose—she too knew that this evening had meant nothing at all, that there hadn't been a wedding. He said with rough kindness: 'Come on. We'll be going', and raised a hand to put it on her arm. . . .

Through these rudimentary gestures of tenderness an impression is imparted to the reader that, if there were any clear hope of salvation for Pinkie, it would come through his relationship with Rose. Certainly throughout the book there is a constant suggestion of what Greene describes in *The Lawless Roads* as 'something outside trying to get in'. This culminates during Pinkie's death-ride in a series of connected images. Throughout what he plans to be the last hours of Rose's life Pinkie is conscious, in a mounting crescendo, of forces of tenderness and pity breaking against his defences. As they drive in darkness and rain out of Brighton along the coast the pressure of pity is as insistent, and as ineffective, as the invisible rollers beating under the cliffs:

> Somewhere, like a beggar outside a shuttered house, tenderness stirred, but he was bound in a habit of hate.

In a pub on the way, even as he loads his revolver, he feels 'the prowling pressure of pity'. When two travellers eye Rose half-heartedly and with contempt for anything so cheap and pathetic, 'tenderness came up to the very window and looked in'. As they drive on again he replies to Rose's timid query by telling her that he does not hate her:

> It was quite true—he hadn't hated her; he hadn't even hated the act. There had been a kind of pleasure, a kind of pride, a kind of—something else. . . . An enormous emotion beat on him; it was like something trying to get in, the pressure of gigantic wings against the glass. . . . If the glass broke, if the beast—whatever it was—got in, God knows what it would do. He had a sense of huge havoc—the confession, the penance, and the sacrament—an awful distraction, and he drove blind into the rain.

At the climax Greene increases the dramatic effect by rapid transitions between the two viewpoints. While Pinkie selfishly fights the force impelling him towards repentance and absolution, Rose selflessly resists virtue which tempts her 'like sin'. She tries to feel the despair which is mortal sin, and of which the supreme expression is suicide, but all she is conscious of is her sense of responsibility for Pinkie:

> He was going to damn himself, but she was going to show them that they couldn't damn him without damning her too.

At the very end the evil forces which control her through Pinkie loosen their hold. When she throws the gun away:

> It was as if somewhere in the darkness the will which governed her hand relaxed.

By contrast, as the shrunken figure of the boy turns and runs from his pursuers out of the light of the dashboard lamp and over the edge of the cliff into the sea, it is 'as if he'd been withdrawn suddenly by a hand out of any existence—past or present, whipped away into zero—nothing'.

The only 'peace' that Pinkie gets is 'annihilation'. Throughout the book he has regarded every act of violence as a further step towards 'security':

> When he was thoroughly secure, he could begin to think of making peace, of going home, and his heart weakened with a

> faint nostalgia for the tiny dark confessional box, the priest's voice, the people waiting under the statue, before the bright lights burning down in the pink glass, to be made safe from eternal pain.

'Give us peace'—the words from the *Agnus Dei* of the Mass are frequently on his lips and nearly always possess ironical force. When he believes he has brought off a scheme to enlist Colleoni's aid in eliminating Spicer, he hums a dance tune to hide a momentary misgiving:

> . . . but as his thoughts circled to the dark, dangerous and deathly centre, the tune changed: 'Agnus Dei qui tollis peccata mundi . . .' he walked stiffly, the jacket sagging across his immature shoulders, but when he opened the door of his room—'Dona nobis pacem'—his pallid face peered dimly back at him full of pride from the mirror.

But Spicer does not die on this occasion—he survives for a later 'accidental' fall from a half-rotten staircase. Hearing him moving about in his room at a moment when he had thought him dead, Pinkie experiences a fear like Macbeth's—'He wanted to ask whether you could do more than hear this Spicer, if he was sensible to the sight and the touch'—and again the words 'Dona nobis pacem' come to his mind with 'a faint nostalgia, as if for something he had forgotten or rejected'. There never is peace or escape. He sees his life as a series of complicated tactical exercises 'thought out on a brass bedstead among the crumbs of sausage roll'. He sets out to escape Nelson Place, but it remains with him in Rose. At the end a thin undernourished boy like himself rises out of the past to remind him of a smoky childhood, 'the cracked bell ringing and the unhappy playground'.

Pinkie's strength is his inability to realize other people, to see through their eyes and feel with their nerves. The thought of pulling plaster from a wound on Spicer's face to see the skin break fills him with pleasure. On the other hand Drewitt, the shady self-tormented lawyer, frightens him by 'coming alive before his eyes'. For once Pinkie sees 'the nerves set to work in the agonized flesh, thought bloom in the transparent brain'. Usually it is music that creates malaise. The blare of seaside music with sex as its main theme is the world's 'wet mouth' (a frequent image in the book) wailing its perverted longings:

> The music made him uneasy, the cat-gut vibrating in the heart; it was like the nerves losing their freshness, it was like age coming on, other people's experience battering on the brain.

The sensation it arouses is the nearest Pinkie gets to sorrow, just as the desire to inflict pain is the nearest he gets to passion. It frightens him because it brings him to the edge of things beyond his comprehension, and it is associated in his mind not only with sex but with his religion. On one occasion, fingering a bottle of vitriol in his pocket—he may have to use it, he thinks, to terrify Rose into silence—he confides to her:

> 'I was in a choir once' . . . and suddenly he began to sing softly in his spoilt boy's voice: 'Agnus Dei qui tollis peccata mundi, dona nobis pacem' . . . Music, it didn't matter what music—'Agnus Dei', 'lovely to look at, beautiful to hold', 'the starling in our walks', 'credo in unum Deum'—any music moved him speaking of things he didn't understand.

Once he has established this fact, Greene uses music at intervals throughout the book to underline the perpetual tension that exists between Pinkie and his environment.

Some words of a half-remembered verse contribute to the pattern of the book in much the same way as the intrusive seaside music and the repetition of 'Dona nobis pacem'. 'Between the stirrup and the ground he something lost and something found', Pinkie quotes and Rose supplies the missing word, 'Mercy'. Frightened and in pain after the razor-slashing intended for Spicer, he proves it a fallacy: 'Between the stirrup and the ground there wasn't time: you couldn't break in a moment the habit of thought.' Rose's prayer not 'to die sudden' is granted in the novel, but Pinkie's last moments are spent in cursing Dallow who has 'betrayed' him and in reaching for his bottle of vitriol. When the vitriol flies back in his face, he runs screaming to his death. Afterwards Rose's confessor talks of mercy—'the appalling strangeness of the mercy of God'—but she says with sad conviction, 'He's damned. He knew what he was about'. She pins her last secret shred of hope to her belief in his love for her, and the book closes as she walks to his lodgings to find proof of it in the gramophone message he recorded on their wedding-day. What he had said then was, 'God damn you, you little bitch, why can't you go back home for ever and let me be?'

Brighton Rock is an extended argument for the reasonableness of the 'terror of life'. Here, as in no other book, Greene uses every opportunity to introduce the macabre or squalid detail: Spicer lying asleep in a stale whisky-filled room, pitifully grey and old, the skin round his mouth in eruption; Rose's parents sitting in 'a mood' on either side of an unlit kitchen stove among unwashed dishes and lavatory smells; Billy, the blind owner of Pinkie's lodging-house, earning a living by pressing clothes while his wife commits adultery with a lodger. There is no quarter given to the living. Spicer's pathetic dream is cut short; Dallow's seedy little Utopia is unrealized; Rose's incautious statement 'Life's not so bad' is a monstrous error. Moreover, we have to reckon with the notion that things do not alter. Life is the same all the way through like the sticks of rock stamped with the name of Brighton. Hell lay about Pinkie in his infancy, it lies about Drewitt in his middle age, and only Rose can remember the missing word for what may be discovered between the stirrup and the ground.

CHAPTER FIVE

THE UNIVERSE OF PITY

The Power and the Glory (1940)
The Ministry of Fear (1943)
The Heart of the Matter (1948)

Les grands sentiments promènent avec eux leur univers, splendide ou misérable. Ils éclairent de leur passion un monde exclusif où ils retrouvent leur climat. Il y a un univers de la jalousie, de l'ambition, de l'égoisme ou de la générosité. Un univers, c'est à dire une métaphysique et une attitude d'esprit.

Le Mythe de Sisyphe, CAMUS

If one knew, he wondered, the facts, would one have to feel pity even for the planets? if one reached what they called the heart of the matter.

The Heart of the Matter, GRAHAM GREENE

I

WHETHER as a result of an interior process of development or of the anxieties, delays and distractions due to the war, or, as is more likely, of both these causes operating together, Greene produced his work much more slowly after 1940. Between *The Power and the Glory* of that year and *The Ministry of Fear* three years elapsed, and between the latter book, an entertainment, and *The Heart of the Matter*, another five years. He published slighter things: an essay, *The British Dramatists*, in the 'Britain in Pictures' series in 1941, and *Nineteen Stories* in 1947. But *The British Dramatists*, in spite of the personal bias that makes him—for example—write down Congreve, can be labelled without too much unfairness intelligent compilation; and *Nineteen Stories* contains nothing later than 1941. When this collection of disappointing short stories appeared some people wondered whether Greene had temporarily written himself out, for *Nineteen Stories* looked to them like a book put together mainly to keep a successful author's name before his public. This supposition was shown to be unnecessary on the appearance of Greene's latest novel. *The Heart of the Matter* has to be bracketed with *The Power and the Glory* for the first place among Greene's books. *The Ministry of Fear*, the entertainment that lies between these two novels, might have made the pessimists cautious: it is written with immense verve and nonchalance, and stylistically and in point of invention it is more attractive than the perhaps finer *A Gun for Sale*. In *The Ministry of Fear* Greene is rather like a window-cleaner, balancing a ladder on his shoulders, who weaves his way in and out of the traffic with his hands off the handlebars of his bicycle. The book is an apparently careless performance, and in some respects it is careless, but one knows that many bits of seemingly arbitrary brilliance are studied.

The Ministry of Fear has a telling reference to '. . . this cardboard adventure hurtling at forty-five miles an hour along the edge of the profound natural common experiences of men'. In the last period of Greene's work it is easy to detect some contempt for the *mise en scène* of the detective story or spy story. By the end of the nineteen-thirties Greene was capable of relating any story with the speed and economy proper to his practice of the thriller. As his violence is never simply a reflection of contemporary violence, but symptomatic of something in the nature of man, ideally he can say all that he needs to say without melodrama. The horror of the fallen world can emerge from the tinkling of tea-cups and the chatter as clearly as from the feuds of race-course razor-gangs or the hole-and-corner sins and despairs of the uprooted. Therefore melodrama can go—and it is less evident in *The Heart of the Matter*—but unhappiness has to remain. 'Point me out the

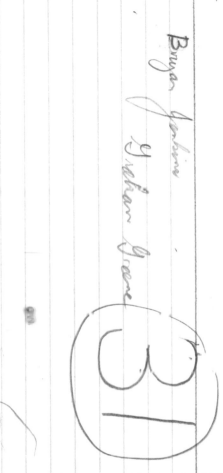

of the Matter, 'and I will
hness, evil—or else an
npossibility in the fallen
iust feel is pity—pity for
g of all kinds, pity even
t the major sentiments
rld of Greene's last three
, just as Mauriac's world
ception (including self-

Blaise Coutûre, Maria
e all of them, if not in
pocrites. In like manner
e Glory, Arthur Rowe of
e Heart of the Matter are
l by pity—it is what
and horrifying emotion
essentially adult virtue
to Greene's ambivalent
g ever diminished pity.
cobie comments in *The*
ully dissects the aberra
be responsible. It leads
his wife and Scobie to
in Rowe and Scobie—
nd responsibility—also
feel. This is the central
ne sharpens it until it is
responsible for an ambiguity about the nature of goodness that has led certain French critics to maintain the existentialist nature of all his fiction.

Perhaps this is not to be taken very seriously—and it may be inspired by no further aim than to dress a Greene translation with a quality of Parisian chic that will commend itself to

French audiences;[1] but several critics have been very cavalier in their treatment of the positions actually taken up in the novels. Greene's emphasis on fixity of character certainly means a corresponding emphasis on situation in the development of his plots, but the line that he discovers between the two abstract halves of the unity man-in-situation is indistinct and wavering. Even Pinkie in *Brighton Rock* is not so completely determined by the accidents of his birth and his childhood in Nelson Place that he does not feel the tidal-pull of goodness at times, particularly on the final death-ride. Rose, too, is there in the novel to show that Nelson Place can breed something very different from Pinkie's perverse egotism, in fact to show that real choices are made by the individual and that the determining force of the environment is not compulsive. Similarly, Padre José appears in *The Power and the Glory* as a foil to the whisky-priest to make clear that the latter could have preferred abject safety to uneasy flight in a circle closed only by the priest's own conscience. Unless Scobie's terrible indecision in *The Heart of the Matter*, most marked in the last scene in the church, is to have no more dramatic value than the mechanical wobblings of a stone on the edge of a cliff before it falls over, then again we must be prepared to admit that 'situation' is not a complete explanation of his behaviour. This view is strengthened if we remind ourselves that in three of the entertainments—*A Gun for Sale*, *The Confidential Agent*, *The Ministry of Fear*—the formula of the chase is not simple, but is complicated by the pursued (Raven, 'D', Arthur Rowe), becoming the pursuer when some tender place in his nature is reached and touched by events. This is clearest perhaps in *The Confidential Agent* when the scholarly 'D', until then almost an acquiescent victim, is roused by the death of Else to become her ruthless avenger. It is quite clear that Greene at this point means us to see 'D' summoning up the resources of his nature to act, choosing

[1] Existentialism itself, says Guido de Ruggiero, 'deals with existence in the manner of a thriller'.

how he will respond to events; it is equally clear that this normal interpretation of meaningful choice is the one that any reader without preconceived notions will put on this part of the action.

If so much is admitted, we should be ready to see the strength of the case for 'situation' (*fatalité*) at the expense of 'character' in the last two novels, so that we may understand why Greene has tipped the balance in this direction. At one moment in *The Power and the Glory*, the whisky-priest, unshaven, cowardly, almost a prey to despair, looks at a faded yellow press-cutting containing a photograph of the round-faced comfortable cleric that he had been before the religious persecutions began. He reflects with amazement on what life and being on the run in the swampy, police-ridden state have done to him. Scobie in *The Heart of the Matter* begins as Aristides the Just (his chief's affectionate name for him), the one official universally regarded as beyond suspicion, but by the end of the novel he has broken his trust as a police officer, committed sacrilege and adultery, and is half-implicated in the murder of a loved and faithful servant. When he says to the Syrian Yusef, 'I've lost my way', and Yusef replies, 'Not a man like you, Major Scobie. I have such an admiration for your character. You are a just man', there is an enormous irony, but the irony only emphasizes that Scobie is recognizably the same man throughout the book. Scobie's degradation, like the whisky-priest's saintliness, seems to be imposed by experience. What turns the well-fed parish priest into the suffering servant and Scobie into an unjust man is a force that appears as something largely outside them.[1] Of course,

[1] The priest is pockmarked by human weakness, but his awareness of his abject state saves him from pride. Pride is Scobie's worst fault, although it takes the unselfish form of seeking to bear the responsibilities of others. Pride persuades him to play the part of a pseudo-providence in the lives of his wife, his mistress and a Portuguese sea-captain. The complete divorce that Greene makes between goodness and respectability is, as always, strongly brought out.

if we wish to be precise, behaviour in each case is the result of internal disposition responding to the pressure of external circumstances, and we can say truthfully that the priest and Scobie are free to behave otherwise than they do. But artistically, weighing the effect of the novels as impartially as one can to distinguish where Greene allows the emphasis to lie, there is no doubt that he leans to the side of 'situation'.

The question we need to ask is why Greene has even risked the possibility of a false interpretation of his later books. The answer is to be found in the obsessional preoccupation with pity as a destructive passion (particularly strong in *The Ministry of Fear* and *The Heart of the Matter*) and the manner in which this idea is linked to Greene's interest in the fact of Péguy's preparedness to accept damnation if any human soul was to be damned. In *Brighton Rock* the priest attempts to console Rose after Pinkie's death by speaking of Péguy. 'He was a good man, a holy man, and he lived in sin all through his life, because he couldn't bear the idea that any soul could suffer damnation. . . . He never took the sacraments, he never married his wife in church. I don't know, my child, but some people think he was—well, a saint.' The thought of Péguy's all-inclusive charity springing from an overwhelming pity has stayed with Greene: in *The Power and the Glory* and *The Heart of the Matter* the central characters are ready to be damned for the sake of others.[1] The priest, agonizing over the inevitable corruption of his illegitimate daughter, prays, 'O God, give me any kind of death—without contrition, in a state of sin—only save this child'. And Scobie is willing to commit suicide and risk damnation rather than decide between the claims on him of his wife and mistress, since to choose

[1] *The Heart of the Matter* has an epigraph from Péguy that repudiates conventional ideas of the meaning of Christianity. 'Le pécheur est au cœur même de chrétienté. . . . Nul n'est aussi compétent que le pécheur en matière de chrétienté. Nul, si ce n'est le saint.' It is a hard saying—only a step from Luther's 'Pecca fortiter'—but the kind of truth the dramatic imagination *wants* to receive.

between them would entail suffering for one of them. If the risk of damnation is to be real, if we are to be aware, for example, that Scobie is theologically in actual danger, then we have to be shown his damnable behaviour. At the same time we must be presented with all the extenuating circumstances if he is to retain our sympathies. There must be a knife-edge balance, and it is this necessity that produces the apparent paradox on the nature of goodness.

The issue of damnation is most nakedly presented in *Brighton Rock*. Greene's reluctance to say that even his most 'wicked' character, Pinkie, is certainly damned leads him to put a huge note of interrogation after the boy-gangster's responsibility. To produce even a marginal sympathy for Pinkie, his responsibility must be whittled down by reminding us of Nelson Place, his ugly childhood, the joyless love-making of his parents, his early association with Kite's gang. But the whole idea of explanation of a character's acts and motives involves for any novelist the tacit assumption that behaviour is determined, just as a biologist—even if he calls himself a vitalist—by the nature of his methods of investigation must tacitly assume the possibility of explaining any phenomenon that may confront him in terms of biological engineering. A novelist, however much he may insist on the freedom of his characters, must in motivating them point to factors in their heredity and environment which limit their freedom and, consequently, their ultimate responsibility for what they do. Greene's obsessional interest in pity compels him to a pains-taking analysis of the reasons for behaviour with the result that the determinism implicit in the idea of explanation becomes explicit. What we have then in Greene's later novels is the whiskery old issue of freedom *v.* determinism brought into prominence by the exactitude of the novelist's examination of Pinkie, the whisky-priest and Scobie.

In this last period of Greene's fiction there is one feature that relates his books more closely to his earliest work than to the novels which lie between. This is the appearance of a major obsession which dims the other obsessions—escape, betrayal, the corruption of innocence, etc. The major obsession of the early novels was found in the divided mind: we have discovered it in the late novels in the idea of pity. This is true of the three books dealt with in this chapter, but more especially and obviously true of *The Ministry of Fear* and *The Heart of the Matter*. In Greene's 'middle' novels the terror of life, the ground of all the obsessions, was rendered through the sombre general picture of a fallen world, and the linked obsessions might only be observed in the situations of comparatively minor characters. When one obsession is aggrandized at the expense of others it is to be remarked that a single character occupies a central position in the book and is the exclusive vehicle for the obsessional theme. Further this character stands in a simple relationship to the author—Andrews in *The Man Within* and Scobie in *The Heart of the Matter* are more direct projections of the author than any characters in *It's a Battlefield* or *England Made Me*. For example, Andrews is young and has the problems of a young man because Greene was still young when he wrote *The Man Within*. Similarly the whisky-priest, Arthur Rowe and Scobie are middle-aged because Greene was middle-aged or approaching middle age when he invented them. The constant return of the priest and Scobie to the father-daughter relationship and the frequent appearances of children in *The Power and the Glory* and *The Heart of the Matter* would also seem to be personal in origin. With 'The Revolver in the Corner Cupboard' in mind, Arthur Rowe's thoughts of suicide and Scobie's death by his own hand offer further support for this conclusion.

It is the adoption of a single character as the vehicle for the main obsessional theme that gives the special flavour of a morality to Greene's later novels. This notion has been discussed in the introductory chapter and only needs to be mentioned here. Since his early books Greene's skill in dialogue, characterization and the intelligent use of background has grown by leaps and bounds, and this obtrusiveness of theme should not be looked on as a weakness (as it must be in the early novels), but as the source of distinct and pleasurable effects. Patterning by the grouping of characters and the repetition of incidents is particularly important in *The Power and the Glory*, the novel in which the atmosphere of the morality is strongest; in comparison with *England Made Me* it is also strong in *The Heart of the Matter*.

Both *The Power and the Glory* and *The Heart of the Matter* have their origin in Greene's travels. Indeed *Journey Without Maps* stands in the relation to *The Heart of the Matter* somewhat as *The Lawless Roads* stands to the Mexican novel. Yet there are differences. Greene visited Sierra Leone briefly as he had visited Mexico, but he lived and worked in the colony later during the war, and there is an important gap between his conception of Freetown as a traveller on his way to Liberia and his view of it six years later as a resident war-time official. In a preface of 1946 to an edition of *Journey Without Maps* he writes:

> I can look back now with a certain regret at the hard words I used about Freetown, for Freetown is now one of the homes I have lived and worked in through all the seasons. I have been able to recognize in myself after a year's sojourn the inertia which as a tourist I condemned so harshly in other people. . . . I have begun to forget what the visitor noticed so clearly—the squalor and the unhappiness and the involuntary injustices of tired men.

The Heart of the Matter does not, of course, forget the squalor, the unhappiness or the injustices, but it is certainly a novel produced from knowing a milieu 'through all the seasons'. A novel from a visitor's viewpoint was begun: 'The Other Side of the Border', the first chapters of an unfinished novel included in *Nineteen Stories*, has already been mentioned. The story opens in England, but in a flashback quickly moves to West Africa and gives us a glimpse of Freetown through the eyes of a pigeon-breasted white preacher of a negro mission, his tin chapel, his attempts at earning a living by third-rate photography, the big tank for baptisms by total immersion. Most of the book would have taken place in Liberia, and one imagines an adult Rider Haggard narrative with some of the overtones of a new *Heart of Darkness*—the first few pages show us the horror of an ingenuous, idealistic youth who returns to England with the idea of telling his employers what has happened prospecting for gold in Liberia away from the checks and restraints of civilization. It is obvious that 'The Other Side of the Border' would have had a basis of adventurous incident almost entirely lacking in the drama of personal relations presented in *The Heart of the Matter*. The experience of Sierra Leone and Liberia as a visitor produced only this novel that never came to full term and a few pieces in *Nineteen Stories*, the germs of which can be found in characters and incidents described in *Journey Without Maps*. For example, the ageing commercial traveller Younger with his slap-and-tickle bonhomie and innocence, depicted in the earlier chapters of the travel-book, reappears transformed in a grim little story entitled 'A Chance for Mr. Lever' (1936). In passing it may be said that many of Greene's short stories are by-products of the imaginative activity initiated by the African and Mexican journeys. Only a few, notably 'The Basement Room' and 'The Hint of an Explanation', are much more than anecdotes or dressed-up fragments of observation. Even these are unimportant: artistically Greene requires more elbow-room.

There is another difference between the relationships of novel and travel-book when we contrast the African and Mexican journeys. The African journey and Greene's wartime spell of duty in Freetown provide the details of *The Heart of the Matter*—the vultures on the tin roofs, the table-legs in enamel basins of water to keep out the ants, the books which grow a mould in spite of daily wiping—just as the Mexican journey gives us the mules and gaseosa stalls, the gold fillings in the teeth, and the deserted churches of *The Power and the Glory*. But, whereas the debt of *The Heart of the Matter* stops short at such details and the nature of its dramatic situations does not depend absolutely on the West African setting, many—perhaps most—of the characters and incidents of *The Power and the Glory* can be recognized as having an earlier existence in the pages of *The Lawless Roads*.[1] There will be a return to this topic in the fuller discussion of the Mexican novel. Here I need only give a single illustration of this dependence. The Lehrs of the novel, the prim, kindly German-American missionaries who give asylum to the priest when he escapes temporarily from the Godless State, are from Chapter Seven of *The Lawless Roads*. Returning from the ruins of Palenque, Greene stopped at Herr R.'s *finca* with its six-weeks-old American newspapers, tulipan tree in blossom, drinkable water and pool for bathing—details that appear faithfully in *The Power and the Glory*, as do Herr R.'s Lutheran distaste for Catholic dogma, his surrender of barren land to the *agraristos* to avoid penal taxation, and half-a-dozen other matters.

There must be a brief comment on the origin of *The Ministry of Fear*. It was begun in Freetown and Graham Greene tells me that he planned it light-heartedly as a thriller of the Michael Innes variety, but if its carelessness and speed derive from this source, its tone is given by the author's injection of autobiographical elements into the memories of Arthur Rowe, the accurate picture of London at the height of the blitz, and the peculiar horror found in an idealism that has taken the wrong turning. Arthur Rowe is the shrinking idealist. He is a man who is unable to see suffering without wishing to remedy it at all costs to himself and others. In a dream in an Underground station during the London blitz he remembers as a boy beating a wounded rat to death with a cricket-bat because he could not bear its pain, and this childhood act grimly foreshadows the later mercy-killing of his

[1] In a note to the second edition of *The Lawless Roads* Greene himself refers the reader to Chapter Five for 'the source of my story, *The Power and the Glory*'. Chapter Five shows us that there was a real whisky-priest who held out despairingly for ten years in the forests and swamps of Tabasco.

wife. For this crime he has been tried, confined during His Majesty's pleasure and then released—the judge, the jury, the prison authorities in turn pitied him. But he cannot pity himself—the release is to a sentence of lifelong isolation. This is the situation when the book opens. What gnaws at Rowe most is to know whether he gave the fatal dose of poison to his wife because he pitied her sufferings or because he could not bear his own. And what the book investigates on the level of its obsessional values is the effect on his character of losing his memory. He comes to new experience confidently with a boy's ardour, but he has a second time to:

> Endure that toil of growing up;
> The ignominy of boyhood; the distress
> Of boyhood changing into man;
> The unfinished man and his pain
> Brought face to face with his own clumsiness....

The investigation is carried out through the machinery of a spy story. If certain reserves have to be made about the conduct of the story when it is considered in cold blood, we have no reserves about the seriousness and tenacity with which the central theme of pity is studied.

Childhood and pity are here brought together. Greene's usual obsessions can be laid bare in *The Ministry of Fear* as in *The Power and the Glory* and *The Heart of the Matter*. In all three books we are again in contact with the ideas about childhood, betrayal, escape and so on with which a study of Greene's novels soon makes us familiar. Sometimes these ideas are treated much as in earlier novels, sometimes they carry a new significance. I showed in an earlier chapter that both Andrews in *The Man Within* and Scobie have a passionate longing for peace, but here it is worth making a distinction. Andrews's longing is mainly for a cessation of fear and never rises beyond a disgust at the inveteracy of man's animal nature. Besides these things Scobie's death-wish contains in itself a kind of acclamation of what is not contingent or transitory. 'It may seem a strange thing to say,' Father Rank remarks to Scobie's wife after his suicide,' -when a man's as wrong as he was—but I think . . . that he really loved God.' The identity in difference of Greene's obsessions, traced through his novels from first to last, is a good example of the concrete thinking of the artist. Newman points out that we can be logically convinced by an argument long before we are persuaded fully, that is to say feelingly, of the truth of an idea. Greene shows his integrity as a novelist both in the fewness of his real ideas—those that have proved themselves in his own experience—and the gradualness of their evolution and enrichment under the discipline of his sense of fact.

II

The Power and the Glory grew out of material Greene assembled when he was travelling in Mexico to investigate the religious situation in 1938. The decision to visit Mexico may have been taken as the result of the execution of Father Pro S.J., who is several times mentioned in *The Lawless Roads*, but the novel would not have been written if Greene had not heard in Mexico of the hunted whisky-priest in Tabasco whose few surviving letters recorded '. . . an awful sense of impotence —to live in constant danger and yet be able to do so little, it hardly seemed worth the horror'.

The nature of Greene's comment on the priest in *The Lawless Roads*—'. . . who can judge what terror and isolation may have excused him in the eyes of God?'—clarifies his handling of the priest's problem in the novel. It is only one indication that, whatever the accidental circumstances of their conception, Greene's novels would have continued to show his concern with Catholic dogma. Greene's question, with its hint of the 'appalling strangeness of the mercy of God' mentioned by the priest in the closing passages of *Brighton Rock*, can be related to a habitual manner of interpreting experience revealed by the description in *The Lawless Roads* of Mexico as an active sector in a universal battle-line:

> The world is all of a piece of course; it is engaged everywhere in the same subterranean struggle . . . there is no peace anywhere where there is life; but there are . . . quiet and active sectors of the line.

In *The Power and the Glory* the nature of this struggle is suggested by the antithetical relationship that Greene establishes between the hunted priest and the police lieutenant who pursues and captures him. The opposition between the two men is more than personal, it is symbolic; and there is a sense in which other characters in the book can also be regarded as symbols: the mestizo, for example, a Judas figure of evil and treachery; the priest's daughter Brigitta, who stands for the early corruption of innocence[1]; and Mr. Tench, who represents 'the huge universal abandonment'.

Whatever the weight of significance Greene may intend his characters to bear, he manages to transfer to the novel much of the immediacy and vitality of their originals in *The Lawless Roads*. Mr. Tench is the dyspeptic embittered Doc Winter, encountered first at Frontera and then at Villa Hermosa, 'without a memory and without a hope in the immense heat'. The mestizo is the half-breed whom Greene disliked in Yajalon for his ugly laugh, his 'curly sideburns and two yellow fangs at either end of his mouth'. Coral Fellows is the fair-haired adolescent daughter of the Norwegian lady who was kind to him. The fat *jefe* with perpetual toothache is the Chief of Police at Villa Hermosa, 'a big, blond, cheery creature with curly hair, dressed too tightly in white drill, with a holster at his fat hip'.

Although much of the hardship and abandonment described in *The Lawless Roads* appears in *The Power and the Glory*, there is no sign in the novel of the hatred that Greene felt for the whole of Mexico at several stages of his journey. Usually

[1] Brigitta is the name the real whisky-priest once drunkenly gave to a boy he baptized. Greene uses this incident and strengthens its meaning by making it an example of his priest's hopeless infatuated tenderness for his illegitimate child.

Greene takes the view that hatred is more enduring than love, but, back in an England of A.R.P. and plans for evacuating children, he found it difficult to remember his hatred. 'It is as if everywhere one loses something one had hoped to keep', he says, and the priest's tragic situation in *The Power and the Glory* illustrates the same truth.[1] The worst things in Mexico take their place beside other causes of pain and are veiled in regret like an unhappy childhood.

Thus in *The Power and the Glory* the world is seen from Greene's customary angle of vision. This had shifted in *Brighton Rock* when disgust altered the focus, but now—even though the author is still dealing with problems besetting the Catholic conscience—disgust and nausea are no longer so exhaustingly present. The Mexican setting and the Catholic situation particularize and alter Greene's vision of life as little as, in his best novel, E. M. Forster's India and its religions alter his.

One idea which does reappear with special force is the sense of 'huge abandonment' in the fallen world. The story of the hunted priest, his pursuit and capture, is set against a background of 'Bystanders' who represent various forms of loneliness and isolation. Out of their predicament Greene constructs a framework for the book. He employs a favourite device at the beginning of the novel when he devotes separate sections of a chapter to each character or group of characters, and he achieves unity here by establishing a common sense of desertion. The pattern is repeated at the end of the book after the death of the priest.

The balance and pattern of the novel is partly determined by an irony analogous to that which shaped earlier work like *It's a Battlefield*. Greene often isolates the element of irony for comment when he discusses writers whom he admires. In *The Power and the Glory*—the story of a hunted priest whose real martyrdom is his consciousness of weakness and sin; whose thoughts on the morning of his death are concerned with

[1] See pp. 180–182.

the uselessness of everything he has done and with the knowledge that the one thing that counts—to be a saint—is beyond him for ever; and whose exiled journeys involve suddenly rejected opportunities of escape, frequent coincidences and strange encounters—there is room to spare for the free play of the ironic sense.

Frequently the emotional significance of a situation is heightened by our consciousness that the result of an action contradicts its original intention. The child Coral and the priest, who trust each other, are indirectly the agents of each other's destruction. The tragic outcome of their meeting gains added force from the link in the priest's mind between Coral and his illegitimate daughter Brigitta. There are other contrasts. Mr. Tench, for example, trapped by lack of funds in the foreign town from which he would escape if he could, watches from the quay the little boat which might carry him away; at his side is the disguised priest, tempted by the opportunity to escape with his life, who has to obey his conscience and remain. There are also the contradictions in the complexities of the priest's feelings: he longs for peace like many of Greene's characters, but peace means either safety outside the state or the finality of capture and death, and neither alternative frees him from the fear of some kind of pain.

In a book where many of the events depend for their full effect on suggestions of paradox and overtones of tragic irony the importance of texture will be considerable. At different points in *The Power and the Glory* this quality may vary from the spareness and economy of the opening sections to the significative symbolism of a central incident like the priest's night in the communal prison cell. The first and last chapters of the novel, which depict the Bystanders' loneliness or degradation, are stripped of all non-essential details. By contrast, in the prison scene, and in some of the incidents of the priest's journey, Greene introduces dreams, reveries, quotations and literary references to suggest the richness of his central meaning and to contribute to the sense the book gives of several simultaneous planes of reality.

Even in the spare, direct opening chapters Greene invests his material with special meaning. The first page picks out Mr. Tench as he walks into the white heat of a blazing afternoon, with the eyes of buzzards gazing down at him, to look for his ether cylinder in the cargo of the *General Obregon* just arrived from Vera Cruz. All the details, the buzzards, the heat, the gaseosa stalls, may be found in *The Lawless Roads*. Even the boat is the *Ruiz Cano*, in which Greene sailed from Vera Cruz to visit Tabasco, and the scene acquires a further dimension in the light of his comment on the original Mr. Tench. Describing Doc Winter skulking abstractedly through the afternoon heat at Villa Hermosa, Greene tells us that 'he loomed during those days as big as a symbol—I am not sure of what, unless the aboriginal calamity, "having no hope and without God in the world"'. In this way Tench, the rootless exile making a bare living out of the decay he has no means to prevent or arrest, becomes an embodiment of the decadence and corruption of 'the evil land'.

We see the priest for the first time through Tench's eyes—a shabby stranger disguised by the dark city suit as the breviary under his arm is disguised by a flamboyant erotic book-jacket. Tench takes the man back to his home—'a phrase one used to mean four walls behind which one slept'. When his guest reminds him that the country was happier before the Red Shirts came because then, at any rate, the people 'had God', Tench can only answer:

> There's no difference in the teeth. . . . It was always an awful place. Lonely. My God. People at home would have said romance. I thought: five years here, and then I'll go. There was plenty of work. Gold teeth. But then the peso dropped. And now I can't get out.

He never will get out. The letter to his wife, delayed for ten years, will remain unwritten. Before the ink is dry on a single line he forgets why he has begun to write. Left alone again when the priest has gone, he turns for reassurance to his 'capital'—'the Japanese drill, the dentist's chair, the spirit lamp and the pliers and the little oven for gold fillings: a stake in the country'.

The theme and the treatment recall *England Made Me*: the careful details define Tench's misery and exile in the same way as Minty's few possessions emphasize his desperate attempt, in the face of ugly fact, to build 'a home from home'. Minty, however, unlike the Catholics in the Godless State, was able to practise his religion. Their predicaments, presented in the same direct style, are on a scale rising from the sense of desertion felt by members of an ordinary Catholic family to the terrible dereliction of the renegade priest José. In the Catholic family the two young daughters respond dutifully to their mother's attempt to bring them up in the old way, but the son Luis, a character who is to carry some of the book's symbolic meaning, is restive. His father tries to explain what it was like 'when the Church was here':

> . . . music, lights, a place where you could sit out of this heat—and for your mother, well, there was always something for her to do. If we had a theatre, anything at all instead, we shouldn't feel so—left.'

When Luis objects to the sentimentality in the martyr's biography that they are reading—an opportunity here for Greene's gift of satirical mimicry[1]—his father refuses to be angry. 'What's the good?' he asks. 'It's not your fault. We have been deserted.'

This man's final remark—'We have to go on living'—is lent tragic force by the fate of the humiliated old priest, Padre José. Sitting alone in the starlight, unmistakably branded by his forty years of priesthood, he is the nightly butt of children

[1] Greene's satire is directed at pietistic journalism, but the parody is also intended to throw into relief the uncomfortable truth about a real saint—a trick for reinforcing reality like that of 'the play within a play'.

who imitate the hideous priest's housekeeper whom he has been forced to marry:

> 'José, José. Come to bed José.' Their little shameless voices filled the patio, and he smiled humbly and sketched small gestures for silence, and there was no respect left for him in his home, in the town, in the whole abandoned star.

Different levels of meaning are brought out by the handling of Padre José's experience, especially when Greene introduces the notion, hinted at in *Brighton Rock* and developed in *The Heart of the Matter*, that God is the good temptation who may be resisted throughout a lifetime. When he is begged by bereaved parents to pray for their dead child—'Tu es sacerdos in aeternum secundum ordinem Melchizedech'—José feels 'the wild attraction of doing one's duty'. The temptation passes, fear comes back 'like a drug', and José returns to the contempt and safety of the house:

> It was as if a whole seducing choir of angels had silently withdrawn and left the voices of the children in the patio—'Come to bed, José, come to bed'—sharp and shrill and worse than they had ever been. He knew he was in the grip of the unforgivable sin, despair. . . .

The seductive angels and the demon children: here the morality pattern is obvious.

Another successful portrait is Coral Fellows, one of a number of children who have parts to play in the novel. She appears after the priest has left Mr. Tench and turned inland to minister to a dying woman. When we next see the priest he is being sheltered by an English child, daughter of an ailing mother and a 'jolly', shallow father who runs a banana plantation. Coral's serious assumption of responsibility is habitual, but, as she helps to conceal the priest in one of the sheds and makes plans for secret meetings and sudden escapes, some quality of the 'Stevensonian adventure' creeps in. This is the only really child-like quality she has been able to retain, and in the light of our later knowledge the fact is weighted with irony. Here again loneliness and isolation are emphatic. Left alone in her turn when the priest has gone, Coral finds the row of small crosses that he has marked low on the wall as he lay on the floor. Sick and dizzy with her first menstrual pain, she crouches down to gaze at them:

> . . . a horrible novelty enclosed her whole morning: it was as if today everything was memorable.

She carries on single-handed with the day's business, she is not afraid of pain, and her matter-of-fact acceptance of it is suggested in a characteristic image:

> . . . it was as if her body had expected it, had grown up to it, as the mind grows up to loss of tenderness.

Coral's integrity and courage contrast with the knowingness and deceit of the younger child Brigitta, the priest's daughter. After leaving the banana plantation the priest decides to make for the village where he had taken refuge during the first stages of the persecution five years earlier. His child had been conceived then in a fit of misery and loneliness after half a bottle of whisky when he had given way to despair. To see her again revives intensely his pitiful sense of guilt and responsibility. He recognizes that he is powerless against the thronged world of terror and lust into which he has brought her. She stands, small and blackly defiant, malicious and already corrupt, between him and God:

> He put out his hand as if he could drag her back by force from—something, but he was powerless; the man or woman waiting to complete her corruption might not yet have been born.

Maria, the child's mother, shelters him, and he celebrates Mass for the reluctant Catholic villagers, who still refuse to betray him. They beg him now to go away for ever and release them from fear. From this moment we watch the priest relinquishing one by one his last links with the normal life that he once had. The process is made clear by a series of small incidents. Here, for instance, he has to abandon on the rubbish-heap his once elegant silk-lined attaché case, a gift from his parishioners on the fifth anniversary of his ordination. When it falls 'a whole important and respected youth' drops among the discarded cans. As he rides away on muleback the priest retains one scrap of paper to remind him of the past. What life has to offer now is his abandoned daughter mocking him beside the rubbish heap and the homelessness of the hunted man.

The next stage of the journey culminates in the loss of this last relic. A mestizo, who guesses his identity and hopes to win a reward by handing him over to the police, contrives to travel some way with him. That night, spent in a hut, the priest resists sleep so that he will not betray himself—he knows he is 'in the presence of Judas'. He smooths out his scrap of paper and deciphers the pencilled notes he once made for a 'bromide' after-dinner speech on the tenth anniversary of his ordination. For a few minutes he sinks back into the past, then he opens his eyes:

> The old life peeled away like a label: he was lying in torn peon trousers in a dark unventilated hut, with a price on his head. The whole world had changed—no church anywhere: no brother priest, except Padre José, the outcast in the capital.

For a while the priest manages to elude the mestizo and becomes 'the man in the shabby drill' hunting for wine in the capital city. He is involved in a series of incidents in the manner of an 'entertainment'—an old beggar acts as guide to the seedy hotel, to the big bare room and the secret cache of liquor in the mattress, while outside in the street the armed police swagger up and down. An episode of rather contrived pathos follows. The disguised priest has to watch with sore, tear-filled eyes a group of 'the godless' drinking to its dregs the wine he has bought for sacramental use with his last *pesos*. The fat Chief of Police is one of the group.

When at last the priest escapes from their company without

money and without the wine, but with a few fingers of the brandy that he has also been forced to buy, he is picked up as an offender against the prohibition laws by some Red Shirts. They set up a hue and cry when he breaks free and runs off into the darkness. He makes for his one possible refuge—Padre José's house—but when he gets there he has to witness his fellow-priest's macabre humiliation.

> 'Go,' José screeched at him, 'go. I don't want martyrs here. I don't belong any more. Leave me alone. I'm all right as I am.' He tried to gather up his venom into spittle and shot it feebly into the other's face. . . . He said 'Go and die quickly. That's your job', and slammed the door to. . . . He caught a glimpse of Padre José peering through a window and then an enormous shape in a white night-shirt engulfed him and drew him away—whisked him off, like a guardian spirit, from the disastrous human struggle.

The police have now overtaken him. The priest opens his fist and drops by the wall of José's house the screwed-up scrap of paper that he has carried with him all this time: '. . . it was like the surrender of a whole past'. He has carried it with him 'because if life were like that once, it might be so again'. The discarding of this last relic suggests the finality of his surrender.

The episodes that follow reinforce our sense of allegory. The priest spends the night in a cramped communal cell deprived of light.

> This place was very like the world: overcrowded with lust and crime and unhappy love: it stank to high heaven. . . .

The crowded unseen figures in the dark seem like shapes from a Doré hell containing every kind of human despair. All the motifs of the book are summarily repeated. The hatred of an illegitimate child for her father and his painful love for her are repeated in the old man's story—a man whose age the priest can only guess, as he crouches beside him, by 'the feather-weight lightness of the bones, the feeble uneven flutter of the breath'. When the man falters out his story, wretchedly resigned to the behaviour of the police in taking his daughter away because she was a 'bastard', the priest is filled with miserable happiness because the word brings his own child nearer. He sees Brigitta again beside the rubbish midden, mocking and unguarded. Then there is the theme of sexual indulgence represented by the two 'lovers' in the darkness wresting pleasure out of their misery. Other prisoners, stirring uneasily throughout the heavy endless night, depict variously religious persecution, the temptation to spiritual pride and to treachery, the sense of pity, the obsessive desire to escape. All these themes figure again symbolically in one of Greene's frequent dream-sequences where the actual and the imaginary merge to represent fantastically the dreamer's plight. The priest falls into disturbed sleep in the middle of a conversation with another prisoner, a self-righteous woman embittered because her sense of religious vocation has been unrecognized and unaccepted:

> His eyes closed and immediately he began to dream. He was being pursued: he stood outside a door banging on it, begging for admission, but nobody answered—there was a word, a password which would save him, but he had forgotten it. He tried desperately at random—cheese and child, California, excellency, milk, Vera Cruz. His feet had gone to sleep and he knelt outside the door. Then he knew why he wanted to get in: he wasn't being pursued after all: that was a mistake. His child lay beside him bleeding to death and this was a doctor's house. He banged on the door and shouted: 'Even if I can't think of the right word haven't you a heart?' The child was dying and looked up at him with middle-aged complacent wisdom. She said: 'You animal', and he woke again, crying.

His inadequacy overwhelms him as he wakes. Every occasion informs against him: his child is corrupt, his presence is a danger to others, his attempts to minister to them fail, his wine is filched by the police; when he is captured he is unable to feel any emotion except fear of pain and death; and now he cannot even find the right words to console the suffering woman at his side. His despair drives him at last into making a kind of bargain with God. If he is allowed to escape detection in prison, he will take it as a sign that he is serving no purpose by remaining in danger; he will leave the district and cross the border into safety.

It seems to him that this sign is given, for he does escape. The lieutenant, with no notion of the identity of the old tramp brought before him, even gives him money before dismissing him with a warning. The amount happens to be the price of a Mass. Receiving the money with astonishment, the priest murmurs, 'You are a good man'. Nobody will betray him. The mestizo, discovered lolling in a cell, refuses to do so because he will be comfortably looked after as long as he keeps up a pretence of being useful to the police. The hostages taken from the villages for his sake are careful to avoid the priest's eyes as they stand among the other prisoners in the morning washing-queue. It is useless for him to pray, 'Oh God, send them someone more worthwhile to suffer for', because God has decided: he has to endure, 'go on making decisions, acting on his own advice, making plans . . .'

So the priest makes for the Fellows' bungalow hoping that Coral will shelter him again. But the place is deserted. Torn-up pieces of Coral's tutorial exercises litter the floor, an abandoned dog prowls through the rooms—the priest fights with it for possession of a bone—and in a dog-eared school anthology of verse he reads Lord Ullin's lament for his lost daughter:

> 'Come back! Come back!' he cried in grief
> Across the stormy water:
> 'And I'll forgive your Highland chief—
> My daughter, O my daughter.'

He feels that all human life is receding from him, that since the night in the cell he has passed into a region of abandonment; that he has died in the prison and now wanders 'in a kind of limbo, because he wasn't good or bad enough. . . .

Life didn't exist any more . . .' Temporarily he has joined the company of Mr. Tench and Padre José.

Into this desolation comes an Indian woman who leads the priest away to her hut in the forest where her child is lying wounded. He has been shot by the police in their attempt to prevent the get-away of a 'wanted' American gunman. When the boy is dead the woman and the priest set off with the body to the mountains on the state border. This sequence, like the prison episode, has imaginative overtones. These derive partly from the dramatic suddenness with which the grove of Indian crosses appears in a calm following rain and lightning, and partly from the intensity of primitive faith which impels the woman to shuffle on her knees across the stony ground, with her dead child on her back, towards the group of rough wooden emblems. A Biblical setting heightens the expectancy of miracle:

> The evening star was out; it hung low down over the edge of the plateau; it looked as if it was in reach: and a small hot wind stirred. The priest found himself watching the child for some movement. When none came it was as if God had missed an opportunity.

After these experiences there is a deliberate slackening of tension. The interlude in the Lehr Mission across the mountains on the further side of the border has something of the effect of Pilgrim's stay in the House Beautiful in *Pilgrim's Progress*. It represents freedom from persecution and the secure routine of an ordered life. There is some comedy in the treatment of the Lehrs: the Lutheran austerity of Mr. Lehr is suggested as he sleeps on his back 'with the thin rectitude of a bishop on a tomb', or discreetly avoids the window when Miss Lehr takes her daily bath in the garden stream.

The breathing-space is short. The priest stays long enough to hear the confessions of the Catholics in the community:

> In three days, he told himself, I shall be in Las Casas: I shall have confessed and been absolved—and the thought of the child no the rubbish heap came back to him with painful love. What

> was the good of confession when you loved the result of your crime?

But Las Casas might be in the fourth dimension –it is further away than Heaven or Hell and the priest knows it. On the morning of his departure the mestizo reappears. He brings, it seems, a desperate summons from the American gunman, who is lying at the point of death somewhere in the Fellows' banana plantation. Though it is obvious that the police are also waiting for him, the priest turns his mule's head away from Las Casas and rides back; he has no doubt now about his duty. On one side of the scrap of paper brought by the mestizo is scrawled the gangster's message 'For God's sake, father . . .' and on the other, in Coral's immature handwriting, part of an essay on *Hamlet*:

> The Prince of Denmark is wondering whether he should kill himself or not, whether it is better to go on suffering all the doubts about his father, or by one blow . . .

The symbolism here is sufficiently complex. The passage from Coral's essay is an oblique comment on the priest's situation and Coral's central position is affirmed, as it is again for the last time when she figures as the stern judge before the high altar in the priest's dream before execution.

The lieutenant and the priest meet at last. Throughout the novel the opposition between these two implies, as I have already suggested, something more than a relationship between pursuer and pursued. The story of the priest's journey is punctuated by descriptions of scenes in the police station at the Capital where, whenever the lieutenant looks up at the 'Wanted' notices and sees the photograph of the once sleek young priest among them, he is stirred by a 'natural hatred as between dog and dog'[1]:

[1] The priest's and the gunman's faces are side by side on posters on the office wall, and the lieutenant's ordinary sympathies are with the 'gringo' gangster. There is a faint twisted echo here of Pilate's 'whom will ye that I release unto you? Barabbas or Jesus which is called Christ'.

> It infuriated him to think there were still people in the State who believed in a loving and merciful God. There are mystics who are said to have experienced God directly. He was a mystic and what he had experienced was vacancy—a complete certainty in the existence of a dying, cooling world, of human beings who had evolved from animals for no purpose at all.

The hatred felt by the lieutenant for the priest seems to breed a kind of intimacy, even a curious identity. The lieutenant has 'something of a priest in his intent observant walk'; his room is 'as comfortless as a prison or a monastic cell'. His sense of mission is strong, he would do anything for children like Luis and his companions—'to eliminate from their childhood everything which had made him miserable, all that was poor, superstitious and corrupt'—but all he has to offer them is 'a vacant universe and a cooling world'. His attempts to ingratiate himself with them are unsuccessful, and with the exception of Luis, who ultimately affirms the priest's superior claim, they hang back afraid. The lieutenant's isolation as he walks away from them, 'a little dapper figure of hate concealing his secret of love', indicates the completeness of analysis that allows a sense of pity to extend to the 'bad' as well as the 'good' characters.

The opposition between the two men and the struggle for Luis's allegiance—the priest is to be unconscious of his influence on the boy—indicates the morality pattern to which all the characters and events contribute in some degree. The measure of achievement in a novel like this is the extent to which the author avoids the appearance of abstraction in spite of the nature of his theme. Sometimes in *The Power and the Glory* the moral or metaphysical significance of the characters, always inescapable, weighs too heavily. Thus the long interchange of ideas between the lieutenant and the priest, which follows the priest's capture and continues throughout the journey to the condemned cell, is, in spite of the ease and naturalness of the dialogue, clearly a form of disputation. The two men become mouthpieces for opposed views of life.

The police lieutenant appears in the door of the hut where the gangster now lies dead and unabsolved—another failure for the priest. The storm-light gleams on his smart leggings—storm and tempest are intermittent throughout the story, underlining emotional tensions—and his hand is on his revolver. His instinct is to kill at once the man whose ideas he hates. But by the end of the long journey back to the town his attitude has changed to a reluctant liking for the priest, a kind of regret that someone who is not bad at heart should be so misguided. He learns that he has twice let the priest slip through his fingers, that the priest has a child, that he regards himself as a bad priest, and that he stayed behind when other priests left first from weakness, then out of pride—'I thought I was a fine fellow to have stayed when the others had gone. . . . I wasn't any use but I stayed.'

> The lieutenant said in a tone of fury: 'Well you're going to be a martyr—you've got that satisfaction.'
>
> 'Oh no. Martyrs are not like me. They don't think all the time—if I had drunk more brandy I shouldn't be so afraid.'

The priest feels guilty of 'a kind of treachery' because he is more afraid of the pain of the bullets which will kill him in three days' time than of judgment afterwards.

But the crux of their discussion turns on what each means by love and pity. The priest challenges the lieutenant:

> 'You hate the rich and love the poor. Isn't that right?'
>
> 'Yes.'
>
> 'Well, if I hated you, I wouldn't want to bring up my child to be like you. It's not sense.'
>
> 'That's just twisting...'
>
> 'Perhaps it is. I've never got your ideas straight. We've always said the poor are blessed and the . . . rich are going to find it hard to get into heaven. Why should we make it hard for the poor man too?'

The inevitability of pain and the absurdity of Utopianism are self-evident facts of life to the priest. But the lieutenant hates the priest's reasons. He cannot accept the idea that pain and suffering may perhaps be good, he wants 'to let his heart speak'. The priest tells him that the heart is always unreliable, that 'a girl puts her head under water or a child's strangled, and the heart all the time says love, love'. Real love, he says, God's love, is another thing altogether:

> 'We wouldn't recognize *that* love. It might even look like hate. It would be enough to scare us—God's love. . . . I don't know a thing about the mercy of God: I don't know how awful the human heart looks to Him. But I do know this—that if ever there's been a single man in this state damned, then I'll be damned too.'

In spite of this declaration the priest in the intervals of his terror in the condemned cell is conscious that he has only once in his life felt a love great enough to move him to beg for his own damnation in place of another's. Through a haze of brandy—the lieutenant has procured him a bottle to help him through his last night—he recalls the image of his daughter beside the rubbish-heap and prays for her salvation:

> This was the love he should have felt for every soul in the world: all the fear and the wish to save concentrated unjustly on the one child. He began to weep: it was as if he had to watch her drown slowly from the shore because he had forgotten how to swim.

We are expected here to remember the reference to Lord Ullin's daughter, and again the two figures of Brigitta and Coral are juxtaposed. It is the quintessential irony that only through his sin does the priest reach anything like the selflessness and devotion he feels to be required of the saint. When he wakes on the morning of his death the only emotion he experiences is an immense disappointment because he has saved nobody, not even the one creature he has loved. It seems to him that with a little more courage, a little more self-control, it would have been quite easy to be a saint.[1]

[1] 'He knew now that at the end there was only one thing that counted—to be a saint.' The sentence is translated literally from Leon Bloy's *La Désespérée*.

He dies in the courtyard outside Mr. Tench's window while the *jefe*, a victim in the dentist's chair, clasps his jaw and moans, 'Oh the pain, the pain'. As the priest's body crumples in a heap against the wall, Tench is overwhelmed by 'an appalling sense of loneliness'. An agitation of loneliness stirs the town: Padre José, who has refused out of fear to hear the priest's last confession, is left to face the laughter of children 'ringing up all round to the disciplined constellations he had once known by name'; the lieutenant, 'without a purpose, as if life had drained out of the world', is left to restless dreams of endless laughter and 'a long passage to which he could find no door'; Coral's bewildered parents face the vacuum produced by their child's death. But that night Luis is roused from his bed by knocking and admits the stranger who has just landed in Tabasco; as soon as he knows that this is another exiled priest, before the other can give himself a name, he makes his gesture of reverence and faith.

Greene's sense of the vulnerability and sensitivity of childhood seems to have led him in this novel to use a number of variations on the theme 'A little child shall lead them . . .' An unknown child comes out of the heart of the Godless State and leads the priest away from the sea and escape into danger and duty; Coral, who shelters him, meets with violent death, though not before she has been influenced by things he has told her. His own illegitimate child, doomed to corruption, is by a paradox the inspiration of his only genuinely selfless desire. The murder of a fourth child leads to a revelation of primitive faith among the crosses in the mountains. Finally, there is Luis, who rejects the lieutenant—aiming a blob of spittle at his revolver butt—and assumes Coral's 'duty' by ministering to the new priest.

We have to take into account the different levels of meaning in *The Power and the Glory*. For instance the significance of the part played by the children, and the full meaning of the sense of desertion and loss felt by characters in the story after the priest's death, may be understood when these things are seen in relation to the symbolic side of the priest's role. Again and again the priest tries to escape. He is first seen near the sea watching a boat which would take him to safety. He nearly escapes again when he crosses the mountains and reaches the Lehrs, but at the last minute he turns back:

> He had tried to escape but he was like the King of a West African tribe, the slave of his people, who may not even lie down in case the winds should fail.

As 'the slave of his people', a scapegoat, the whisky-priest becomes capable of heroism to which as a comfortable cleric he could never have attained.[1] Yet there is also a level of the book on which the priest may be said to represent convincingly the struggle of an ordinary man against bad habits and simple weaknesses. On this less abstract plane many of the other characters have equal vitality. In a few instances, however, subordinate characters who have to be regarded symbolically as well as realistically lose their convincing actuality when their behaviour is manipulated in order to illuminate some aspect of the book's theme. Luis is as convincing when he rejects the sentimentalism and responds to the heroics in the story of Juan the Martyr as he is when with half-reluctant fascination he fingers the lieutenant's gun. But our sympathetic response suffers when his behaviour at the end of the story seems to be contrived to establish the enduring nature of the values represented by the priest. This is not to argue that a novelist has to refrain from making his characters and their experiences symbolic of his vision of life; but it does suggest that the nature of his vision may sometimes prevent the rescue of material from the dangers of abstraction.

Only infrequently do these dangers imperil Greene's characterization. His eye for the typical gesture, his ear for

[1] Rayner Heppenstall in *The Double Image* assumes that Greene owes a debt to Bernanos in *The Power and the Glory* on the strength of the whisky-priest's role as a scapegoat. Greene's confessed lack of partiality for the novels of Bernanos inclines me to believe that resemblances are 'purely coincidental'.

the exact colloquial phrase, and his talent for describing personal oddity lend vitality to people as diverse as the police lieutenant, the Chief of Police, the renegade priest José, and the two children Coral and Brigitta. When the book is closed we remember vividly the small figure of the lieutenant expressing even in his intent observant walk his concentrated hatred and his sense of mission; Brigitta, alternately mocking her father and crying with mortification because he does not work in the fields like other villagers and is 'no good for women'; Coral's peevish mother, Mrs. Fellows, turning restlessly on her bed, her wretchedness increased by her permanent terror of death; Captain Fellows singing at the top of his voice as he chugs down the river in his boat, persuading himself that he is a happy man; Coral herself, supervising the unloading of bananas, keeping accounts because no one else will, and working painstakingly in the heat at her correspondence-school tutorials.

At the same time the book creates memories of another kind. There are moments when Greene manages to produce symbols of extraordinary poetic power: for example, in the communal cell sequence, or during the journey across the mountains when it seems that even the miracle of resurrection may occur until the priest asks, 'Why, after all, should we expect God to punish the innocent with more life?' There is the priest's sudden bewildered discovery, in the midst of fever and exhaustion, and after years of persecution, of a church with its doors still open:

> He asked: 'The barracks?'
>
> 'Father . . . it is our church.'
>
> 'A church?' The priest ran his hands over the wall like a blind man trying to recognize a particular house, but he was too tired to feel anything at all . . . he sat down suddenly on the rain-drenched grass, and leaning against the white wall, he fell asleep, with home behind his shoulder blades.

Such moments remind us that many incidents in *The Power and the Glory* are really stages of a spiritual *via crucis*. The whisky-priest is driven to sin and despair; he is made to lose everywhere 'something he had hoped to keep'. After the night in the prison, when his bargain with God reveals his distrust, his discovery of desolation in the Fellows' house signifies his entry into a spiritual desert; the comparative calm of his sojourn with the Lehrs is the doldrums of self-deception; his return with the mestizo to the banana plantation represents his heroic reawakening to duty. But there is no operatic grand finale. The martyr does not die in a blaze of faith. He goes out wretchedly, smelling of the brandy which has failed to drown his fear, with an enormous sense of anticlimax and a feeling that he has 'missed happiness by seconds at an appointed place'. The world ends—it is the only conceivable ending—'not with a bang but a whimper'. The whimper hall marks the heroism.

III

The title of *The Ministry of Fear* is capable of two interpretations corresponding to the entertainment's two levels of spy story and 'sermon on pity'. At one point in the book Arthur Rowe (the central character through whose eyes the whole action is seen), now without adult memories as the result of a bomb explosion, has the war and Nazism explained to him by a young idealist, Johns. Johns, the assistant of a Dr. Forester at the luxury nursing-home where Rowe is a patient, tells him what is meant by a Fifth Column and how it can be recruited from misguided enthusiasts and from those who can be blackmailed. Almost everyone has something to hide, Johns argues, and the Nazis have card-indexed people very thoroughly:

> They formed, you know, a kind of Ministry of Fear—with the most efficient under-secretaries. It isn't only that they get a hold on certain people. It's the general atmosphere they spread, so that you feel you can't depend on a soul.

Towards the end of the story the second broader significance of the title is made explicit by a reflection of Rowe's. His memory has been restored, he is once again a 'whole man', and he has to conceal from Anna Hilfe, whom he loves, the fact that he has regained self-knowledge. He feels himself pledged to an anxious deception for the rest of his life. Anna must never find out that he knows he has been tried and imprisoned for the mercy-killing of his wife.

> A phrase of Johns' came back to mind about a Ministry of Fear. He felt now that he had joined its permanent staff. But it wasn't the small Ministry to which Johns had referred, with limited aims like winning a war or changing a constitution. It was a Ministry as large as life to which all who loved belonged. If one loved one feared.

John's other phrase 'the general atmosphere . . . so that you feel you can't depend on a soul' can also be evoked in the wider context so that it comes to represent the human situation. The lonely isolation of Arthur Rowe—'One attended cinemas at ten in the morning with other men in macintoshes who had somehow to pass the time away'—is the fundamental isolation and loneliness of every man.

In an entertainment Greene allows himself more freedom than in a novel, but the liberties taken in *The Ministry of Fear* are nearly impudent. He incorporates greater incoherence than is usual in his plot and simultaneously invests his exciting, loosely knocked-up narrative with much of the seriousness of attitude expected in his novels. The result is a certain ungainliness: means and ends are not adjusted to each other. In comparison with *A Gun for Sale*, *The Ministry of Fear* has a ramshackle look. Where it is superior to *A Gun for Sale* and the other entertainments is in fertility of invention, the pinpointing of detail, the reality of the ungrotesque minor characters—Henry Wilcox, for example—and the confidence with which Greene drives the narrative forward at high speed when the emphasis is on action. The speed seems to have had an exhilarating effect on Greene's style. The colour and particularity of the writing alone are enough to remind us that we are not to read this entertainment as we would a Michael Innes or an Agatha Christie.

Another matter noticed very quickly is Greene's success in using recurrent phrases to elucidate the various heads of his sermon on pity. Properly speaking the theme of the book is not simply the nature of pity, but the nature of pity understood in relation to its origin in the disappointment of childish expectation by experience. This is established in various ways—one of them is by references to reading in childhood. In the first chapter we are told of Arthur Rowe's memories of fêtes and bazaars to which he went romantically as a boy hoping to pick up a talisman or a magic ring, but from which he returned carrying only a copy of Charlotte Yonge's *The Little Duke* or an old atlas. Later in the same chapter, back in Rowe's grim lodgings, we find that he reads and re-reads two novels by Dickens 'because he had read them as a child and they contained no adult memories'. Reading in boyhood and *The Little Duke* come to symbolize the state of innocence when the ideal and the actual have not yet been found to be separated by a saddening rift-valley. So that in Chapter Seven Greene can refer to adult experience with the words '. . . the little duke is dead and betrayed and forgotten', and later again a reference to 'a book called *The Book of Golden Deeds* by a woman called Yonge' at once supplies the emotional key of a reflective passage. There are half a dozen other references, variously weighted, to reading in childhood. And there are other similar recurrences pointing at different aspects of the central theme. The device is therefore a structural one and a means by which the entertainment gives an impression of unity in spite of its looseness of plot.

Ordinarily the reader is prepared to meet an author half-way. In an entertainment he will not cavil at an abrupt solution of difficulties in the plot or dispute an elaborate use of coincidence, if he feels assured that this poetic licence will be used to sustain interest at a high pitch by a series of plausible minor excitements and surprises. In *The Ministry of Fear* Greene does succeed in keeping the reader's interest. Consequently we are not seriously worried about the reasons for hiding the micro-films of a naval secret in a cake and allowing the cake to be obtained by a stranger, Arthur Rowe, who happens to hit accidentally on the correct password in a fortune-teller's booth at a garden fête. Nor do we boggle at the inadequately motivated change of mind that causes Willi Hilfe, the spider at the centre of the web of Nazi espionage, the pitiless man opposed to Arthur Rowe in whom pity is overdeveloped (rather as the priest and the police lieutenant are antithetically conceived in *The Power and the Glory*), first to frame Rowe for a non-existent murder so that he will go underground and keep out of the way of the police, and then very shortly afterwards attempt to kill him in earnest. But we are made uneasy by the portrait of Willi Hilfe. Not that he is in a straightforward sense unreal: on the contrary he has at once too much life for the spy story and hardly enough for his significance in the expression of the main theme of pity. To have made the beauty and evil of Willi Hilfe, the ruthless moral anarchist who is a leader precisely because he is incapable of feeling the pain of others, thoroughly convincing at this second level, Greene would have had to describe part of the action from Hilfe's viewpoint. He would have had to create the character from within, to endow him with some of the demonic quality of a Stavrogin; and the plot, good enough for a thriller, barely good enough for an entertainment, would have been blown into fragments under the pressure of imaginative actuality. This is another way of saying that some of the implications of characters and incidents in *The Ministry of Fear* hardly seem to belong to the world of the entertainment, and the fault imputed is one of confusion of 'kinds'.

The rejection of Willi Hilfe as a mouthpiece for any part of the action in *The Ministry of Fear* made the adoption of a single point of view nearly inevitable. At once monotony of story-telling became a possibility, and Greene went to work very cleverly to avoid it at all costs, dividing his story into four blocks of narrative, four books, and shifting the main focus of interest from book to book. The emphasis falls now on physical action and suspense and now on character and motive, and these differences are carefully exaggerated by pronounced changes of tempo. Thus in a block of narrative where action is of chief importance we tend to rabbit-jump breathlessly from one incident and background to the next, while in another block, where questions of motive are explored, the background may remain unchanged and incidents will be developed to match the slow pace of a character's process of self-discovery. Apart from such shifts of interest with their consequent variations of tempo, the feeling of a second point of view is simulated when Arthur Rowe loses his memory, and variety is also arrived at by comment intruded on the action (in imitation of Mauriac) and by various forms of patterning. These remarks will be plainer from the account of the story that follows.

The Ministry of Fear, it has been said, is divided into four books. The first, 'The Unhappy Man', set against a background of bombed streets in the London blitz, piles complication on complication and mystery on mystery at story level, while it introduces us to the personality of Arthur Rowe and describes the experiences in childhood, adolescence and later life that have made him an outlaw. Released from imprisonment for the mercy-killing of his wife, who had suffered from a cruel incurable disease, he finds himself without friends, he is unable to get a job even in civil defence, and he is driven to discover his isolation with special force because of the stronger community-sense of war-time. This part, and only this part, of *The Ministry of Fear* resembles a Michael Innes thriller, and it is distinguished by the careless display of fancy that carries Rowe from a garden fête in aid of the 'Free Mothers' to Mr. Rennit of the Orthotex Private Inquiry Bureau, to a meeting with the charming 'refugees' Willi and Anna Hilfe, thence to Mrs. Bellairs, who holds séances, and finally—through a book auction and an A.R.P. funeral in Battersea—to a suite in the Regal Court Hotel where a bomb explodes and destroys his memory and he saves Anna Hilfe's life. This is a kind of rake's progress for Greene: he is enjoying his irresponsibility in setting himself puzzles somehow to be solved before the end of the novel.

These successive milieus are brilliantly put before us and the various transitions are generally made plausible, though once or twice the machinery creaks badly. For example, the furtive little bookseller with black carious teeth, the expert on eighteenth-century landscape gardening whom Rowe meets on the Embankment, by his claim of a weak heart—a claim that automatically stirs a hyper-sensitivity to pity—persuades Rowe to carry a heavy suitcase into the Regal Court Hotel and up to a particular suite. Greene himself seems to jib a little at this device, for Rowe reflects that he feels that he is being pushed around by a 'surrealist imagination'. A more serious fault in the first book is that Chapter Five[1], 'Between Sleeping and Waking', is not in harmony with the other chapters of active melodrama. This section, describing Rowe's dreams and half-dreams with their fantasies, symbols and distorted reminiscences of childhood, is given a home in an underground Tube station packed with Londoners sleeping through the disturbances of a night raid. The extended dream-soliloquy is done with considerable skill, but it is another example of the incompatibility of the demands made by the spy story and the sermon on pity.

The second book of the entertainment is entitled 'The Happy Man'. As Richard Digby, the victim of a bomb accident, Rowe is being cared for in Dr. Forester's nursing-home in the country. He remembers nothing of how he came there; indeed his memories back to the time of childhood have now been wiped out. In place of his gloomy London rooms and the half-lit Underground platform whining and moving with the distant explosions of German bombs,

[1] Misnumbered Chapter Four in the original edition.

there are 'conversations in Arcady', sunlight, primrose covers on the beds, advanced reading in the functional bookcases and early daffodils in Swedish-glass vases. Instead of self-torture and self-condemnation, here 'the great thing, you see, is not to worry'. In this book the interest shifts from detection to psychology. We are soon in possession of the truth about the spy plot and we recognize Dr. Forester as a traitor behind his smooth front of the great, once-misunderstood healer. Since mystery breaks down as a source of interest on the story-level —except for the question of the identity of the chief Nazi spy— another source of tension at the same level is substituted: will Rowe regain his memory and, if so, by what means; and how will he then act?

In *Journey Without Maps* Greene writes: 'I find myself always torn between two beliefs: the belief that life should be better than it is and the belief that when it appears better it is really worse'. Not to worry is to be sub-human. It is with a kind of devout hatred, therefore, that Greene sets out to reveal the ugliness, squalor and cruelty that lie behind the spick and span nursing-home. Venturing like a schoolboy into the sick bay where dangerous lunatics are said to be restrained, Rowe encounters stone floors, threadbare drugget, dust and the squalid masculinity of Poole's quarters. Poole is the keeper, a hulking cripple with enormous twisted shoulders, and Greene pictures his room with some of the disgusted intensity that Rimbaud put into such a poem as 'Les Pauvres à l'Église'. Everything is in a chosen disorder: the place smells, the dirty bed is unmade, clothes have been left lying about, and a cheap alarm-clock and a teapot serve as book-ends for lives of Napoleon and Cromwell and Carlyle's *Heroes and Hero-Worship*. 'It was like the underside of a stone: you turned up the bright polished nursing-home and found beneath it this.' Or, as Rowe reflects, it was as if 'something were disappointing his expectations'.

Rowe in his role of Digby, it must be remembered, is an adolescent with the obstinate idealism and the unflagging energy of youth. Continually he recalls his boyish ambitions and wonders what he did become in the life that Dr. Forester keeps from him for 'medical' reasons. 'I was very fond of African exploration. One might look up some old Colonial Office lists.'[1] Irony is used to good effect here. He says to Anna Hilfe, his only visitor at the nursing-home, that he must have lost all his friends; and to her question, 'Did you have a great many?' he answers, 'I suppose—by my age—one would have collected a great many'. Puzzling again over his job in the world, he thinks of the law. 'Was it law, Anna? I don't believe it. I can't see myself in a wig getting some poor devil hanged.' He rejects medicine too. 'Too much pain. . . . It made me feel ill, sick, hearing of pain. I remember—something about a rat.' After turning down all the careers that seem to have been open, the crowning irony is reached when he adds in a puzzled voice, 'I suppose in a way I wanted to lead—a good life'. Anna, thinking both of the tie between herself and her brother and of Rowe's secret, gently reminds him, 'People don't always become what they want to be'.

The discrepancy between our hopes and achievements is measured by a later speech of Rowe's after he has escaped from Dr. Forester's home and is talking to Mr. Prentice, a tweedy man with 'the fainéant air of Arthur Balfour' who is engaged in counter-espionage. Rowe is painfully relearning the facts of life.

> 'Is life really like this? . . . I thought life was much simpler and grander. I suppose that's how it strikes a boy. I was brought up on stories of Captain Scott writing his last letters home, Oates walking into the blizzard, I've forgotten who it was losing his hands from his experiments with radium, Damien among the lepers. . . . There was a book called The Book of Golden Deeds by a woman called Yonge . . .' He said: 'If you were suddenly taken from that world into this job you're doing now you'd

[1] One of Greene's ambitions after reading *King Solomon's Mines* as a boy was to enter the Colonial Service.

feel bewildered. Jones[1] and the cake, the sick bay, poor Stone—all this talk of a man called Hitler . . . your files of wretched faces, the cruelty and meaninglessness. . . . It's as if one had been sent on a journey with a wrong map.'

The last phrase reminds us of the autobiographical element in *Journey Without Maps* and of the parallelisms that Greene contrives between personal and geographical exploration. The ideals taught in the classroom or from the pulpit of the school chapel seem to have no bearing on life as it happens in the world outside. Map and country mapped are in flat contradiction. Indeed the gap between ideal and real explains the two selves of characters in Greene's earlier novels: 'the man within' is in some sort nourished by pictured ideals and, were it not for him, the ordinary instinctive man would find it easier to come to terms with actuality.

In the first book of *The Ministry of Fear* the interest is divided between the detective plot with its fancy puzzles and rapid action, and the gradual revelation of Rowe's character to the reader in the thoughts and dreams of the past provoked in Rowe by the circumstances of the present. Although these interests can be distinguished, the means of stimulating them is usually the same. Greene kills two birds with one stone by making a move in the detective story precipitate a memory of Rowe's past. Economy of effect, which implies pattern, will always delight if it does not offend probability too grossly, and fortunately our sense of probability (as Conrad knew) is fairly elastic. Thus we find it satisfying that Rowe on his return from the fête with the all-important cake, and visited in his rooms by the malignant cripple Poole, should lift his cup of tea to his mouth in the middle of a discussion on the war and the intellectual's attitude to it and taste hyoscine. 'Life struck back at him like a scorpion, over the shoulder', for it had been an overdose of hyoscine that he had given his wife to end her pain. He feels outraged that this should happen to him, the

[1] Jones is the private detective hired by Arthur Rowe from the Orthotex Private Inquiry Bureau.

'professional'. The incident not only gives us a piece of information about the past (how Rowe's wife died) and an effective moment of melodrama in the present, but it also reveals how monstrous the act of killing seems to Rowe and therefore demonstrates how vast his sense of pity must have been to screw him to the point of poisoning his wife's bedtime cup of milk.

There is a further illustration of the same kind of economy in the séance scene at Mrs. Bellairs's house. Rowe has always feared the dark for a childish nightmare of a cupboard door opening and something unknown and terrifying coming out—the nightmare is Greene's and has been noted earlier. He does not want to stay for the séance, but Willi Hilfe, posing as a friend, jollies him into the séance-room to take his place in a circle of joined hands. Sometimes, he thinks, it is more difficult to make a scene than to die—he is frightened that he may be attacked for his investigations of the cake mystery—and immediately his thoughts go back to his dead wife. He has never known whether she guessed that he was going to poison her.

> A memory came back to him of someone else who wasn't certain, wouldn't make a scene, gave herself sadly up and took the milk.

This detail adds enormously to the horror of the séance-scene when the voice of the medium in a trance calls out, 'Arthur, why did you kill . . .?' before the lights are switched on and one of the company is found apparently murdered by Rowe's own pocket-knife. Rowe's foolish humility here, his desire not to be the central figure of a Bateman cartoon, recalls Fred Hale's desperate attempt to seem normal in *Brighton Rock* when Pinkie and the razor-gang are after him. In response to Ida's cheery 'What's the matter?' Hale pretends that there is nothing wrong and forces himself to little phrases and acts of cockney gallantry to keep her in his company, although he is feeling physically sick and in terror of his life.

In the entertainment's second book, it has been said, the story-interest turns on whether or not Digby will find out that he is Rowe and what he will do if he succeeds. On the upper level of meaning the interest is concentrated on the feelings of a man who is able to drop overboard the accumulated load of guilt of his adult years and face existence with the pitiless freshness of youth. It is the schoolboy element in Rowe revolting against petty restrictions that drives him to the sick bay. He has been forbidden the newspapers—stupidly and arbitrarily, he thinks, though in fact Dr. Forester is worried about some too intelligent guesses made to the assistant Johns concerning the temporary disappearance of Defence documents from a Ministry. These guesses might lead Rowe to stumble on part of the truth of the spy business and possibly to recover his memory. A Minister in the House of Commons has denied the loss of any documents, according to the Press, but in terms ambiguous enough to cover their temporary disappearance, and, from his eager reading of old news to fill the vacuum of his memory, Rowe recalls that a similar case had occurred a few months earlier. 'The thing to do', he suggests, 'would be to follow up the first case . . . to find the point of failure.' This is another phrase doing double duty, for the exploration of Rowe's childhood is Greene's following up of Rowe's case 'to find the point of failure'.

This banning of newspapers is one sign that the nursing-home is not the Garden of Eden, and Rowe, to whom it had at first occurred to wonder whether the sick bay had 'more reality than the conception of Hell presented by sympathetic theologians—a place without inhabitants which existed simply as a warning', now sees patients removed there and the terror of restraint that poisons pleasure in the hygienic amenities of the home. He begins to wonder whether something equally sinister may not live behind Dr. Forester's 'noble old face'. Out of boredom he turns to the books on the shelves in his room, books belonging to Dr. Forester—a minor irony since Rowe's act is the result of the banning of newspapers—

and in these 'iron rations of old men' he finds a copy of Tolstoy's *What I Believe* with rubbed-out pencil marks in the margin. There are marks beside 'the gross fraud called patriotism and love of one's country', and he senses ignobility behind the careful but incomplete erasure.

The Ministry of Fear is a book written in war-time and here Greene offers us, I think, something of his own views on war, patriotism and pacifism. Rowe-Digby wonders:

> . . . why does he write as if the worst thing we can do to our fellow-man is to kill him? Everybody has to die and everybody fears death, but when we kill a man we save him from his fear. . . . One doesn't necessarily kill because one hates: one may kill because one loves. . . .

The irony of this is not left to speak for itself, for Greene adds, 'the old dizziness came back as if he had been struck over the heart'. Rowe defends taking part in war:

> Wasn't it better to take part even in the crimes of people you loved, if it was necessary hate as they did, and if that were the end of everything suffer damnation with them, rather than be saved alone?

Tolstoy, Rowe decides, was 'too busy saving his own soul'. A link with more obvious passages in Greene's novels connected with Péguy's willingness to be damned is clear in this quotation, and the remark about Tolstoy is echoed at the end of the book when it is said of Rowe, 'He wasn't interested in saving his own soul'.

There is in the treatment of the sources of Dr. Forester's treason, I feel, a flavour of war-time highbrow-baiting. At moments it is glib, on a par with the sentimental remark Greene allows himself about Winston Churchill, but mainly it is a serious if tendentious examination of the temptation of power to the idealist, the 'emancipated' man, and that this is intended to support and run parallel to Rowe-Digby's investigation of himself is evidenced by the figure of the military man Stone, Rowe's fellow-patient in the nursing-home. Stone is portrayed sympathetically and uncritically. He is something of a blimp, certainly not an intellectual, and he suffers from a chronic fear of treachery. He has seen men digging by night on a small island on an ornamental lake in the grounds of the nursing-home, and his poor twisted brain converts the diggers into traitors and Nazis. He tries to occupy the island for the Allies, walking into the muddy pond with 'his very clear blue eyes and the bristling military moustache and the lines of care and responsibility'. This is too much for Dr. Forester, who has concealed the remains of Jones, the murdered private detective, on the island; Stone disappears into the sick bay, and it is reported that he has had a relapse. In this part of the entertainment Stone is intended to capture our admiration to the same degree that Dr. Forester is intended to earn our contempt. Like Scobie Stone accepts responsibility —'That was the thing you learned in this place: that a man kept his character even when he was insane. No madness would ever dim that military sense of duty to others'. Stone is white as Dr. Forester is black, the atmosphere is charged with the one-sided implications of a parable, and we want to argue as we do mistakenly when we confuse a parable with a short story.

What causes the trouble is not Greene's requiring two different responses from the reader in rapid succession, one in which freedom to think all round the subject is permitted by the context, and one in which this freedom is narrowly circumscribed: it is the failure of artistic tact that makes the change of response difficult for us by such obvious weighting of the scales. The 'military sense of duty to others' has its limitations, but they do not appear. On the other hand Dr. Forester is not only an internationalist, but a cowardly one; not only a scientist embracing a Utilitarian ethic, but a man to whom these beliefs will allow the murder of innocent people. Greene's heroes are solitaries, but Greene himself dislikes the isolation of the intellectual; and here prejudice seems to have stampeded him into accepting herd-warmth at almost any price. Poole, the keeper of the sick bay, is Dr. Forester's colleague in treason, and earlier in the book he has argued with Rowe in the latter's London lodgings. 'I was thinking . . . that it's intellectuals like ourselves who are the only free men. Not bound by conventions, patriotic emotions, sentimentality . . . we haven't what they call a stake in the country.' The rootlessness of the highbrow is one thing, and a proper subject no doubt for good, clean fun, but it is alarming to see Greene giving, however obliquely, even a gramme of support to the 'Catholic' nonsense of Colm Brogan and other like-minded journalists.

Rowe goes to the sick bay with vague suspicions, but mostly out of schoolboy bravado and in the hope of talking to Stone. He finds him in a strait-jacket, feels an appalling movement of pity—'he felt capable of murder for the release of that gentle tormented creature' (another sentence with overtones)—and, caught by Dr. Forester on the way back, blurts out that he has visited and talked to Stone. In spite of the protests of the good-natured, hero-worshipping Johns, Dr. Forester cold-bloodedly makes Rowe a present of his real name and shows him a recognizable newspaper photograph with the correct name in the caption. He tells Rowe that he is a murderer, not caring whether this revelation drives him to insanity or suicide. But he has not reckoned on Rowe's resilience of spirit—'It wasn't all fear he felt: he felt also the untired courage and chivalry of adolescence. He was no longer too old or too habit-ridden to start again.' Bits of his past float up to Rowe from the depths of his shaken mind as he stands alone in his bedroom where he has sought solitude like a sick animal; he clings to the furniture as he remembers the hunched shoulders of Poole in his shabby lodgings, then Forester's face at the séance and the bleeding figure of a man—he knows now, he thinks, why he has been called a murderer—finally the sad face of a woman. Rowe cannot interpret all these pictures, but he is tortured by them to the point of agony. Greene has devised a situation in which the 'terror of life' makes its maximal impact, because it is no longer a matter of a gradual resignation to a conviction, but of an 'instantaneous conversion'. The familiar image of the pains of childbirth, used to make real Raven's death in *A Gun for Sale*, is brought into service to show how Rowe is torn at this moment: '. . . his head was racked with pain as other memories struggled to get out like a child out of the mother's body', Greene writes, and again, '. . . his brain reeled with the horror of returning life'.

Rowe's escape from the nursing-home brings the second movement of *The Ministry of Fear* to an end. Books Three and Four, entitled 'Bits and Pieces' and 'The Whole Man', do not like the earlier books constitute distinct movements of the narrative, since both are equally concerned with laying bare for inspection the works of the spy plot and the completion of Rowe's self-knowledge. Indeed the two sections are continuous in action. At the end of 'Bits and Pieces' Rowe is telephoning a London number that will bring him to the leader of the spy ring, which has been broken up by Mr. Prentice's inquiries. At the beginning of 'The Whole Man' he is travelling to the address behind the number with the realization that Anna Hilfe's brother is the wanted leader, and—a touch that belongs to the *Boy's Own Paper*—glad that he has kept the number to himself. Rowe's secretiveness is explained by further references to his artificial 'adolescence'. Here Greene's tongue is very firmly in his cheek. The justification, then, for the division of the last movement of *The Ministry of Fear* into two books is to be found in simple convenience. 'Bits and Pieces' is a picaresque retracing of some of the ground covered in 'The Unhappy Man', while 'The Whole Man' concentrates on the triangular relationship between Rowe, Anna Hilfe and her brother Willi, and in its earlier scenes makes use of a much slower tempo.

At the beginning of the third book Rowe goes to Scotland Yard to give himself up for the murder of the business man Cost at Mrs. Bellairs's séance. He finds that no such murder is on record and is handed on to Mr. Prentice, who convinces him that Cost under another name is alive, and that the story of the nursing-home involves treason as well as cruelty. In these explanatory interchanges, a necessary preliminary to the melodrama of later scenes, detection is the most prominent interest, but it is closely enough associated with Rowe's further (but still incomplete) discovery of himself to produce some effective ironic play. For example, with the removal of the suspicion of having murdered Cost, Rowe's spirits rise and he tells Prentice, who knows all about the mercy-killing and the time in prison, how much it means to him to feel innocent.

The following scene in 'Cost's' tailor's shop, probably Greene's finest piece of *grand guignol*, is the first of a series of incidents like those of the first book of the entertainment, but handled with even more virtuosity and with Rowe now a hunter, no longer a hunted man—the favourite variation on the chase pattern noted earlier in *A Gun for Sale* and *The Confidential Agent*. At the shop Cost, a tape-measure round his shoulders, realizes that the game is up as he is silently confronted with witnesses who are able to identify him. He refuses to break down. Deferentially he excuses himself to telephone to his chief on the plea of ringing a client ('I find at the last moment that we shall not be able to repeat the trousers. . . . Personally, sir, I have no hope. No hope at all'.), then borrows the cutting shears and—before his intentions can be grasped—walks evenly to his Roman death in a fitting-cubicle before a triple mirror.

Rowe is unmoved by Cost's suicide. In the taxi on the way to visit Mrs. Bellairs Prentice comments on this and brings forward again the entertainment's main theme. 'Pity is a terrible thing. People talk about the passion of love. Pity is the worst passion of all: we don't outlive it like sex. . . . You don't feel it, do you? Adolescents don't feel pity. It's a mature passion.' Pity and cruelty are the two sides of a coin. We are reminded of Prentice's pity for the victims of the spy ring as we watch his smooth calculated brutality in dealing with the fake medium in her suburban home. He is entirely convincing. Smashing an ornamental lamp and breaking expensive cups by dropping them on the floor in search of the micro-film of Defence secrets, he tells her crudely to get in touch with Cost and ask him why he cut his throat, advises her not to believe the story that they don't hang women spies in Britain.

Rowe is as unaffected by Mrs. Bellairs's tears as by Cost's suicide. As Prentice and he drive through the twilight and early evening to the nursing-home, he is drunk with 'danger and action'. This is life as imagined by a boy, helping in a great cause, knowing that things will work out well:

> He didn't worry very much about Stone: none of the books one read as a boy had an unhappy ending. And none of them was disturbed by a sense of pity for the beaten side . . . the remains of an iron bedstead on the third floor of a smashed tenement only said: 'They shall not pass', not 'We shall never sleep in this room, in this home again'. He didn't understand suffering because he had forgotten that he had ever suffered.

The further reference to boyhood reading is followed by another use of a recurrent image—that of a map. Earlier an incorrect map symbolized the impossible ideals with which we have to tackle experience. Now Rowe sees the narrow space on either side of the road lit by the headlamps of the car as the 'coloured fringe along the unexplored spaces of a map'; what is going on in the darkness are 'the profound natural common experiences' to which the 'adolescent' Rowe is a stranger. But it is part of his education that he is soon to lose his feeling of the heroic and learn that 'happiness should always be qualified by misery'. Things have not worked out at the nursing-home as they would have done in a boy's story. Stone is dead—chloroformed by Dr. Forester while still helpless in a strait-jacket; Dr. Forester is dead—shot in despair by the hero-worshipping Johns; a small box of clips and buttons and a watch are dug up on the island—all that remains of Mr. Jones of the Orthotex Private Inquiry Bureau. Rowe is left in the sick bay with the smell of anæsthetic in the air, learning 'that there weren't always happy endings' and feeling 'cruelty waking beside pity, its old and tried companion'. It is there that he decides to follow up alone the clue of the telephone number noted in the tailor's shop. This private investigation provides the material of the fourth book.

'The Whole Man' opens in the Hilfe apartment with a scene of some emotional subtlety as well as melodramatic excitement. Anna's betrayal of her brother because she loves Arthur Rowe is to be considered in a context of earlier Greene betrayals, and the portrait of Willi, the entirely selfish amoralist, found asleep 'deeply and completely at peace, and so defenceless that he seemed to be innocent', again emphasizes that not to worry, not to suffer, is to be something more or less than human. Beside him on the bed is an open volume of Rilke's poems concealing a revolver. Perhaps this conjunction sums him up too neatly. Love, pity and cruelty are linked once more when Anna has to decide to crack her brother's wrist with a wooden candlestick to prevent him taking charge of the situation with his gun. Her bitterness as she turns on Rowe and pushes him out of the room, because she has had to reject and injure Willi for him, is conveyed with exact insight. So are the different kinds of understanding of her feelings by the two men.

Anna, almost in tears, has promised Rowe that she will not let Willi escape and that she will obtain the micro-film from him. She intends to let her brother go, and her bitterness is partly due to her knowledge that she is acting in this way not for Willi's sake, but for Rowe's. She does not want Rowe once more to become the 'unhappy man' obsessed with guilt about his wife's death. Willi also understands why she is letting him escape and automatically cheats. He is on his way to Paddington and the Irish boat train when Rowe takes the film from Anna and finds that it is not the all-important negative. From this point to the end the tempo quickens.

Greene winds up his story with two brief scenes on the

waiting boat-train and in the men's lavatory at Paddington. They are typical of his entertainment manner. Rowe finds Willi in a carriage helping a deaf old lady to wind wool—his good looks and his pose as a gallant refugee have always made him a great favourite with old ladies. Disarmed while he is helpless, Willi still tries to bargain with Rowe—the film-negative and Rowe's 'past' against his own escape—while the anti-aircraft guns go into action against the German bombers in another air-raid, and the old lady, placidly knitting, turns her head at the loudest explosions as if she is dimly aware of something she cannot account for. Rowe is consumed with curiosity about the lost years of his life, but he will not bargain. He forces Hilfe to leave the train and they take shelter in the 'Gentlemen's' as the bombs begin to fall. The film is handed over as the urinals flush, the floor whines and the dust of explosion settles. Willi now offers to complete Rowe's memory at the lower price of the revolver and a single bullet to commit suicide. The offer is refused. With a sense of spiteful amusement that he can still cause people to suffer—in the train listening to the German bombers he had said wistfully, 'What fun they are having up there'—Willi tells Rowe about his trial for the murder of his dead wife. The lost years are recovered and Rowe, once again a 'whole man', can spare enough pity to throw his enemy the gun and a penny to open a closet, so that he may kill himself out of sight as Rowe goes to telephone the police.

This résumé of *The Ministry of Fear*, lengthy as it is, in several respects does less than justice to the book. It fails to suggest the richly concrete presentation of the complexities of the main theme; the economy with which different situations and atmospheres are established and at the same time subordinated to dramatic intentions; and the successful treatment of the 'normal' minor characters. This last point needs to be expanded because it is something new. The minor figures of Greene's early novels agree with a worn popular convention that supporting characters may be 'flat'—because they have not engaged the author's interest they lack even a momentary life; they are simply a convenience to him like uncounted small change. The successes of the middle period are chiefly in the vein of the satirical or grotesque minor character: Minty in *England Made Me*, 'Creepy' Billings in 'The Other Side of the Border'. There are grotesques in *The Ministry of Fear*, such as Rennit and Poole, and there are characters, like Dr. Forester and Stone, who are wanted chiefly for their symbolic part in the development of the book's meaning; but many of the minor characters—a Johns, a Mr. Prentice, a Henry Wilcox—are drawn with a new kind of assurance that anticipates Greene's sobriety and certainty of touch in *The Heart of the Matter*. Perhaps this fact is connected with a passage in Rowe's reflections as he talks to Rennit at the Orthotex Private Inquiry Bureau:

> The grand names stood permanently like statues in his mind: names like Justice and Retribution, though what they both boiled down to was simply Mr. Rennit, hundreds and hundreds of Mr. Rennits. But of course if you believed in God—and the Devil—the thing wasn't quite so comic. Because the devil—and God too—had always used comic people, futile people, little suburban natures and the maimed and warped to serve his purposes. When God used them you talked emptily of Nobility and when the devil used them of Wickedness: but the material was only dull shabby human mediocrity in either case.

From one point of view this is an apology for the gargoyles of Greene's novels, but the means of justification implies a fresh tendency to concentrate on what is normal and therefore more sympathetic in people. The new minor characters have an immediate authenticity because they have been found interesting for their own sakes. Henry Wilcox illustrates this conveniently.

Wilcox has only two appearances in *The Ministry of Fear*, but these appearances, in the first and third books, build the impression of a character in process of growth who would be different again if he were to appear a third time. We meet him first in Battersea when he is broken by grief at his wife's death. He has been a friend of Arthur Rowe in the old days, a timid chartered accountant with a masterful athletic wife. Rowe arrives to cash a cheque and is welcomed by Wilcox, who thinks it nice of him to come to the funeral. His mother-in-law is present and her sense of propriety is outraged at the appearance of a 'murderer', but Wilcox now understands intuitively some part of Rowe's present and past misery. His own grief is not simple. His useless rage against his wife's heroism—she has lost her life in a bomb-incident—which emerges when he looks at her row of silver cups for athletic triumphs and says, 'I suppose . . . she thought she'd win another of those blasted pots', is a complication speaking of an earlier state of feeling divided between admiration and jealousy. When the funeral party is ready he says that he won't go. But as the grim little cortège of A.R.P. workers, rescue officials and neighbours lumbers off out of step, he cannot help following. He has always depended on his wife; he forgets about cashing Rowe's cheque as he trots bareheaded to overtake the procession. Greene emphasizes the absoluteness of Rowe's loneliness by making it clear that the bewildered, deflated widower still has some position, some relationships.

The scene with Henry Wilcox in the third book is excellent ironic comedy. Rowe's memory is, of course, incomplete and he carefully explains to Wilcox that he is not a murderer. Rowe simply means that the muddle of Cost's supposed murder has been cleared up, but Wilcox naturally assumes that Rowe no longer feels his earlier guilt about his wife's death. 'You brood too much', he says. 'A thing that's done is done.' The phrase suggests his own recovery from grief.

> 'But this was never done, you see. I know that now. I'm not a murderer.'
>
> 'Of course you aren't, Arthur. No friend of yours—no proper friend—ever believed you were.'

A little puzzled, Rowe asks if there was much talk, and

Wilcox replies, 'Well—naturally', with a hint of surprise at his friend's insensitivity. But instantly he returns to seeing the position in terms of his own loss and recovery from it. 'It's no use mourning someone all your life', he says. 'That's morbid.' The suspicion of jauntiness reveals the emancipation that Henry Wilcox has found in his widowerhood, but his remarks to Rowe all bear on his own case and describe the guilt he still feels in being free of his masterful wife. Henry Wilcox exists as a 'round' character for us apart from his function of stressing Rowe's isolation at the beginning of the book, and later the fixity of obsession so different from his own 'natural' adjustment to grief.

IV

The Heart of the Matter is a Catholic novel (at least in Greene's sense of a novel written by a Catholic) and its theological implications have been teased out at great length by many amateur theologians and anti-theologians, not to mention a few professionals, most of whom too readily forget that they are dealing with a piece of fiction, not an actual case-history. If Scobie's fate is ambiguous, it is because the facts given in the novel admit of several interpretations. In life there would be the hope of unearthing further data which might conceivably determine the bearing of the facts already known. But in dealing with a character in a novel there can be no new facts to discover; and for this reason most of the exercises in casuistry are as irrelevant to a valuation of *The Heart of the Matter* as a Victorian essay on Hamlet's obesity to literary criticism of the play. Similarly the attempts to transform Scobie into the hero of an Existentialist novel seem to me beside the point. Discussion of the meaning of *The Heart of the Matter* is doomed in advance to sterility if it does not take into account that the words composing the book have been organized primarily with an artistic, rather than a philosophical or theological, intention.

Certainly one of Greene's aims in his novel is to make Scobie's goodness and fall equally convincing: without this his fable must lack tragic intensity. He writes as a sensitive and intelligent Catholic: that is, as a man for whom the moral law exists, but who does not always find its application easy—a position stated in Father Rank's words after Scobie's death: 'The Church knows all the rules. But it doesn't know what goes on in a single human heart'. Greene has not worked out the precise worth of his characters by a kind of moral calculus; he has simply seen them. He has presented a story, presented it, perhaps he would feel, *sub specie æternitatis*; but no amount of weeding will turn a garden into an asphalt barrack square. Is a more conclusive summary of the unravelling of Scobie's history to be asked for than these words of John Donne?

> Thou knowest this man's fall, but thou knowest not his wrastling; which perchance was such that almost his very fall is justified and accepted of God.

What is *The Heart of the Matter* about? One answer is given concretely in Greene's book with its complex of incidents and characters carefully arranged to produce a response that is the total meaning. If we try to give another answer we necessarily simplify, and we may simplify wrongly. The obsessional theme of *The Heart of the Matter* is pity, 'the terrible promiscuous passion which so few experience', and this associates it with *The Power and the Glory* and even more closely with *The Ministry of Fear*; but it is not enough to observe this likeness—we must also observe the differences accompanying the likeness and pick out the distinct note of *The Heart of the Matter*, a note I would characterize as one (for Greene) of severity.

This severity needs to be described, but momentarily let us consider some of the peculiarities of the ruling conception of pity in the novel. Pity is still held to be the mark of the feeling adult mind as in *The Ministry of Fear*, but it is no longer the origin of pity in childhood that is dwelt on. The principal characters are largely realized for us in their immediate present—Scobie, Wilson, Louise, Helen. If Helen Rolt refers to her schooldays, it is because she has recently left school and, like all the other characters, draws on recent memories. Greene satisfies his preoccupation with childhood, as in *The Power and the Glory*, not by study of the state of childhood, but by the essential part given in the development of the action to the memory of a child: the whisky-priest's daughter and Scobie's dead child, Catherine, have a similar function in the two books. In *The Heart of the Matter*, again as in *The Power and the Glory*, the notion of responsibility is brought alongside the main theme of pity and illuminates it. Responsibility enters into *The Ministry of Fear*, where Rowe's guilt is a form of it owed to his crime, the mercy-killing of his wife, but *The Heart of the Matter* shows Scobie burdened with a primary sense of responsibility that leads him into crime. As in *It's a Battlefield* Greene's responsible man is a policeman —'There was no other profession for a man of my kind', Scobie says. Responsibility for others to the point of endangering the self is common to the whisky-priest in *The Power and the Glory* and Scobie—Greene's derivation of the idea from Péguy has been indicated; but Scobie's reflection, 'One should look after one's own soul at whatever cost to another, and that's what I can't do, what I shall never be able to do', reminds us at once of Rowe's scornful criticism of Tolstoy in *The Ministry of Fear* and makes it apparent that the linkage of pity and responsibility was in Greene's mind throughout that entertainment. Again, it is in *The Ministry of Fear* and *The Heart of the Matter* that the dangers of an indiscriminate and too easily stirred pity are stressed, but the emphasis on the link with cruelty is not the same. *The Ministry of Fear* hints that the man most conscious of a sadistic streak in his own nature is the man most capable of pity—this comes near to extrapolation, but still seems a just comment. The cruelty worked by Scobie's compassion may not be incidental, but he is quite unaware of any sadistic impulse in himself.

The difficulties of this analysis, illustrated by the haphazardness of the distinctions drawn, are an argument for the inseparability of theme from the characters and situations in which it is embodied, and from the methods employed in putting both in front of the reader. For example, the obsession with pity in *The Heart of the Matter* is also developed in association with ideas about escape and betrayal, ideas met in earlier Greene fiction including *The Power and the Glory*; but what may be called the vibration of each of these ideas can only be determined, and then approximately, by an extended 'practical criticism' of *The Heart of the Matter*, which is of all Greene's novels the one in which the system of cross-references, qualifying the meaning at any moment, is most subtly elaborated.

There is a single element in the presentation of the theme of pity that is unforeshadowed in the earlier fiction of Graham Greene: the problem of reconciling the existence of suffering with an omnipotent and merciful providence is now raised explicitly for the first time. In *It's a Battlefield* the Commissioner, Greene's responsible man, finds human and divine justice equally incomprehensible, but he is not a devout man like Scobie, nor is pity an important factor in his character. It is the thought of waste that shrivels him. But in *The Heart of the Matter* the incomprehensibility and the apparent heartlessness of the scheme of things are deeply felt by Scobie. His objection in round terms would be to the paradox of a creature more compassionate than its Creator. There is only 'the hint of an explanation—too faint to be grasped'. The phrase becomes the title of a short story published in 1949 and points to a new preoccupation connected with the 'terror of life' that may still be growing in Greene's mind. The relative importance of the notion in *The Heart of the Matter* is again a matter better examined in its context, a scene which is a nodal point for many of the novel's significances and includes some of Greene's finest writing. The death of the child in the hospital at Pende is made actual with a pathos that puts me in mind of some of the most disciplined of John Crowe Ransom's poems.

With the earlier letter of the Portuguese sea-captain to his married daughter, it is beyond argument one of Greene's major imaginative successes.

The severity described as the distinctive note of *The Heart of the Matter* has several causes. One may be a watchfulness about melodrama. No incident is exploited for a passing exciting effect, no character is allowed to take the bit between the teeth, however interesting he or she may be, and become out of hand in relation to the whole. But the most general explanation of the severity—and anxiety about melodrama is really an aspect of this—is Greene's desire to rely for his total effect only on the drama of human relations presented with a minimum of comment. The proportion of dialogue to narrative, description and comment is significantly high.

In 'The Revolver in the Corner Cupboard' Greene has told us that after a psycho-analysis in his adolescence he could for many years 'take no æsthetic interest in any visual thing at all'. There is certainly no pausing over landscapes in any of Greene's novels (after his early 'unsuccessful' ones), but here a special disposition is consciously strengthened. It is not until one hunts to discover how the trick has been worked that one is aware with what economy the background of the West African port—the wharves, the police offices, Cape Station and the shanties of Sharp Town—has been built up. At the sensuous evocation of place Greene is deficient, unlike Conrad and Mauriac, two novelists whom he admires, but in *The Heart of the Matter* this weakness is made to contribute to a planned spareness of dramatic incident.

Similarly there is a direct avoidance of colour and cleverness —except possibly in the pages describing Scobie's reading of *A Bishop among the Bantus* to the small boy in the border hospital. The deliberate casualness and unforced quiet manner are admirable, but occasionally a piece of understatement is self-defeating. A single example will make this plain. Scobie's work-colleague Fraser is always humming a song picked up on leave:

What will we care for
The why and the wherefore
When you and I
Are pushing up the daisies.

It is only mentioned once early in the novel, but we are expected to remember it and accept the ironic application, after more than a hundred intervening pages, when Scobie returns from Helen's Nissen hut after becoming her lover. 'In the wet and noisy darkness he had even lifted his voice and tried out a line from Fraser's song, but his voice was tuneless.'

The special note of the novel owes much, too, to Greene's prudence in the employment of imagery and to his adoption of various minor stylistic devices. The necessary lift that is given by metaphor to the ordinary language of narrative is supplied, without destroying unity of tone, by using many recurrent and 'extended' images, and further by choosing imagery in many cases subdued to the scene and characters by a special aptness. The stylistic devices all aim at economy. They range from an idiosyncratic use of punctuation, often aimed at producing a simultaneity among several impressions, to verbal collocations of different types but of the general order instanced in the following examples. When Greene writes, 'They watched their separation anchor in the bay' of the arrival of the liner that is to take Scobie's wife to South Africa, or 'Silence and solitude were being hammered away' of her return to her home, he is attempting—these attempts are not always well-chosen—to do two things at once: he is mentioning in the same breath a physical event and the observer's emotional response to it.

The activity of the imagery is too important to be passed over so briefly. Recurrent images may be used, rather like tracer-elements in medicine, to make visible the structural links between various scenes in the novel; to direct our attention to repetitions of mood; or in connection with the appearances of particular characters. An example in the last category, which also illustrates aptness of metaphor, is to be found in a series of images concerning Scobie and related to his job as deputy-commissioner of police. Scobie and his wife Louise walk into the lounge of the white Station club where she dreads to go 'like a couple of policemen on duty'; to Scobie Helen's worn look is 'like handcuffs on his wrists'; another character, Wilson, feels 'an odd elderly envy for Scobie, much as an old lag might envy the young crook serving his first sentence'. Cognate with this series is another, appropriate in a novel about a colony and protectorate in war-time, involving words such as 'territory', 'border', 'country'.[1] When Scobie comes home to find Louise sick:

> He stood very still like a spy in foreign territory, and indeed he was in foreign territory now.

When Wilson, infatuated by Louise, is asked to shut the window of her bedroom, he feels that he has no right to be there:

> . . . his employers had never taught him that he would find himself in a country so strange to him as this.

Sometimes this type of image carries a further typical significance—we recall the divided loyalties of home and school at Berkhamsted as 'life lived on the border'; the title of the abandoned 'The Other Side of the Border'; the idea of Mexico as 'an active sector of the line' in the conflict between good and evil. When Scobie decides to stand by his mistress, Helen Rolt, he feels:

> . . . as though he were turning his back on peace for ever. With his eyes open, knowing the consequences, he entered the territory of lies without a passport for return.

And again, when he is refused absolution by a priest:

[1] The authorities, it has to be remembered, are worried about the smuggling of industrial diamonds over the border—this is a matter with important repercussions in the plot—and relations are strained with their Vichy French' neighbours in the first place.

It seemed to him that he had only left for his exploration the territory of despair.

Extended images are used more sparingly, but also act to preserve unity of tone. The term 'extended image' is not self-explanatory, and the shortest way of making my meaning clear is to quote a short passage, italicizing the key phrase and its extended elements. The passage occurs when Louise returns from South Africa and puts the photograph of her dead daughter back on the dressing-table:

> [Scobie] went upstairs and from the doorway saw the face in the white communion veil staring back at him again: *the dead too had returned.* Life was not the same without the dead. The mosquito-net hung, *a grey ectoplasm*, over the double-bed.
>
> 'Well, Ali,' he said, with the *phantom* of a smile which was all he could *raise* at this *séance*, 'Missus back. We're all together again'.

Any apparent affectation here, it should be said in justice to Greene, is quite invisible at the correct temperature of the original context.

These preliminary remarks do not call for much to be said about characterization and structure. The whisky-priest and the lieutenant at one important moment in *The Power and the Glory* are too obviously mouthpieces for opposed philosophies of life to be fully convincing as individuals; and in *The Ministry of Fear* two characters, Dr. Forester and Stone, never have much life apart from their symbolic function. By contrast all the principal characters of *The Heart of the Matter* are consistently 'round'. Scobie himself, his wife Louise, his enemy Wilson, the Syrian Yusef, are satisfactorily complex, and in the second and third cases, it may be said, further complexity is suggested than the novel finds time to explore. Understandably Helen Rolt is less complicated, but for the most part her pathos and gaucherie ring true. I am not quite sure that Greene worked hard enough with her, but failure would certainly be too strong a word for the limitations of this portrait. The minor characters, too, are either actually or potentially round. There are no grotesques among them, unless we count the mildly caricatured Harris. The others—the Catholic Syrian, Tallit, the bitter self-important bandy-legged Captain Perrot, Ali—are drawn with varying degrees of fullness, but their predictability is more than mechanical. Perhaps Father Rank and the Commissioner come nearest to being author's conveniences.

An obvious feature of the novel's structure is Greene's use of the point of view. The greater part of the action is seen through Scobie's eyes, but from time to time Wilson's is the recording consciousness. On the surface Wilson is a 'U.A.C. clerk' given the job of checking the distribution of the trading company's goods in the colony and keeping an eye open for possible dishonesty: actually he is a Government spy investigating the smuggling of industrial diamonds. His true job is known to Scobie's chief and a few other officials, and it is guessed by Yusef; but for a long time it is not even suspected by Scobie. We must be given some explanation of Wilson's behaviour—Scobie is puzzled by him—and we must be introduced to events outside Scobie's knowledge. These are the practical reasons for using Wilson's point of view. But the relevant sections have other uses. They give us Scobie unsympathetically from the outside and, by reducing his scale, prevent too simple a response to the action; they also serve to remind us of the continued existence of other people with their jobs and leisure activities—censorship, pink gins, cockchafer-hunts, letters to school-magazines.

There are indications that at first Greene intended to make more use of this method of construction than he does in the printed novel. Chapter II (Book I, Part II) begins rather abruptly with the return of Louise and Wilson from a walk to find Scobie about to set off on a mission to Bamba. It is a short chapter mostly in dialogue, and the action, seen from Wilson's point of view as the few comments make clear, could less strictly be described as observed by an ideal spectator.

Parenthetically, it may be noted, this is a means by which the author can reduce or increase emphasis: he can raise or lower our degree of identification with the character who is our window into the action. Consequently a section that is technically from a particular point of view may in fact approach the objectivity of third person narration.

Greene explains the abrupt beginning of the chapter in terms of the excision of an earlier chapter describing Louise's and Wilson's walk. Tact is needed in deciding how long you can remain with one point of view in a novel using multiple presentation, and here Greene came to the conclusion that the narrative would lose shape if a further chapter from Wilson's viewpoint (and without Scobie's presence) were to be included. Greene has also informed me that he played for a time with the idea of a third point of view (Louise's), but finally—wisely, I think—decided against it. This would have endowed Louise with too much importance in Book I unless the action was to be seen in Book II from Helen Rolt's viewpoint. With this further complication the final book, involving four viewpoints, would have been very difficult to write, and the desired meaning might well have been blurred.

Reduced to bare bones the story of *The Heart of the Matter* is the story of Scobie, a deputy-commissioner of police in Sierra Leone, and his relations with two women, his wife Louise and his mistress Helen. For them he sins and commits crimes, and for them finally he dies. He is a man of nearly fifty and has outlived his earlier passion for his wife, whom he now thinks of with worried affection and compassion. They share the memory of a dead child, Catherine. Pity and responsibility for others—particularly where the others are weak, unattractive or defenceless; a hopeless longing for peace, seen as a freedom from anxiety; a solid practicality; a sincere and serious belief in his religion—he is a convert to Catholicism while his wife is a 'cradle' Catholic: these are his dominant characteristics. From his responsibility and practical sense springs his inability to deceive himself. Scobie is logical—and in this connection a remark by Rostenne is worth quoting: 'Ce qui garde des plus graves péchés et du désespoir les chrétiens médiocres, c'est . . . la légereté et l'aisance avec lesquelles ils vivent dans l'illogisme. . . .'

During his wife's absence in South Africa, Scobie is betrayed by his sense of pity and becomes the lover of Helen Rolt, a bewildered nineteen-year-old girl widowed in the shipwreck that brings her eventually to Sierra Leone.[1] He finds that the love-affair involves him in responsibilities that conflict with his private vow on Louise's behalf 'during the horrible little elegant ceremony among the lace and candles, that he would always see to it that she was happy'. It also involves him in sacrilege—to avert Louise's suspicions on her return he has to pretend that everything is normal and practise his religion. He is as helpless as Buridan's ass between the claims of Louise and Helen, for he will make neither unhappy by turning wholly to the other. He can, of course, elect to remain as he is, but even this position soon becomes intolerable. He would rather damn himself by self-murder than continue the acts of sacrilege, which he sees as 'a continuous shower of blows' rained on the bruised face of Christ. The women, he thinks, will soon forget him after his death. He studies the symptoms of angina pectoris so that his suicide may appear a natural death, and poisons himself with the Evipan tablets prescribed by a doctor for the imaginary complaint.

Helen's grief is real, but we know it will not last; and we know, too, that her mood of nihilism will probably drive her to give herself to a R.A.F. handlebar-moustache of a convincing silliness, who talks of 'no time like the present for a prang' when he wants to go to bed with her. Louise is left embittered. Ironically, she had returned to Freetown because

[1] Helen Rolt has a little of Lucia's ridiculous innocence in *England Made Me*. There is the same 'daring' and the same romantic use of cliché. Scobie thinks of Helen that she has not 'read the best books like Louise'.

of her knowledge of the love-affair, but her suspicions had been lulled, and she had supposed that Scobie had broken with Helen, from his face-saving performance of his religious duties. After Scobie's death she finds out the 'truth'. She has no inkling of the suffering that he has endured, and she thinks of him as a bad and dishonest Catholic. Wilson hints at the possibility of suicide, a final horror to her for it means that she must think of her husband as damned. When she brings herself to accept Wilson's argument, she is left as empty of feeling as Helen.

So much of the story is enough for understanding the novel's division into books. Book I sets the West African scene, establishes the relationship between Louise and Scobie, and leads up to Louise's departure for South Africa. Book II introduces Helen Rolt, describes her growing intimacy with Scobie and the early course of their love-affair, and concludes with the telegram announcing Louise's unexpected return. In time it covers the rainy season. These two books are like the major and minor premisses of a syllogism: the third book describes the conclusion that Scobie draws from the two incurred responsibilities—suicide.

The further division of the three books into parts, chapters and sub-sections, which are the smallest units of narrative, requires us to know how Scobie's life is crossed by Yusef, Wilson and Ali. The triangular relationship of Scobie and the two women is one side of the main story, but both Wilson and Yusef are necessary for the 'degradation' of Scobie's character which is another reason for the self-disgust that predisposes him to suicide. By the end of the novel Scobie feels that he is contaminated by evil and contaminates others merely by continuing to exist. A dream shows this—dreams are used with the frequency customary in Greene's fiction. Scobie sees himself:

> . . . drifting down just such an underground river as his boyhood hero Allan Quartermain [sic] had taken towards the lost city of Milosis. But Quartermaine [sic] had companions while he was

> alone, for you couldn't count the dead body on the stretcher as a companion. He felt a sense of urgency, for he told himself that bodies in this climate kept for a very short time and the smell of decay was already in his nostrils. Then . . . he realized that it was not the dead body that smelt but his own living one.[1]

The climax of self-condemnation comes with the death of Ali. Ali dies because Scobie no longer trusts him, and the chief ground for distrust is that the appearance of trustworthiness is not enough. 'Wouldn't many people gamble on my honesty and lose their stake? Why should I lose my stake on Ali?' Scobie is known as a just man—even Wilson, who hates him, bursts out with, 'Oh, you are unbearable. You are too damned honest to live'—yet all the time he is sadly aware of his corruption. With the revelation of the extent of his fall on Ali's death, he no longer wishes to live. The 'terror of life' has become too great.

The 'syllogistic' structure already described is complicated by the structure resulting from Scobie's relations with Yusef and Wilson. This structure traces the progressive stages of Scobie's downfall from complete, almost wooden rectitude by a series of tied and contrasted scenes. The two aspects of the story are interdependent. For example, to mention two of many links, it is from Yusef that Scobie borrows money to send his wife abroad, and Wilson hovers near the Scobie-Helen-Louise triangle by his furtive, uneasy passion for Scobie's wife.

Wilson is an interesting study. 'His profession was to lie, to have the quick story ready, never to give himself away . . .', but this perpetual need to be on guard is partly inborn. It might be said that the profession of spy chose him.

[1] Rider Haggard's spelling is Allan Quatermain. Apart from revealing self-disgust this passage brings out Scobie's loneliness in the love-affair—'. . . you couldn't count the dead body on the stretcher as a companion'. Helen is carried into Scobie's life at Pende on a stretcher, but they cannot understand each other in spite of becoming friends and lovers. They are separated by thirty years and inhabit different worlds of belief.

He feels his inferiority and tries hard to be indistinguishable from good mixers by wearing his moustache 'like a club tie' and talking loudly of Edgar Wallace. His secret vice is late Romantic poetry. He carries with him a *Golden Treasury*, from which he gives himself guiltily hypodermic shots of Longfellow and Mangan. He distrusts himself profoundly; and because of this he must distrust others. Scobie's rectitude must be found hollow. Like Iago he is furiously afraid of a 'daily beauty' in his enemy's life that makes his own life ugly. His is a Judas rôle and this may explain the humiliations that he has to undergo—the wrong kind of tropical suit, the nose-bleed, the shrinking agony of realizing that he has walked home with his shirt-tail hanging out. In *The Power and the Glory*, it may be remembered, Greene remarks on the aptness of turning 'the world's traitor' into 'a figure of fun'.

His need to prove Scobie a sham compels him to believe that his enemy is in league with Yusef for the smuggling of industrial diamonds. In reality Yusef is quite uninterested in what he contemptuously calls 'gravel', and is only concerned with the smuggling of gem stones out of the colony as an insurance against British defeat in the war. Yusef's affection for Scobie, which Wilson finds so suspicious, has grown from amazement at finding a completely honest official. There is in it the amusement of the adult for a rather absurd innocence, but Yusef has the same serious need to feel the solidity of Scobie's worth to be rock-like that Wilson has to find it a cardboard theatrical pretence. This balancing of Yusef against Wilson in relation to a central figure reminds us unobtrusively of the Morality, and is one feature of a pattern defining imaginatively the novel's meaning.

Wilson's enmity towards Scobie is fed from another source. To the clubmen at Cape Station, Scobie's wife is known as 'Literary Louise', and from a shared interest in poetry a queer friendship develops between her and Wilson. On her side it is no more than tolerance produced by boredom, but Wilson manages to work up a tormented romantic feeling. Even in intimacies he is tortuous. Jealous of Scobie and longing to be taken seriously by Louise, he writes a bad poem and has it printed in his school-magazine. Then—to impress her—he clips out the page and pastes it on a blank sheet of paper so that he may tell her that it has appeared in a highbrow weekly. She is unimpressed—her tastes are for Virginia Woolf and the younger 'pylon' poets—and he experiences 'a nausea of self-disgust'.

Scobie's downfall is the direct result of his compassion. His failure to secure the reversion of the Commissionership of Police is too much for Louise, pathetically insecure in her relations with others and neurotically aware that she is a source of amusement to some of the officials and their smart wives.[1] She demands to be sent to South Africa. Scobie's feeling that he has somehow failed in manhood is increased by an unsuccessful attempt to secure an overdraft from his bank. He turns to Yusef for a loan—Yusef is always trying to press gifts on him: a roll of silk, a refrigerator, a case of whisky. The imprudence of the act is underlined by Scobie's failure to report the loan, as he tells Yusef he will do, to the Commissioner, but any price is cheap for Louise's happiness:

> He had always been prepared to accept responsibility for his actions, and he had always been half-aware too, from the time he made his terrible private vow that she should be happy, how far *this* action might carry him. Despair is the price one pays for setting oneself an impossible aim. It is, one is told, the unforgivable sin, but it is a sin the corrupt or evil man never practises. . . . Only the man of goodwill carries always in his heart this capacity for damnation.

His imprudence over the loan has been anticipated in the

[1] Scobie and Louise recall Fellows and his wife in *The Power and the Glory*. Scobie is quite unlike Fellows (except for feeling happiest alone), but Louise and Mrs. Fellows are both inclined to suffer from 'nerves' and be irritable. Coral Fellows corresponds to the dead daughter, Catherine. The likeness is marked enough to suggest that Greene derives both groups of characters from the same source, literary or otherwise.

novel by his behaviour to the Portuguese captain on board the *Esperança*. Scobie is too ready to play the part of a pseudo-providence, to forget under the sway of pity 'what experience had taught him—that no human being can really understand another, and no one can arrange another's happiness'. He goes out to the *Esperança* with the Field Security Police to search for diamonds, but, left alone in the captain's cabin, finds a letter hidden in the lavatory-cistern addressed to a Frau Groener in Leipzig. Frau Groener is the captain's daughter. The captain throws himself on Scobie's mercy, begs him to open the letter to assure himself that it is quite innocuous. Scobie replies briefly that he must leave it to the censorship, but pity is already at work:

> The man had lowered his bulk on to the edge of the bath as though it were a heavy sack his shoulders could no longer bear. He kept on wiping his eyes like a child—an unattractive child, the fat boy of the school. Against the beautiful and the clever and the successful, one can wage a pitiless war, but not against the unattractive: then the millstone weighs on the breast.

The image in the first sentence of this passage at once recalls another in the concluding paragraph of the previous chapter, when Scobie, having wrestled with his wife's misery in the hot small hours under the mosquito net, promises that he will find some way of sending her to South Africa.

> He was surprised how quickly she went to sleep: she was like a tired carrier who has slipped his load. . . . The load lay beside him now, and he prepared to lift it.

Here the use of recurrence serves a frequent purpose of linking the similar elements of two situations. The particular image is a common one and further instances of it will be noted.

Immediately before the passage quoted from the night scene between Scobie and his wife, Louise has remarked, 'After all . . . there's nobody to save for . . .' with bitter reference to the death of their daughter Catherine. Only

Louise had been with the child in England when she died, and for years Scobie has felt guilty about this as if he had purposely avoided a necessary occasion of suffering. When the Portuguese captain complains, 'If you had a daughter, you'd understand. You haven't got one,' Scobie agrees quietly, but the blow disables him. On his return to his office he opens the letter. Greene makes clear what is happening:

> Scobie against the strictest orders was exercising his own imperfect judgment.

By one reckoning he is the prey to his compassion, by another the proud, self-sufficient man. He will not trust the censor to behave mercifully if the letter is innocent. The function of this decision is to pre-figure the final important occasion when he will refuse to trust anybody, even God, with the responsibility for the happiness of his wife and mistress. Scobie acknowledges to himself that he has been corrupted by sentiment; and he goes on to isolate the cause. The pathos and unattractiveness of the captain had counted for less than the thought of Frau Groener, 'a stout young Portuguese woman as graceless as himself'.

> What a fool. He owed his duty to Louise, not to a fat sentimental Portuguese skipper who had broken the rules of his own company for the sake of a daughter equally unattractive. That had been the turning point, the daughter.

The degree to which almost any important scene in *The Heart of the Matter* is involved with all the others, by an organization in depth of parallel emotional relationships and correspondences of phrase and image, can be shown from this interview on the *Esperança*. Because the scene is the first step in Scobie's downfall, it calls up the later steps: the loan from Yusef; adultery with Helen Rolt, which in turn forces him to smuggle a package of diamonds for Yusef; acts of sacrilege; his nearness to conniving at Ali's murder; suicide. The smuggling incident is more closely linked than any of the others, because it again involves the Portuguese captain; and a comparison of the two scenes on board the *Esperança* is a measuring-rod for determining the extent of Scobie's degradation in the time-interval between them. In the first Scobie is the beginner in wrongdoing, moved by pity for another to a venial breach of the law. In the second he has to humiliate himself before the captain by asking a return for his charity. Yusef is blackmailing Scobie. To keep the knowledge of his infidelity from his wife he must now break the law more seriously and for 'selfish' reasons. As he searches the cabin he sees the captain's face in a mirror and barely recognizes it.

> Momentarily he wondered: who can that be? before he realized that it was only this new unfamiliar look of pity that made it strange to him. He thought: am I really one of those whom people pity?

The handy-dandy of the two cabin scenes italicizes, as it were, our perception of what has changed.

Similarly the various scenes with Yusef signpost Scobie's descent. Near the beginning of the novel Scobie gives the Syrian a lift in his car and warns him to be careful in his dealings. Yusef brushes the warning aside, but asks for friendship: 'That is what I should like more than anything else in the world'. The wish is repeated in a later scene at Bamba when Scobie laughs at the suggestion that Wilson is spying on him and adds: 'I don't think the time's ever likely to come, Yusef, when I shall need *your* pity. If you do want to do something for me, though, go away and let me sleep'. The remark is already ironic at their next meeting soon after Louise's sailing to South Africa. Scobie has wanted something more from Yusef—the loan of the passage money. He welcomes Yusef into his house and gives him a drink to the latter's surprise, but he explains very carefully that his commitments are restricted to the loan and the interest on it. 'You are going to get nothing but four per cent.'

These interviews with Yusef all occur in the first book of

the novel. Two scenes in the second book are particularly effective. The earlier of these takes place in an inner room of Yusef's bungalow, which consists of 'a succession of small rooms identically furnished with sofas and cushions and low tables for drinks like the rooms in a brothel'. On information from Yusef Scobie has moved against Yusef's Syrian business rival, Tallit, only to discover that Tallit has been framed. Scobie feels betrayed and visits Yusef to tell him that any real relationship between them is now at an end. The various similes and metaphors used—one has been quoted above—together compose an extended image of sexual infidelity, suggestive of the less than guilty, but more than innocent, tie between the two men. By accepting the loan two months ago, Scobie reflects, 'he had lost his integrity'—the thought of the loan is like 'the memory of an adultery'. But the quarrel is unreal, like 'a lover's quarrel', and Scobie says good-bye amiably enough in a room 'as anonymous as a hotel bedroom':

> 'Goodbye, Yusef, you aren't a bad chap, but goodbye.'
>
> 'You are wrong, Major Scobie. I am a bad chap.' He said earnestly, 'My friendship for you is the only good thing in this black heart. I cannot give it up. We must stay friends always.'

When Scobie refuses this appeal, Yusef stares brazenly at him and threatens to go to the Commissioner with the story of the loan. Then he takes back the threat.

> 'Of course I shall not go. One day you will come back and want my friendship. And I shall welcome you.'

'Shall I really be so desperate?' Scobie wonders. The earlier certainty has gone—it is a question now.

The later scene takes us back again to Scobie's house and contrasts strongly with the scene in the house following Louise's departure. At the first of these meetings Scobie had been able to say, 'You are going to get nothing but four per cent', but now his hands are tied. He is Helen Rolt's lover and she is infuriated by the secrecy and his caution. 'You come here after dark and you go after dark. It's so—so ignoble.' Out of pity he writes a foolish letter, carefully signed with his full name, confessing his love and his adultery, and slips it under Helen's door. She does not find it. They pretend to think that it has been swept up as waste paper, but it has come into Yusef's possession.

Obscurely distressed at having to blackmail Scobie, but never for a moment doubting that by his code he must do so, at first Yusef simply begs Scobie to take a packet of diamonds to the captain of the *Esperança*—'Nothing for the Germans. Nothing that will hurt your country. . . . Major Scobie, I implore you.' When Scobie is unmoved, he, too, becomes formal; but again friendship conflicts with business.

> 'Oh, Major Scobie, what made you write such a letter? It was asking for trouble.'
>
> 'One can't be wise all the time, Yusef. One would die of disgust.'

Finally he makes it clear that the letter will be handed to Louise as she lands if Scobie refuses to help him. Scobie has to yield, to pay more than four per cent, but Yusef is complicated enough to know that his success is also a failure.

> 'I am the base Indian.'
>
> 'The base Indian?'
>
> 'Who threw away a pearl', Yusef sadly said. 'That was in the play by Shakespeare the Ordnance Corps gave in the Memorial Hall. I have always remembered it.'

The power of this scene, it should be observed, is increased by Scobie's unwillingness (which is our unwillingness) to attend initially to what Yusef has to say. Scobie and Helen have quarrelled about Louise's return, and Yusef's first remarks are crossed with the reading of a misspelt and childish letter from Helen swallowing all her pride. This device camouflages the obviousness of the Yusef development and even gives it a fraction of surprise.

The final interview between Scobie and Yusef in Book III of the novel begins with a simple remark, 'This is the first time you have ever honoured my office, Major Scobie', which is again a kind of compass-bearing to Scobie's present plight. He has come for help and Yusef's help can only be of a dubious kind. Tangled every way and burdened with guilt, he has such a longing to ease his shoulders for a moment that he shows a dull failure to be suspicious when Yusef claims that Ali can be made 'quite trustworthy'. At Yusef's bidding he sends a message to summon his servant and waits for whatever may happen.

To Yusef the time is one of unalloyed happiness. At last his 'friend' is with him, relying on him, bound to him in intimacy over a shared secret. To Scobie the interval is agonizing as Yusef drones on:

> 'I just wanted to say, Major Scobie, that you need not worry about me. I want your good, nothing so much as that. I will slip out of your life, Major Scobie. I will not be a millstone. It is enough for me to have had tonight—this long talk in the dark on all sorts of subjects. I will remember tonight always.'

It is the essence of the irony in this scene that Yusef, who is genuinely persuaded that Scobie's goodness can link him with the moral life (for which he has such a simple, 'impersonal' respect), should commit his first thoroughly wicked action of which we have certain knowledge—the planning of Ali's murder—out of the purest friendship. Yusef's love is quite unselfish, but, because it is unselfish without reference to any values but that of loyalty to the object of devotion, it is murderous. The cross-reference to Scobie's equally unselfish and unlimited pity is unmistakable. Together, Yusef's devotion and Scobie's pity lead to Ali dead on the wharf.

Other paired scenes and scene-sequences help in the design of *The Heart of the Matter*. Corresponding to the two scenes on the *Esperança* are scenes early and late in the bank manager's office; and Scobie's various dialogues with the Commissioner or with Father Rank, though less important, are comparable in structural function to his interviews with Yusef. Without this elaborate symmetry there are numerous other cross-references that make for architectural unity. For example, there is a distinct parallelism between Scobie's scenes with the overwrought Louise and those with Helen after the secrecy of her position has begun to tell on her nerves. If he shuts his eyes, Scobie thinks, Helen's voice is that of Louise—a younger Louise 'perhaps less capable of giving pain'. With his mistress as with his wife he finds himself apprehensive, telling small comforting lies, directing the conversation away from dangerous places—'He wondered sadly whether love always inevitably took the same road'. Parallelism is pointed by the imagery. Turbulence of emotion is identified with storms of weather when Scobie thinks of Louise's sudden calm as 'the quiet centre of the storm'; and when, after a quarrel with Helen, he notices inwardly, 'the pillar had wheeled on its course: the storm was involving others now: it had passed beyond them'.

Another parallel between Louise and Helen is drawn when, on two like occasions, Scobie finds that an object of his care has suddenly come alive: in each case this revelation of independent personality only sharpens his sense of pity and awakens further responsibility. Expecting an outburst from Louise, he finds that she has guessed his feelings—'I'm not going to bait you now'. And when he thinks about it, lying awake in bed:

> It occurred to him, as it hadn't occurred to him for years, that she loved him: poor dear, she loved him: she was someone of human stature with her own sense of responsibility, not simply the object of his care and kindness.

With Helen the comment is implicit. Driving to her Nissen hut in the fury of self-revulsion after Ali's death, he meets her walking down the hill, hatless in the sun, her face defeated and broken. It has not struck him that Ali's death may also be the last straw for her. She becomes real; and as Louise's awareness of his feelings in the earlier incident makes it even more imperative that he should find the passage money to send her away, so this time Helen's despairing courage ('I can't go on ruining you any more. . . . I'm going to go away—right away') destroys his own determination to end their relationship.

Once or twice a scene seems to have been included in the novel simply to complete a pattern. Thus Wilson's visit to the native brothel, a good scene in itself, is unnecessary except to afford a contrast between Wilson's and Scobie's attitudes to sexual love. Wilson, the gangling romantic, with his bad poetry and his absurd idealization of Louise, must pay for his fine sentiments with a compensating animality. Greene's intention is undisguised when he makes Wilson reflect that he will be able 'to write another poem to Louise' once he has had a native girl. By contrast the basis of Scobie's feelings for Louise and Helen is affection. With Louise the physical bond has ceased to be important; with Helen it had seemed to be ruled out by their difference in age. The comment on their surprised mutual surrender to desire illustrates this: 'What they had both thought was safety proved to have been the camouflage of an enemy who works in terms of friendship, trust and pity.'

The necessary link between Wilson's fluctuations of lust and romanticism is provided by an image used in the brothel scene and later in an interview with Louise when he declares his love. In the narrow cubicle of the native brothel 'the dim and wayward light' reminded Wilson of 'a vault newly opened for another body to be let down upon its floor'. In the scene with Louise, Wilson's nose bleeds and he has to lie on the floor to stop it.

> She stood over him as though he were a corpse. . . . They neither of them heard the car stop or the footsteps up to the threshold. It was strange to both of them, hearing a third voice from an outside world speaking into this room which had become as close and intimate and airless as a vault.

Both images may perhaps be related to the fear of the body

evident from the beginning in Greene's fiction and strongest in *Brighton Rock*, but much less strident in the last group of novels. In *The Heart of the Matter* it can be traced in certain images describing women. For example, Louise:

> His wife was sitting under the mosquito-net, and for a moment he had the impression of a joint under a meat-cover. But pity trod on the heels of the cruel image and hustled it away . . .

the black girl whom Wilson meets in the brothel:

> . . . he saw a girl in a dirty shift spread out on the packing-cases like a fish on a counter . . .

and Helen lying asleep beside Scobie:

> She lay in the odd cramped attitude of someone who has been shot in escaping. It seemed to him for a moment even then, before his tenderness and pleasure awoke, that he was looking at a bundle of cannon fodder.

The idea has, of course, its connection with the obsessional 'terror of life', the notion that unhappiness is natural, expressed here not only in Scobie's settled conviction that life is 'immeasurably long', but also, more explicitly, in his reflections on suffering in the hospital scenes at Pende; and, more plainly and familiarly, in the feelings significantly associated with a school childhood like Greene's—of a minor character, Harris:

> The walls of Downham—the red brick laced with yellow, the extraordinary crockets, the mid-Victorian gargoyles—rose around him: boots beat on stone stairs and a cracked dinner-bell rang to rouse him to another miserable day. He felt the loyalty we all feel to unhappiness—the sense that that is where we really belong.

The mode in which Greene's preoccupation with childhood acts in *The Heart of the Matter* has so far only been glanced at in the first *Esperança* scene where Scobie's memory of the dead Catherine stirs his pity for the captain with the unattractive married daughter. Scobie's memory of his daughter, jogged daily by the photograph on his wife's dressing-table of 'the little pious nine-year-old girl's face in the white muslin of first communion', has a similar instrumentality in other situations. The relationship with Helen Rolt develops because Scobie at once feels protectively responsible for the widowed nineteen-year-old girl who in age could have been his own child—her stamp-collecting and her eagerness to talk about 'crushes' on schoolmistresses and not being good at trigonometry show how recently she has left school. At their second meeting Scobie tells her of Catherine's death. He is touched into being paternal by her amazing innocence when she patronizes her father, a clergyman, for believing in 'God and heaven, all that sort of thing', and thinks it daring that 'John and I—went together, oh, a fortnight before we married'. The substitution of Helen for his daughter in Scobie's mind is the more plausible for an accusation by Louise in a wrangle with her husband—'You've never loved anyone since Catherine died'.

In the Pende section of the novel, which deals with the transfer from French to British hands of some of the survivors of a torpedoed ship who are finally washed ashore after weeks adrift in open boats, the reference to Scobie's daughter is more complex. Among the hospital-cases transferred are Helen Rolt and a six-year-old girl who has lost both her parents at sea. The phrases used to describe Helen as she lies unconscious on a stretcher establish the parallel with Catherine—'Her arms as thin as a child's . . . the wedding ring loose on the finger, as though a child had dressed up'—but temporarily it is the six-year-old orphan who confuses past and present for Scobie and haunts his mind.

The doctor has said that the child will die by morning, and Scobie feels drawn irresistibly to the temporary hospital. This is the emotional centre of the book. The 'terror of life' appears in a reflection on human misery and the inevitability of pity:

> What an absurd thing it was to expect happiness in a world so full of misery. . . . Point me out the happy man and I will point you out either egotism, selfishness, evil—or else an absolute ignorance.

Then the thought widens until it is a question whether universally peace is not an illusion, the result of short-sightedness:

> Outside the rest-house he stopped again. The lights inside would have given an extraordinary impression of peace if one hadn't known, just as the stars on this clear night gave also an impression of remoteness, security, freedom. If one knew, he wondered, the facts, would one have to feel pity even for the planets? if one reached what they called the heart of the matter.

At the back of Scobie's soliloquy is the posing of the problem of suffering in what is usually held to be its acutest form—the suffering of a child.

> He thought: It would need all Father Brûle's ingenuity to explain that. Not that the child would die—that needed no explanation. Even the pagans realized that the love of God might mean an early death . . . but that the child should have been allowed to survive the forty days and nights in the open boat—that was the mystery, to reconcile that with the love of God.
>
> And yet he could believe in no God who was not human enough to love what he had created. 'How on earth did she survive till now?' he wondered aloud.
>
> The officer said gloomily, 'Of course they looked after her on the boat. They gave up their own share of the water often. It was foolish, of course, but one cannot always be logical. And it gave them something to think about.' It was like the hint of an explanation—too faint to be grasped.[1]

[1] Greene suggests that the child's suffering may be the opportune means of the parents' salvation. Similarly evil is made to work for good in the short story 'The Hint of an Explanation' (1949), where a Catholic boy who takes his faith matter-of-factly discovers a vocation to the priesthood by observing the seriousness of an atheist's blasphemy.

The identification of Catherine and the dying child is obvious as soon as Scobie enters the hospital. He is asked by the missionary's wife to watch by the bedside while she goes to dispense, and he accepts unwillingly as by 'a trick of the light on the pillow and a trick of his own mind' he sees a white communion veil over the child's head. He realizes that after all he has not escaped seeing Catherine die. The image of carrying a load, noticed earlier, recurs here:

> He could hear the heavy uneven breathing of the child. It was as if she were carrying a weight with great effort up a long hill: it was an inhuman situation not to be able to carry it for her.

Like the whisky-priest in *The Power and the Glory*, Scobie prays, 'Father, give her peace. Take away my peace for ever, but give her peace'. The child's eyes open and she repeats, 'Father'. With the sweat pouring off him he recovers a memory that 'he had carefully buried', and he uses his handkerchief to make a rabbit's shadow on the pillow until Mrs. Bowles returns and tells him harshly that the child is dead.

The simultaneous identification of his dead daughter with Helen and the six-year-old is made later in the novel, when, after Louise's return, Scobie's sense of his two contradictory responsibilities begins to oppress him. He is preparing for confession:

> He prayed for a miracle, 'O God convince me, help me, convince me. Make me feel that I am more important than that child [Helen]'. It was not Helen's face he saw as he prayed but the dying child who called him father: a face in the photograph staring from the dressing-table: the face of a black girl of twelve a sailor had raped and killed glaring up at him in a yellow paraffin light.

And again, after Ali's death, the same idea of substitution is at work when Scobie identifies parting from Helen with Catherine's death in England—'I missed that one death and now I'm having them all'. So that, looked at in an odd light, Scobie's suicide at the end of the book is not simply a means of securing Helen's and Louise's happiness, but an act of atonement satisfying his irrational guilt at having failed to suffer enough directly for his daughter's death. This is to be blunt where the exact shades of meaning necessarily escape definition, but it is at least an approach to the complexities of the novel's significance. And, if there is in Scobie's pity an element of neurotic compulsion, this may explain—if any explanation is needed for fluctuations of human feeling on the rack of an intolerable situation—the 'doubleness' of his attitude to his own behaviour. In the long final monologue, which he addresses to God in church, he will not accept all the guilt:

> If you made me, you made this feeling of responsibility that I've always carried about like a sack of bricks.[1] I'm not a policeman for nothing. . . . There was no other profession for a man of my kind.

Yet, ordinarily and more typically, he accepts entire responsibility for his actions: 'O God, I am the only guilty one because I've known the answers all the time.'

Appreciation of the meaning of Scobie's suicide, however, is incomplete without attention to two familiar Greene obsessions—those of escape and betrayal—which have a comparatively minor role in the novel. In Greene's work the idea of escape is invariably associated with the longing for peace. Since to live is to feel pity and responsibility, absolute peace is unobtainable. 'I can't bear to see suffering, and I cause it all the time', Scobie says to Helen, 'I want to get out, get out.' Suicide is the final escape; short of it, happiness is most nearly achieved when we are freest of commitments and have reduced our personal needs to a minimum—when we are nearest to nullity. After Louise has sailed to South Africa and before he has become entangled with Helen, Scobie momentarily achieves this negative state of being:

> Except for the sound of the rain, on the road, on the roofs, on the umbrella, there was absolute silence: only the dying

[1] The final recurrence of this image.

moan of the sirens continued for a moment or two to vibrate within the ear. It seemed to Scobie later that this was the ultimate border he had reached in happiness: being in darkness, alive, with the rain falling, without love or pity.

'Later' is the operative word in this quotation: true happiness has to be carefully distinguished from our sensation of it, a fact indicated by a comment as Scobie comes away from his first visit to Helen's Nissen hut:

> He walked away, feeling an extraordinary happiness, but this he would not remember as happiness, as he would remember setting out in the darkness, in the rain, alone.

If Scobie's 'longing for peace', explained in this way, can be regarded as a kind of psychological preparation for his suicide, it has also to be remembered that as a Catholic he regards suicide as 'the unforgivable sin'. Corresponding to the scene of his death in the third book, important scenes in the first and second books, which are supported by a host of lesser references, emphasize in the one case the psychological revolution that has to take place before he can accept the idea of suicide for himself, in the other his open-eyed acceptance of the Church's teaching on the subject.

At Bamba in the first book he has to investigate the death of the assistant district commissioner, a pimply charmless youth called Pemberton, who has got into debt to Yusef's storekeeper and taken 'the easy way out' by hanging himself. There are conversations with the local Catholic priest, who 'hopes' it may prove to be murder since suicide 'puts a man outside mercy'. Scobie disagrees. 'If you or I did it, it would be despair—I grant you anything with us. We'd be damned all right because we know, but he doesn't know a thing.' And when the priest reminds him of the Church's teaching, he bursts out, 'Even the Church can't teach me that God doesn't pity the young'—a phrase that recalls Father Rank's consolatory words to Louise after Scobie's death. Shortly after his arrival in Bamba he goes down with malaria, and in a feverish dream he again rejects the possibility of his own suicide. He dreams that Louise is crying upstairs and that he is writing a farewell letter to her. Then, as he turns to find a weapon, he realizes that for him the act is impossible:

> Suicide was for ever out of his power—he couldn't condemn himself for eternity—no cause was important enough.

His confidence acquires in retrospect the same irony as the early light-hearted dismissal of Yusef's offered help and friendship.

In the novel's second book a dinner party recalls Pemberton's suicide. Louise's telegram announcing her return from South Africa has been received by Scobie, and he has to break the news to Helen. The general conversation, which runs on ways of committing suicide and the Catholic attitude to self-destruction, need not be described in detail: it is adroitly put together, but still has some air of contrivance. It is here that Scobie learns from a woman doctor how easily the symptoms of angina can be faked. It is here, too, that he has a crushing retort for the nonentity who cheerfully claims that Hell won't worry him if it simply consists of 'a personal sense of loss'. 'Perhaps you've never lost anything of importance', Scobie replies.

Scobie's suicide is the climax of the third book. His care on the night of his death that Louise shall detect nothing unusual in his manner brings to mind Rowe's behaviour in *The Ministry of Fear* when he poisons his wife out of compassion and reluctantly leaves her to die alone—there must be no break in routine. After Louise has gone upstairs to bed, Scobie takes the Evipan tablets and tries to pray, but words escape him. In the last paragraph of the chapter we have Mauriac's 'good temptation' in an image, used earlier in *Brighton Rock*, of a force trying to break in and make communication:

> It seemed as though someone outside the room were seeking him, calling him and he made a last effort to indicate that he was

here. He got on his feet and heard the hammer of his heart beating out a reply. He had a message to convey, but the darkness and the storm drove it back within his breast, and all the time outside the house, outside the world that drummed like hammer blows within his ear, someone wandered, seeking to get in, someone appealing for help, someone in need of him. And automatically at the call of need, at the cry of a victim, Scobie strung himself to act. He dredged his consciousness up from an infinite distance in order to make some reply. He said aloud, 'Dear God, I love . . .' but the effort was too great and he did not feel his body when it struck the floor or hear the small tinkle of the medal as it spun like a coin under the ice-box—the saint whose name nobody could remember.

Scobie commits suicide fully aware what he is about, but at the end it is left an open question whether he can be regarded as 'finally impenitent'. He has betrayed God because Louise and Helen are the realer victims to him, but as he dies he struggles to take responsibility again 'at the cry of a victim'. That God is his victim here recalls an earlier moment when Scobie returns to his empty house after becoming Helen's lover, and thinks wearily of the lies to be told, the multiplied responsibilities:

> . . . he felt the wounds of those victims who had not yet bled. Lying back on the pillow he stared sleeplessly out towards the grey early morning tide. Somewhere on the face of those obscure waters moved the sense of yet another wrong and another victim, not Louise, not Helen. Away in the town the cocks began to crow for the false dawn.

The double reference to Genesis and to Peter's denial of Christ is obvious enough. Scobie betrays his job, Ali, Helen and Louise, but the full height of the argument is that he loves where he betrays, and he also loves and betrays God.

BIOGRAPHICAL NOTE

Graham Greene was born at Berkhamsted on October 2nd, 1904, *and educated at Berkhamsted School (of which his father was headmaster) and at Balliol College, Oxford, where he won an exhibition in Modern History. His first book*—Bubbling April, *a collection of verse—was published by Basil Blackwell in* 1925. *After a short period of apprenticeship to journalism in Nottingham, where he became a Catholic in February* 1926, *he moved to London to take up the post of a sub-editor on the staff of the* Times. *He married in* 1927 *and has a daughter and a son. After the publication of his first novel in* 1929 *he left the* Times *and lived by his writing. Between* 1935 *and* 1939 *he travelled to Liberia and Mexico and was film-critic for the* Spectator (*and for* Night and Day *of which he was part-editor during its brief career in* 1937). *For a few months in* 1940 *he worked at the Ministry of Information, and he was literary-editor and dramatic critic of the* Spectator *in* 1940–1. *In December* 1941 *he went out to West Africa to work for the Foreign Office. He spent three months in Lagos and was then transferred to Freetown, where he remained until February* 1943. *On his return to England he worked in a department of the Foreign Office. From* 1941 *to* 1948 *he was a director of Messrs. Eyre and Spottiswoode, taking an active part in publishing from* 1944. *He now lives in London and is at present at work on a new novel.*

BIBLIOGRAPHY

I. BY GRAHAM GREENE

All works by Graham Greene are published by William Heinemann Ltd., unless otherwise indicated.

1. *Novels and Entertainments*

	The Man Within	1929
	The Name of Action	1930
	Rumour at Nightfall	1931
E	*Stamboul Train*	1932
	It's a Battlefield	1934
	England Made Me	1935
E	*A Gun for Sale*	1936
	Brighton Rock	1938
E	*The Confidential Agent*	1939
	The Power and the Glory	1940
E	*The Ministry of Fear*	1943
	The Heart of the Matter	1948
E	*The Third Man*	1950

Titles marked 'E' are entertainments. Novels and entertainments are now being issued in a uniform revised edition.

The Third Man, though labelled an entertainment, consists of two stories—'The Third Man' and 'The Fallen Idol'—which have been made into films by Carol Reed; together with a note by Greene describing the changes made necessary by their translation from one medium to another. 'The Fallen Idol' is the short story 'The Basement Room', already published twice (see under 2 below). 'The Third Man', hitherto unpublished, is the original story-treatment for the film of the same name.

2. *Short Stories*

The Bear Fell Free, limited edition of a single short story (Grayson & Grayson, 1935).

The Basement Room (Cresset Press, 1935).

Nineteen Stories (1947).

Nineteen Stories contains the eight stories originally printed in *The Basement Room*, ten other stories (not including *The Bear Fell Free*) and the fragment of the unfinished novel 'The Other Side of the Border'. The American edition omits one story, 'The Lottery Ticket', and adds 'The Hint of an Explanation'.

3. *Travel and Miscellaneous*

Babbling April, poems (Basil Blackwell, 1925).

The Old School, essays by divers hands. Edited, with a short introduction and an essay, 'The Last Word', by Graham Greene (Jonathan Cape, 1934).

Journey Without Maps (1936).

The Lawless Roads (1939).

British Dramatists ('Britain in Pictures' Series, Collins, 1942).

Why do I Write? An exchange of views between Elizabeth Bowen, Graham Greene and V. S. Pritchett (Percival Marshall, 1948).

4. *Articles in Books, Introductions*

'Henry James—An Aspect', contributed to *Contemporary Essays*, 1933, edited by Silva Norman (Elkin Mathews and Marrot, 1933).

'Henry James', contributed to *The English Novelists*, edited by Derek Verschoyle (Chatto and Windus, 1936).

'Fielding and Sterne', contributed to *From Anne to Victoria*, edited by Bonamy Dobrée (Cassell, 1937).

'Subjects and Stories', contributed to *Footnotes to the Film*, edited by Charles Davey (Lovat Dickson, 1937).

Selection of Film Criticisms, reprinted in *Garbo and the Night-watchman*, edited by Alistair Cooke (Jonathan Cape, 1937).

'Convoy to West Africa', contributed to *The Mint No. 1*, edited by Geoffrey Grigson (Routledge and Kegan Paul, 1946).

Introduction to *The Portrait of a Lady* by Henry James, contributed to World's Classic edition (Oxford University Press, 1947).

'The Short Stories', contributed to *Tribute to Walter de la Mare on his Seventy-fifth Birthday* (Faber and Faber, 1948).

Introduction to *Oliver Twist* by Charles Dickens, contributed to Novel Library Edition (Hamish Hamilton, 1950).

5. *Uncollected Poems, Short Stories, Essays, etc.*

'François Mauriac: La Pharisienne: An English View', article contributed to *France Libre* (1945).

'The Revolver in the Corner Cupboard', autobiographical essay contributed to *The Saturday Book 6*, edited by L. Russell (1946).

'Heroes are Made in Childhood', broadcast talk printed in *The Listener* (27 March, 1947).

Speech to the Grande Conférence Catholique at Brussels, printed in *La Table Ronde* (February, 1948).

Speech to the Centre Catholique des Intellectuels Français ('Le Chrétien est-il de la Terre?'), printed in *Foi en Jésus-Christ et Monde d'aujourd'hui* (Editions de Flore, Paris, 1949).

'The Hint of an Explanation', short story contributed to *The Month* (February, 1949).

'Behind the Tight Pupils', poem contributed to *The Month* (July, 1949).

This is a select list of items of interest. See also the files of the *Spectator* (1935–41) and *Night and Day* (1937).

II. ON GRAHAM GREENE

Allen, Walter, 'The Novels of Graham Greene', *Penguin New Writing 18* (July–September 1943). Reprinted in *Writers of Today* (1946), edited by D. Val Baker.

Allen, Walter, *Reading a Novel.* This short book contains a criticism of *The Power and the Glory.*

Engel, Claire Eliane, *Esquisses Anglais* (Editions Je Sers, Paris, 1949). Contains essays on T. S. Eliot, Greene and Charles Morgan.

Grubbs, Henry A., 'Albert Camus and Graham Greene', *Modern Language Quarterly*, Vol. X, No. 1 (March, 1949).

Lemaître, Henri, 'Un romancier chrétien de l'absurde: Graham Greene', *Culture Catholique 4* (Paris, 1949).

Madaule, Jacques, *Graham Greene* (Editions du Temps Present, Paris, 1949).

Marshall, A. Calder, 'Graham Greene', contributed to *Living Writers*, edited by G. H. Phelps (1947).

Rostenne, Paul, *Graham Greene, témoin des temps tragiques* (Les Témoins de l'Esprit, Julliard, Paris, 1949). This book contains a prefatory letter by Greene.

Woodcock, George, *The Writer and Politics* (1948).

Zabel, Morton Dauwen, 'Graham Greene', contributed to *Forms of Fiction*, edited by W. Van O'Connor (University of Minnesota, 1948).

INDEX

2

PR
6013
.R44
Z6

Allott, Kenneth.

The art of Graham Greene, by Kenneth Allott and Miriam Farris. New York, Russell & Russell, 1963.

253 p. illus. 23 cm.

Includes bibliography.

1. Greene, Graham, 1904– I. Allott, Miriam (Farris) joint author.

PR6013.R44Z6 1963 823.912 63–15146 ‡

Library of Congress [5]